LightFoot Guide to t

Pilgrimage Route to Santi
in Franc

Le Puy-en-Velay to Ronceveaux

by Angelynn Meya

Auvillar © Alexia Adamski

LightFoot Guide to the Via Podiensis: Pilgrimage Route to Santiago de Compostela in France, From Le Puy-en-Velay to Roncevaux

2nd edition, January 2017
www.pilgrimagepublications.com

Photographs:
By Alexandra Huddleston, Alexia Admaski and Angelynn Meya.
Cover photo: Le Sauvage © Alexandra Huddleston

Cover and book layout design: Marie Engelhardt

Maps: Paul Chinn.

Map data based on openstreetmap.org © OpensStreetMap contributors.

The GR® hiking routes described in this guide have been reproduced with the permission of the FFRP.

www.ffrandonnee.fr

ISBN: 978-2-917183-37-3

Pilgrimage Publications welcomes any comments or corrections that could improve this guidebook. Please write to us at mail@pilgrimagepublications.com

Pilgrimage Publications is a not-for-profit organisation dedicated to the identification and mapping of pilgrim routes all over the world, regardless of religion or belief. Any revenue derived from the sale of guides or related activities is used to further enhance the service and support provided to pilgrims.

PREFACE

In the Middle Ages, pilgrims from across Europe converged upon the Spanish sanctuary of Santiago de Compostela, where James, one of Jesus' 12 apostles, was believed to be entombed. To reach the Iberian peninsula, they often had to first cross France. And the via Podiensis, the oldest of the French pilgrimage routes, was one of the main trails that they used.

The via Podiensis starts in the city of Le Puy-en-Velay, in south central France and ends approximately 750 kilometres later at the foot of the Pyrenees near the Spanish border. From there, it joins the *Camino Francés*, the famous main pilgrimage route that runs across northern Spain to the Cathedral of Santiago de Compostela.

Because of its dramatic landscapes, cultural and culinary richness, historical heritage and well developed infrastructure, today, the via Podiensis remains not only an important pilgrimage route but is also one of the most popular hiking trails in France.

This guidebook is intended to provide modern pilgrims with all of the information they need to successfully complete this journey and to meet their personal goals. Regardless of your motivation to walk the via Podiensis, or *"Le Chemin"* (in pilgrim-speak), it promises to be an enriching human, spiritual, cultural and linguistic adventure.

In preparing this guidebook, I would like to thank the many pilgrims whom I met along the Chemin, and who shared their stories, comments and recommendations. I would also like to thank my friends Alice Mignon, Rick Sherfey, Matthieu Warnier, Rime Sabbah, Diane Jalles and Rosanna Decicco for their help in verifying much of the information herein, as well as Alexandra Huddleston and Alexia Adamski for their moving photographs and the Mignon family for their kind support.

Changes will inevitably occur within the life-span of this edition. If you have comments or corrections to improve this guidebook for future users, we would be grateful to hear from you. Please write to us at: mail@pilgrimagepublications.com.

Bon Chemin!

Angelynn Meya

CONTENTS

Stages. This book divides the 774 kilometre route from Le Puy-en-Velay to Roncevaux into 34 stages that average 23 kilometres in length (or about 5 3/4 hours of walking per day at a moderate pace of 4km/hr).

Each stage includes a route summary, detailed instructions, map, elevation profile, historical and cultural overviews and information about accommodation.

Generally, stages end in larger villages or towns that have basic amenities, commerce and cultural sites. But this is not always the case. Some stages end in villages with limited resources or accommodation. In these cases, plan in advance to secure accommodation and food.

The stages in this guide are suggestions. You should feel free to create your own stages based on your own rhythm and needs. Accommodation is available all along a stage and has been listed in this guide. But if you are just starting your pilgrimage, we recommend that you walk not more than 25km per day.

Instructions and Map. While the route is very well way marked, each stage in this guide includes a map and detailed route instructions. Each route instruction corresponds to a GPS waypoint marked on the map and provides the number of metres to the next waypoint, detailed directions, a verification point, a general compass direction and elevation. GPS waypoint data can be downloaded for free at www.pilgrimagepublications.com. In addition to waypoints, the maps also indicate facilities.

Shells before Saint-Jean-de-Laur

When to go? The Le Puy route is practicable from April until the end of October, with the most popular months being May, June and September. May is an ideal month to cross the Aubrac plateau, when wild orchids are in blossom. Those seeking a more solitary experience often set off in October.

Leaving in July and August will generally be hot. In August, the French go on holiday, meaning that there are more tourists and vacationers along the route and accommodation may be harder to come by. For those planning to go all the way to Santiago de Compostela in one go, leaving from Le Puy in April or May is best, as this means crossing Spain in June or July, before the August heat.

When not to go? Best to avoid the route in winter, from November through March, as there may be significant snow cover and the route is not easy to follow. Crossing the Margeride, the Aubrac Plateau or the Pyrenees could be dangerous. Moreover, much accommodation will be closed, the days are shorter, and with colder temperatures you would need to carry more materials and more weight.

Our Lady of Le Puy © Alexia Adamski

How long will it take? The length of your trip depends on how much time you have as well as your physical stamina. The trip from Le Puy-en-Velay to Ronceveuax described in this guide takes 34 days, excluding rest days. Continuing on to Santiago de Compostela from Roncevaux would take an additional four weeks, which means more than two months of walking.

However, few are those that have the luxury of so much time. Those that do, tend to be students, retirees or people in between jobs. Most pilgrims tend to make the journey in segments thus completing the pilgrimage over several years. Each year they walk for a week or more starting in the place at which they ended the previous year. Others choose to do only certain sections for cultural or spiritual reasons. For example, the most popular section of the route is the 10 day walk from Le Puy-en-Velay to Conques, after which the number of pilgrims diminishes significantly.

When planning your trip, try to remain flexible and to not over plan. You may regret being tied down to a fixed schedule, when you find that you want to linger a bit longer in a certain place.

Solo. Walking the route alone is a safe and enriching journey. It is also easy to make friends. Solitude after all is a choice. Going solo will also mean that it is much easier to find accommodation and tailor your trip to suit your own tastes.

Groups. Travelling in groups of three or more will require some forward planning to secure accommodation.

Children. Travelling with children is generally not recommended, unless they are sufficiently independent and old enough to walk and carry their own backpacks. Some families travelling with smaller children use donkeys to transport children and equipment.

Bicycles. Many of the stages of the via Podiensis are not practicable by mountain bike, or require a high level of expertise, this is particularly the case in the stages that cross the Massif Central, from Le Puy-en-Velay to Cahors which are steep and rocky both on the descent and ascent. If you do wish to do the via Podiensis by bike, there are alternative routes that follow roads. These routes are described in other guide books and further information is available on the Internet.

Dogs. It is not recommended to take your dog. This is because dogs, particularly larger breeds, have a hard time handling day-after-day long distance walking. Moreover, not all accommodation is dog friendly. If you nevertheless wish to take your dog, you will need to adapt your journey to suit the dog's needs, including walking shorter distances, taking rest days, avoiding heat and certain sections of the route (e.g. those that pass through open cow pastures), and organizing logistics (booking dog-friendly accommodation, transporting food, etc.). You should also consult your veterinarian before heading off and purchase specialized equipment, if needed (such as dog shoes or paw cream).

Horses and donkeys. Some pilgrims make the journey by horse or donkey. Forward and logistical planning will be needed, particularly for accommodation. There are a number of companies that provide horse and donkey rentals, including fully equipped animals. There are certain portions of the path that are not practicable by horse, but alternative routes are available.

Donkey in Sant-Côme-d'Olt

The via Podiensis' infrastructure is well developed and varied, with the furthest distance between accommodation being about a two hour walk (or 8km). The choice of accommodation depends on budget, preference and location. The accommodation listed in this guidebook has been carefully selected based on personal experience and recommendation. Accommodation for each stage as well as a short distance beyond the stage end and is of the following types:

Pilgrim Hostels and **Religious Hostels.** Pilgrim Hostels represent a minority of hostels on the Chemin. They are considered special places that embody the "spirit" of the route and are often either family run hostels or Christian organisations, operated by volunteers, many of whom are former pilgrims. A number of these ask no more than a donation of whatever the pilgrim can afford and are sometimes called *donativos*. Religious hostels are often housed in operating convents or monasteries and offer the possibility to take part in religious services.

Statue of Mary © Alexia Adamski

The principle behind *donativos* is that they offer lodging and meals to pilgrims, who in turn donate a sum that they think appropriate or which they can afford. The money left by pilgrims one day covers the costs of pilgrims staying the next day, and so on. *Donativos* also permit those with financial difficulty to accomplish the Chemin, and thus they embody a kind of solidarity. They are not for profit organisations and do not receive public subsidies. The general rule is to pay an amount of money that reflects both your means and the market rate. In other words, if possible pay what you would have paid for equivalent services at a commercial hostel. For example, half board at a commercial hostel would cost around €35; an equivalent amount should be left at a *donativo* for the same services, if possible.

Commercial and Municipal Hostels (*Gîte d'étapes*): These represent typical pilgrim accommodation. Accommodation is basic, and includes a dormitory or shared bedrooms, bathrooms and kitchen and often a washing machine, which can be used for an additional charge (around €3). The majority of *gîtes* are clean and well maintained. Sheets are not generally provided, though blankets usually are. The average price varies from €15 to €25, per night. Reservations can usually be made between 24 and 48 hours in advance, unless you are travelling in a group, which will require greater notice. Most *gîtes* do not open before the afternoon (around 2p.m.), so there is no need to rush to arrive early. They often offer an option of half-board (called "*demi-pension*"), which will include dinner and breakfast. Dinners are usually communal and a good opportunity to meet other pilgrims.

Hotels and Bed & Breakfasts (*chambre d'hôtes*): Bed & breakfasts are a step up in the accommodation ladder. Here you will stay in someone's house and have your own room (usually a double or family sized room), clean sheets and private bathroom. Breakfast is included in the price. Bed & breakfasts require advance reservations. Hotels are not the usual places that pilgrims stay; but now and again you may want to splurge.

Camping: In addition to spaces for tents, many camp sites offer mobile home or cabin rentals. Hot showers, toilets, groceries and restaurant facilities are often available during the summer season. Campsites are, however, usually located off the main route. A few people opt for *camping sauvage*, or camping discretely off the route in unauthorised areas. While this can be a beautiful experience, it is important to follow the Leave No Trace Principles developed by the Centre for Outdoor Ethics (www.lnt.org).

Equestrian Centres. In addition to providing facilities for horses, equestrian centres often offer a hostel or the ability to camp on site.

Tourist Offices (*Offices de Tourisme*). Most towns and large villages have Tourist Offices with staff that speak English and can assist with finding and booking accommodation. This is a great resource for anglophones.

Reservations: It is best to reserve in advance if you are more than one person. Reservations can usually be made 24 to 48 hours in advance. Reservations are particularly recommended between Le Puy-en-Velay and Figeac, one of the most frequented sections of the route.

Pricing: Each year prices increase by approximately 10%. This book lists 2016 prices.

Budget: Budgets depend on your financial situation, needs and preferences. The two main costs to consider are accommodation and food. The average daily cost of a comfortable pilgrimage on the Via Podiensis, staying in pilgrim hostels is around €35-€40/day. The average cost of a commercial hostel is between €13 and €25 per night. B&Bs and hotels are significantly more expensive. Pilgrim hostels often provide meals, including breakfast, dinner or both for an additional charge (around €15). Restaurants may also propose pilgrim menus at a reduced price. It is possible to lower overall costs, by preparing your own meals, in which case budgeting €12/day for food, should be sufficient. Costs can be further reduced by camping.

This guide includes not only the main pilgrimage route, the via Podiensis, from Le Puy-en-Velay to Roncevaux, but also a number of alternative routes, that may be particularly attractive to certain pilgrims. The via Podiensis route and the main alternative routes are described below.

Via Podiensis. The modern via Podiensis is the main route that is taken by pilgrims. It is clearly way marked with the white and red bands of the French long distance hiking routes known as the *Grande Randonées*. This book follows the hiking route numbered GR®65, which is oriented nearly constantly in a south-westerly direction. The route starts in the volcanic mountains of Velay, crosses the solitary Aubrac Plateau, passes through the Lot river valley and the brandy vineyards of Armagnac to end in the Basque region of the Pyrenees. It passes through several medieval villages that have been selected for inclusion in the association of the Most Beautiful Villages of France (*Les Plus Beaux Villages de France*). Like the *Camino Francés* in Spain, several sections of the Chemin are identified on the UNESCO world heritage list, which recognizes its "key role in religious and cultural exchange and development in the later Middle Ages." The most challenging section of the route is the first 10 days, where the climbs and descents are the steepest.

Abbey of Bonneval Alternative Route. After Aubrac, there is an alternative route that leads to the remarkable Bonneval Abbey, a Cistercian abbey founded in 1147, and then re-joins the GR®65 in Espalion. It adds no extra time to the hike, unless you wish to spend an extra day at the abbey (recommended). The route, which is not well frequented, is challenging, with some steep descents. It is marked by light blue way markings and crosses spectacular plateaus and forests before arriving at the abbey, which is hidden in a forest valley. The abbey is self-sufficient and today houses a Cistercian convent and a small chocolate factory. The sisters also offer board to pilgrims. For the more adventurous, spiritually oriented or nature loving, this detour is recommended.

Rocamadour. The alternative route through Rocamadour takes six days (as opposed to four on the main GR®65) and uses the red and white way markings typical of the GR®. Rocamadour, revered for its miraculous black Madonna, has been an important Christian pilgrimage destination since the Middle Ages. Today, this stunning village built into the cliffs is the second most visited site in France. This route, which is less popular than the via Podiensis, is well marked. From Figeac it follows the GR®6 north through the villages of Cardaillac, with its lovely medieval centre, and Gramat. The approach to Rocamadour through the valley of Alzou is particularly stunning. From Rocamdour, the path then heads south on the GR®46 through the Causses of Quercy Nature Reserve, before re-joining the Lot River in the village of Vers. There, the route takes the GR®36, which runs alongside the Lot River to the city of Cahors, where it reconnects with the main Chemin (GR®65).

Célé Valley. From Figeac, the alternative route through the Célé Valley, which also uses red and white way markings takes five days (as opposed to four days on the GR®65), despite being about 10 kilometres shorter than the main route. It is generally considered more beautiful than the main route, as it crosses the limestone hills typical of the Causses region, passes beautiful villages built into the cliffs and follows the refreshing Célé river. The route, known as the GR®651, begins at Mas-de-la-Croix (after Figeac), where it descends into the Célé Valley to the lovely medieval village of Espagnac. From there, it climbs and descends along the limestone cliffs, in dry and often difficult and rocky terrain, passing through several historic villages on the Célé River, before re-joining the Lot near the village of Bouziès. There, the route takes the GR®36, which runs alongside the Lot river to the city of Cahors, to reconnect with the main Chemin (GR®65). In Bouziès it is also possible to make a day trip (recommended) to Saint-Cirq-Lapopie, considered one of the most beautiful villages in France, and which is a lovely four kilometres walk south along the Lot river.

Way markings. With the exception of the blue way markings of the Bonneval Abbey alternative route, all of the routes described in this guide are very clearly way marked with the white and red bands of the French long distance hiking routes known as the *Grande Randonées*. These markings appear regularly on trees, rocks, walls and posts, and particularly at forks or crossroads. There are four marks to look for:

Keep straight on	Turn right
Turn left	Wrong Way

In addition, the Chemin is often way marked by a stylized scallop shell of Saint James, where the lines represent the roads of Europe leading to Santiago de Compostela. Frequently, there are signposts indicating the number of kilometres to the next village.

The Chemin sometimes crosses other routes, which are often way marked with other colours, such as yellow bands. These can be ignored. Stay focused on the red and white markings of the GR®s.

WHAT TO TAKE?

Traditional wisdom is that your backpack should weigh no more than 10% of your body weight. For example, if you way 75 kilos (165 pounds), your backpack should not weigh more than 7.5 kilos (16.5 pounds). Bear in mind that you will also have to add the weight of water (about 2 litres or 2 kilos.)

Mental preparation for your trip begins when reflecting on what is truly essential to take. The more weight the tougher the walk.

PACKING CHECKLIST

Backpack (35-40 litres): Your backpack should be suited to your morphology and have a rain cover.

Sleeping bag liner or super thin sleeping bag: Many hostels provide blankets so that a liner is generally sufficient.

Foot wear: (1) Light-weight hiking shoes that are water resistant, but breathable. No need to take hiking boots, which are too heavy and ill-suited for long distance walking and (2) flip flops or sandals, for the evening

Walking poles (optional)

Water bottles (at least 2 litres) or Camel-Bak (optional)

Documents: Identity Card/Passport, Insurance Card, credit cards, Pilgrim Passport, and ziploc bag to put them in.

Miscellaneous: Safety pins (to hang clothes to dry), knife, headlamp, basic sowing kit, adapter/converter, cell phone and charger, camera (optional)

Clothing: Invest in clothes that are specifically adapted to hiking or sport, and are breathable, lightweight and quick-dry:
- 2 quick dry T-shirts
- 1 long sleeved shirt
- 1 fleece or sweater for cool evenings
- 1-2 pairs shorts (quick-dry)
- 1 hiking pants
- 1 rain paints
- 1 ultra-light rain coat
- 3 underwear
- 3 pairs of hiking or running socks, which allow for ventilation and reduce friction
- Swim wear
- Pyjamas

Accessories and toiletries:
- Sun: hat, sunglasses, sun screen
- Toiletries: Quick-dry towel, shower gel/shampoo, toothbrush and tooth paste, moisturizer, nail clippers, comb/brush
- Earplugs (snoring protection)
- Soap/detergent for washing clothes.
- Health: First aid kit, blister prevention foot cream (applied before walking to reduce friction), 2nd skin blister patches, such as Compeed®, which is available in French pharmacies.
- Other medicines, as needed

Walking in autumn or early spring will require taking additional warmer, but breathable clothes, as well as a hat, gloves and scarf. This will add weight to your backpack.

Pilgrim Passport (*Carnet du Pèlerin* or *Crédential*). The pilgrim's passport serves as proof that a pilgrim has undertaken a pilgrimage on the Way of Saint James. All along the Chemin, pilgrims collect passport stamps (*tampons*) from the places they spend the night, churches, museums, cafes, etc. The passport is then presented at the Pilgrim's Office in Santiago de Compostela as proof of their journey in order to receive a Compostela, or a certificate attesting to the successful completion of the pilgrimage.

While in Spain it is mandatory to have a Pilgrim Passport in order to stay in public hostels, this is not the case in France. In France, the passport is primarily required for *donativos* and Christian hostels. A Pilgrim Passport can be obtained from numerous pilgrims associations ahead of your trip, in Paris (from La Société Française des Amis de Saint Jacques de Compostelle, www.compostelle.asso.fr), from the Confraternity of Saint James ww.csj.ork.uk or at the Cathedral in Le Puy-en-Velay gift shop. To standardize the various passport models and to ensure that prices are affordable, the passport must be of a type approved by the Pilgrim's Office in Santiago.

Physical Fitness. No special training is required to do the Chemin if you are in generally good health and routinely exercise. Nevertheless, it is recommended that you start doing long distance hikes at least a couple of months before you set off. This will help you to develop endurance and strength, as well as to test your equipment (shoes and backpack). It will make the first days of your hike easier. Your capacities will quickly improve after a few days of walking the Chemin.

Boots © Alexia Adamski

Fountain © Alexandra Huddleston

Water. There are watering points all along the route. Take advantage of these to fill up your water bottles and avoid dehydration and related injuries, such as tendinitis. Cemeteries also generally have water spouts with drinkable water.

Eating. For an additional charge (around €5), hostels usually propose breakfast starting at 7 a.m. Breakfast usually consists of coffee/tea and baguette with marmalade. To supplement this light start of the day, consider carrying snacks (fruits, nuts, etc.). Lunch is served from 12:30 to 2 p.m. Most cafes and restaurants will serve a *plat du jour,* which is an inexpensive way to enjoy a hearty meal. Alternatively, it is easy to put together a picnic by buying goods at a local market (*marché*) or grocery store (*épicerie*). Dinner is generally served from 7:30 p.m and consists of three courses and wine. Many hostels serve dinner, as part of a half-board. Another option is to use the communal kitchen to cook your own meals. This may be the best choice if you have dietary restrictions or are on a limited budget. An increasing number of lodgings offer vegetarian meals. Ask in advance (i.e., when making your reservation) if this option is available.

The Chemin also represents a gastronomic journey. The cuisine changes regularly as the route passes through various regions - from Le Puy to the Basque country. In descriptions of the regions, this guide notes culinary highlights, which we encourage you to explore.

Business Hours. Business hours are generally from 9:30-12:00 and 14:00-18:00. Most private and public establishments close for two hours at midday. In small towns, shops are often closed on Sunday and Monday, though larger supermarkets may be open.

Baggage transport. Several companies offer services to transport backpacks from one stage to the next. In the morning, pilgrims leave their backpacks at the hostel, indicating where they plan to be that evening. A van picks up the baggage in the morning and drops it off at the destination. The hostels work with different transport companies and are generally happy to organise this service. Many people transport their bags daily while others use this service when they need a break. Transport costs between €5 and €10 per bag.

Arrival and Departure.

Plane. Le Puy-en-Velay is accessible by flying into Paris, Geneva or Lyons, and thereafter continuing by train or car.

Train. There is regular train service between Paris and Le Puy-en-Velay, via Lyon, Clermont-Ferrand or St-Etienne. The journey takes about 4.5 hours. Trains also run from Charles de Gaulle airport in Paris to Le Puy-en-Velay (about 5.5 hours). If travelling from the UK, in summer, Eurostar trains run from London to Lyon. There are also regular train connections between Geneva and Le Puy. From Saint-Jean-Pied-de-Port, return trains to Paris pass through Bayonne and Bordeaux. Return trains to Geneva are difficult. If in France, trains can be booked at www.voyages-sncf.com. If outside of France, we recommend registering and using the following website: www.captaintrain.com.

Car-share. An affordable and fun alternative is to travel by car, using the car sharing site www.blablacar.fr, which connects drivers and passengers willing to travel together between cities and to share the cost of the journey. You can register and create a profile on the website (in French).

Telephone. It is best to have a cell phone in France, mostly to be able to make reservations and in case of emergency. If you have an unblocked cell phone, you can purchase a SIM card for your phone once in France, such as at stores run by Orange or SFR (telecommunications companies). The phone store can register the SIM card (take your passport) and get your phone working. This can be done for example in Le Puy-en-Velay. Additional phone credits can be bought at *Tabacs* (tobacconists) along the route.

Medical Insurance and Assistance. EU citizens should have a European Health Insurance Card, a free card that simplifies access to medically necessary, state-provided healthcare during temporary stays in any of the 28 EU Member States. Contact information for doctors can usually be obtained from pharmacies, town halls or tourist offices. In France, patients generally pay for doctors' visits and medication out-of-pocket. These expenses may thereafter by partially reimbursed by insurance companies once proof is provided.

Banking and Cash. Along the route, and certainly in the larger towns, there are ATMs where you can withdraw cash. You should carry sufficient cash to pay for accommodation, as often these do not accept credit cards. Standard banking hours are Monday-Friday: 9:30-12:00 and 14:00-16:00, Saturday 9:30-12:00.

Internet. Wifi or wireless internet is available in many commercial hostels, but not always. Wifi is often available in cities (such as Le Puy-en-Velay, Figeac, Moissac or Cahors), while in rural areas, chances are slim.

Emergency numbers. The Europe-wide emergency number is 112 (fire, police, ambulance, coastguard, search and rescue). In France: police: 17; fire: 18, or 15: ambulance.

Pilgrimage in the Middle Ages

Pilgrimage to holy places is common to all major religions. In Christianity, if life is a physical journey towards an eventual union with God in the afterlife, pilgrimage becomes a metaphor for that journey. In other words, by physically journeying towards a holy place, pilgrims make a spiritual journey towards God. In medieval Christendom, pilgrimage was also a redemptive act, whereby pilgrims' sins were forgiven. For example, making a pilgrimage to Santiago de Compostela during a Holy Year (when Saint James' feast day (25 July) fell on a Sunday), would mean release from purgatory in the afterlife.

During the Middle Ages, there were three major pilgrimage destinations: Jerusalem, Rome and Santiago de Compostela. The foremost of these was Jerusalem, which was linked to Christ's life and scenes from the Bible. However, when Jerusalem fell to the Arabs in 637 AD, pilgrimage to the Holy Land became less accessible, resulting in the growth of alternative pilgrimage sites, such as local shrines, relics brought from the Holy Land and the tombs of saints. Rome was a second important pilgrimage destination, as it housed the tombs of Saints Peter and Paul and the seat of the Catholic church.

The third destination was Santiago de Compostela, located in a remote corner of north western Spain, where it was believed that Saint James, one of Jesus' 12 Apostles, and brother of Saint John, was entombed.

According to the New Testament of the Bible, James the Greater, son of Zebedee, left being a fisherman on the sea of Galilee to follow Christ, and witnessed, amongst others, Christ's Transfiguration on Mount Tabor. He was also believed to have evangelized in Spain. Upon returning to Jerusalem from Spain, he was beheaded by Herod Agrippa I around 44AD. According to legend, James' followers placed his decapitated body in a rudderless boat that, guided by providence, made its way through the Mediterranean sea up the Atlantic coast to the coastal village of Iria Flavia (now known as Padron), on the northwest corner of Spain. In an account from the 12th century, the body was taken by oxcart for burial at a site known as Compostela. During the reign of the Bishop Theodomir of Iria Flavia (circa. 820-830), a hermit was led by a star to the field where the relics were rediscovered. The name "Compostela" could refer to the field of a star (*campus stellae*) although it is more likely a reference to the Latin word, burial (*compositum*).

Thereafter, the relics were placed in a reliquary and churches were successively built on the site. Santiago de Compostela's transformation from a local to an international pilgrimage destination is suggested by evidence of pilgrims coming from other countries, including Bishop

St James - Le Puy cathedral

Goldescalc, the bishop of Le Puy-en-Velay, who arrived in Compostela in 951. By the 12th century, pilgrims from abroad were regularly journeying to Santiago, with the pilgrimage being promoted by the Bishop of Santiago, who recognised the political and religious importance of the shrine.

One of the most important texts to emerge from this period was the 12th century Codex Calixtus, attributed to Pope Calixtus II. It was a spiritual and physical guide to pilgrimage to Santiago de Compostela. The Codex contained five sections: (1) sermons, prayers, songs and hymns for the Saint's feast, (2) a narration of the 22 miracles performed by Saint James, (3) stories of the Saint's life and legends about the transport of his body from Jerusalem to Spain and the discovery of his tomb; (4) a history of Charlemagne's campaigns against the Moors in the 8th century, and (5) the Liber Santi Jacobi, a guide to the pilgrimage routes to Compostela through France and Spain.

The creation of the Codex and a magnificent church in Santiago de Compostela testified to the importance of Saint James by the 12th century. While the lack of records limits knowing how many pilgrims travelled there each year, annual visitors likely numbered in the thousands. Other evidence of the cult's importance were the images of Saint James in artwork along the pilgrimage routes.

Some churches were also dedicated to other saints and were pilgrimage destinations in their own right. These churches often contained a saint's tomb or relics, as in the case of Conques. The Codex encouraged "visiting" these Saints.

During this period, societal customs promoted religious pilgrimage. Laws were enacted to protect pilgrims and an infrastructure of hostels or hospices, bridges and other support services, including financial ones, developed to meet pilgrim's needs.

Pilgrimage to Santiago declined after the Renaissance. However, by the 21st Century it would experience an incredible resurgence, with more than 260,000 pilgrims a year arriving at the Cathedral of Santiago de Compostela.

Shells © Alexandra Huddleston

The Via Podiensis and modern pilgrimage

Like the Camino Frances, the Via Podiensis traces its historical heritage to medieval texts. The earliest recorded pilgrim to Santiago from beyond the Pyrenees was Bishop Godescalc of Le Puy-en-Velay who travelled in 950-951AD. According to a prayer included in a 10th century manuscript that tells of his pilgrimage, Godescalc was born on and was ordained a bishop on Saint James' feast day, suggesting that he personally identified with the Saint.

The second text that described the Le Puy route was the fifth book of the Codex Calixtus, which was the earliest guide to the pilgrimage routes to Compostela. The guide was written in Latin around 1140 by a Frenchman, and described four main pilgrimage routes in France, including one starting in Le Puy. According to the Codex, pilgrims from Burgundy and Germany would take the Le Puy route, along Roman roads, passing through Le Puy, Conques and Moissac.

However, during the Middle Ages, Le Puy was foremost a pilgrimage destination in its own right, rather than the starting point of the route to Santiago. Over the centuries, thousands of pilgrims flocked to the sanctuary to pay devotion to the Black Madonna, which was brought to Le Puy by Saint Louis, on his return from the crusades. To accommodate the multitudes, a new hospital (*Hotel-Dieu*) was built in the 15th century.

Indeed, the fact that Godescalc had travelled to Santiago was only rediscovered in 1866 when the 10th century manuscript described above was found in the National Library in Paris. Equally, historians question the lack of evidence for the supposed hundreds of thousands of medieval pilgrims that purportedly followed in Godescalc's footsteps to Santiago.

That Le Puy is the starting point for pilgrims bound for Santiago, was largely a 20th century phenomena, underpinned by the creation in the 1970s of a long distance hiking route, the GR®65, that recreated the pilgrim route from Le Puy to the Spanish border.

Thereafter, in 1987 the Council of Europe launched its Cultural Routes Programme and declared the Santiago de Compostela Pilgrimage Routes the first such cultural routes. The Council considered these routes "highly symbolic in the process of European unification," and appealed to public authorities, institutions and individuals to revitalize them. It concluded with the aspiration that travel along these routes could help to "build a society founded on tolerance, respect for others, freedom and solidarity." Significant efforts to revive the French pilgrimage routes, notably the via Podiensis, were made in the 1990s, led by the French Hiking Federation (*Fédération Française de la Randonnée Pédestre*). By 1998, seven sections of the via Podiensis as well as numerous monuments along the way were registered on UNESCO's World Heritage List. Consequently, since the 1990s the route has been very well developed.

The 21st Century has witnessed the true upsurge of pilgrimage. Never before have so many pilgrims walked to Santiago de Compostela, including on the via Podiensis. Each year tens of thousands set off from Le Puy, which has also become an important point of convergence for pilgrims coming from the east, such as from Switzerland, Austria and Germany. And these numbers are only likely to increase.

The region of Velay makes up the south-eastern part of the Massif Central, the mountainous area in south-central France that comprises about 15 percent of the country. It is a volcanic region that was formed some 14 million years ago and is dotted with numerous small volcanoes and spires that rise above a wide basalt (volcanic stone) plateau. It is bound in the west by the Allier river (crossed in Stage 2), which has etched deep gorges that separate Velay from the granite massif of Margeride to the west. The region's capital is Le Puy-en-Velay, the starting point of the Via Podiensis, and a city famous for being a Catholic sanctuary, for its lentils and other local products (such as, bobbin lace and the digestive liquor, Verveine, which is made from 32 different herbs).

Le Puy-en-Velay, rue des Tables © Alexandra Huddleston

DISTANCE **23.5km**

ASCENT **736m**

DESCENT **546m**

FROM LE PUY **0km**

TO RONCEVAUX **774km**

Route - The path is well-marked with the red and white way markings of the GR®65, as well as wooden signposts and the shell of Saint James. The route gradually climbs along country roads, farm tracks and hiking trails across fields and villages. After Montbonnet there is a steep climb into the woods of the volcanic Mount Déves, followed by a steep descent into Saint-Privat-d'Allier, which can be slippery when wet. Note the lovely views of Le Puy, when leaving the city, the chapel of Saint Roch before Montbonnet and the views while descending to Saint-Privat-d'Allier.

Pointers - From Place du Plot, pay attention to correctly follow the way marking for the GR®65, as Le Puy is the starting point for several GR® routes. **Pilgrim's Passport (*La Crédential*):** You can obtain a pilgrim's passport and stamp from the Cathedral gift shop (after the pilgrims mass and blessing at 7a.m. or during opening hours). **Reservations:** Most people set off from Le Puy on the weekends, often resulting in accommodation being fully booked during the summer months. It is best to reserve accommodation in Le Puy in advance or set out on a weekday. **Choice of routes:** After Tallode, you have the choice to take the main GR®65, or take a historic variant passing through Bains and Fay, which will add approximately 2km to your walk. Both routes are equivalent in terms of difficulty, however, the variant is less frequented. **Advance planning:** If you don't plan on stopping for lunch in Montbonnet, you should shop for lunch the evening before as there are limited facilities on the route and shops won't be open early in the morning when you leave. Fill up on water before you set out and as you pass watering points. **Market:** There is a lively and colourful market at Place du Plot each Saturday morning, featuring local and regional produce and goods.

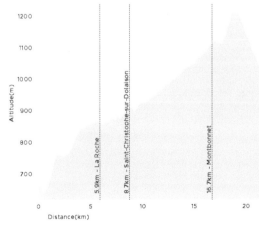

Le Puy-en-Velay

The city of Le Puy-en-Velay (popl. 18,600, alt. 630m) (or Le Puy, from the Latin word *podium*, or elevated structure) sits in a four million year old volcanic basin, from which several volcanic spires emerge; these are the remains of volcanic necks that once ejected lava. In Le Puy, several of these spires are capped by Catholic monuments, such as the Cathedral of Le Puy, the Chapel of Saint Michael of Aiguilhe or the 84 metre rose-coloured statue of Our Lady of France.

Cathedral of Our Lady of Puy (*Cathédrale Notre-Dame-du-Puy*)

Le Puy en Velay cathedral ©Alexandra Huddleston

The Cathedral of Our Lady of Puy is an UNESCO world heritage site. It traces its origins to a 5th century sanctuary, though the present structure was built in the 11th century, and was thereafter renovated on several occasions. It is an impressive Romanesque monument that has rich oriental influences, including a façade of alternating dark and light brick work and an inscription on the wooden door frame at the entrance to the cathedral in pseudo-Arabic script, which states: "There is no other God but Allah." Historians attribute these oriental features to influence from Moorish-Spain, including through pilgrimage, as well as from the crusades.

The church is accessible through an imposing staircase that rises into a series of three porches and gradually narrows into what is called the womb staircase, which emerges into the central nave of the cathedral directly opposite a 17th century black Madonna. An original Madonna was brought to Le Puy in 1254 by St Louis upon his return from the crusades and was highly venerated in the Middle Ages; it was, however, burned in 1794 during the French Revolution. The black Madonna's wardrobe includes 25 dresses, the oldest of which is from the 14th century and is on display in the cloister museum. The cathedral also has a several million year old flat volcanic rectangular stone called the *Pierre des fieves*, or apparition stone, which is believed to have healing powers and which relates to a legend from the 3rd century about the apparition of Mary.

Except for the winter months, mass is held daily at 7:00 a.m., followed by a pilgrim blessing that takes place in front of the 16th century polychrome stone statue of Saint James. The blessing ends with the singing of the Salve Regina, a Latin hymn dedicated to Mary which some believe was written in Le Puy in the 11th century.

Cloister and Treasury

Built in the 11th and 12th century, the cloister is an excellent example of Romanesque architecture, and is notable for its columns and polychrome decoration. It also has one of the oldest examples of ironwork in France - a 12th century wrought iron gate with patterns that resemble Arabic latticework. The cloister museum has an exceptional collection of liturgical embroidery from the 14th to 20th century.

Our Lady of France (*Notre-Dame de France*)

Standing on the highest volcanic peak, called Corneille Peak, Our Lady of France is an imposing 16 metre rose-coloured statute of the Madonna and child, which was completed in 1860, following the Crimean War (1853-1856). The war posited France, Britain and the Ottoman Empire against Tsarist Russia, and concerned the rights of Christian minorities in the Holy Land as well as power over the waning Ottoman Empire. The monument was made from 213 canons taken during the battle of Sebastopol (1854-1855), a final siege in the war which ended when the Tsar sued for peace in 1856. This is one of the most visited monuments in the region.

Chapel of Saint Michael of Aiguilhe *Montbonnet*) (*Chapelle Saint-Michel d'Aiguilhe*)

Saint-Michel d'Aiguilhe

The Chapel of Saint Michael sits on an 82 metre volcanic spire that can be reached by 220 steps. The views alone are worth the climb. Built in 961, following Bishop Goldescalc's return from pilgrimage to Santiago de Compostela and dedicated to Saint Michael, the chapel was itself a pilgrimage destination. There are three oratories placed on the stairway leading to the chapel. In its vaulted interior are beautiful 10th/11th century frescoes, including of Christ in Majesty (seated as a ruler on a throne, as described in the Book of Revelation) and an original altar.

Place du Plot/Saturday Market

Place du Plot is the traditional starting point of the Via Podiensis. In 1548, local consuls set up a pillory here, where drunkards were put on display and endured public shaming. The Bidoire fountain dates from the 13th century and is the oldest in Le Puy. Today, Place du Plot holds a lively farmers' market on Saturday mornings. Of note is the local farmers' cheese (*fromage fermier de Velay*) and the famous green lentils of Le Puy.

Saint-Christophe-sur-Dolaison

Saint-Christophe-sur-Dolaison (popl. 1,000, alt. 900m) has a small 11th century Romanesque church that was built from the reddish volcanic stone of the region and which has a four-arched bell tower and a wooden altar depicting Saint Christopher, patron saint of travellers. Near the church are the remains of a communal oven, which was once a mainstay of village life. Families would take turns heating the oven with wood and baking bread. Along the route, several villages have communal ovens, some of which are still in use.
Saint Roch Chapel (*Chapelle Saint-Roch de*

Chapel of Saint Roch

Built in the 11th century by the powerful Montlaur Family (their coat of arms is on the vaulted ceiling), this Romanesque chapel was first dedicated to Saint Bonnet and later to Saint Roch. According to legend, Saint Roch was born in the 14th century into a wealthy French family. But he gave up his possessions and went on pilgrimage to Rome where he tended to victims of the plague. After performing several miraculous cures, he succumb to illness and withdrew to the forest. There, he was cured by an angel and was supplied with water by a spring and with food by a local dog. In art, he is often depicted as a pilgrim showing a left leg infected by the plague and accompanied by a dog.

Saint-Privat-d'Allier

Privat-d'Allier © Alexandra Huddleston

The village of Saint-Privat-d'Allier (popl. 400, alt. 875m) is built on a rocky spur overlooking the Allier valley. Its 13th century castle (privately owned) played a strategic role in controlling the road to Gévaudan (the historic territory of the Gabali, a Celtic people, and which is today part of Margeride). The village's Romanesque church dates from the late 12th century and the priory (a religious house for clerics) is mentioned in a 12th century papal bull (letter from the Pope).

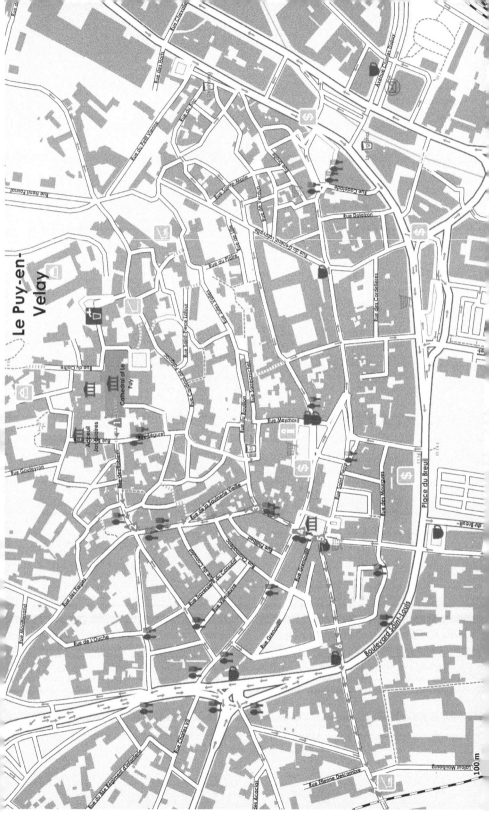

Le Puy-en-Velay

Waypoint	Total(km)	Directions	Verification	Compass	Altitude(m)
1	0.0	In **Le-Puy** descend Cathedral staircase and continue straight on rue des Tables.		W	686
2	0.1	Turn left onto rue Raphaël.	Pass the 15th century Fountain des Tables before turning left	S	686
3	0.3	Turn right onto rue Chénebouterie		SW	676
4	0.4	Continue straight crossing **Place du Plot**	Pass fountain de la Bidoire to the left	SW	654
5	0.4	From Place du Plot turn right onto rue Saint-Jacques.	Coloured ceramic relief of Saint James to the left	W	650
6	0.5	Cross boulevard Saint Louis/N102 and continue straight on rue des Capucins		W	649
7	0.7	Continue straight on rue des Capucins climbing hill.	Pass under bridge	SW	642
8	0.9	At the end of rue des Capucins turn right onto rue de Compostelle.	Small park with statute of St. James to the left	W	643
9	1.0	Keep left on rue de Compostelle	Continue climbing hill	SW	643
10	1.3	Turn right off rue de Compostelle onto foot path	Pass sports complex on the right	S	653
11	1.4	Turn right rejoining rue de Compostelle	Follow row of hedges lining road to the right	SW	670
12	1.8	Leave main road and turn left onto track called the Ancienne route de Saugues	Signpost	SW	714
13	1.9	Continue straight on track	Pass stone wall on the left	SW	715
14	2.6	Continue straight on Ancienne route de Saugues	Cross of Jalasset (1621) on the left and picnic area to the right	SW	754
15	3.5	Continue straight on Ancienne route de Saugues and climb hill	Pass farm on right	SW	761
16	4.6	Cross the D589 departmental road and continue straight on track.		W	830

Leaving Le Puy-en-Velay

17	5.4	At crossroads turn left in the direction of La Roche	Signposts indicate GR®65	SE	856
18	5.7	Cross the D589 departmental road and continue straight through village of La Roche	Village of La Roche visible ahead	S	862
19	5.9	Take a sharp right in the hamlet of La Roche and descend on foot path		SW	864
20	6.0	Continue straight on the road	Pass **communal oven** on the left	SW	864
21	6.2	Turn left onto footpath heading towards valley	Picnic bench and information point to the left	W	866
22	7.0	Leave foot path turning left onto track	Head towards farm	SW	873
23	7.2	Turn right onto track	After passing cross on the left with valley views. Yellow sign post	SW	880
24	8.3	Continue on tree-lined footpath		S	888
25	8.5	Pass mobile snack bar on the right		S	900
26	8.6	Enter village of **Saint-Christophe-sur-Dolaison**		S	907
27	8.7	Turn right at Place de l'eglise and cross Saint-Christophe-sur-Dolaison	Church of Saint-Christophe and Auberge du Grand Chemin on the right	SW	908
28	8.8	Turn right onto rue du Château	Head away from the town hall (la Mairie)	SW	911
29	8.9	After leaving village centre, turn right onto small road towards Tallode	Pass castle on the right	W	914
30	9.1	Pass under D906 departmental road and stay to the left towards Tallode	Underpass	W	912
31	9.6	Enter hamlet of **Tallode**	Brown stone farmhouse to the right	SW	917
32	9.8	Continue straight on road leaving Tallode	Pass cross on the right	W	927
33	10.1	Continue straight on main road. The alternative route to Bains departs on the right (signpost)	Pass cross on left and follow signs towards hamlet of Liac	SW	928
34	10.7	Enter hamlet of Liac and keep left on main road	Pass stone cross on right	W	930
35	10.8	Turn right onto footpath in village centre	Signposts	W	931
36	10.9	Leave village of Liac. Continue straight on foot path		W	932
37	11.0	Continue straight on footpath	Stone walls and pastures	SW	932
38	11.6	Continue straight towards the hamlet of Lic	Pass picnic area on the left	SW	961
39	11.8	After leaving Lic, turn right on footpath	Farm and signpost	NW	965
40	12.1	Stay to the left on track	Signpost	W	977
41	12.4	Cross asphalt road and continue straight towards village of Montbonnet	Asphalt road	SW	987
42	12.8	At intersection continue straight on footpath following stone wall	Stone wall	W	993
43	13.1	At intersection continue straight	Hills visible straight ahead	W	1003
44	13.6	Continue straight on foot path	Farm visible straight ahead	W	1016

stage 1

45	14.0	Turn right onto departmental road D621 towards centre of Ramourouscle	Hamlet visible to the right	NW	1026
46	14.2	In hamlet centre at fork and fountain, turn left towards Montbonnet	Cross of Ramourouscle (1631) on left, fountain and signpost	SW	1034
47	14.6	Stay right on asphalt road	Pass farm on left	W	1043
48	15.5	Continue straight on asphalt road	Pass picnic area on the left. **Saint Roch Chapel** ahead	NW	1069
49	15.8	Stay to right on asphalt road	Village of Montbonnet visible ahead	NW	1074
50	16.5	Turn left onto route de Saugues/ D589 towards centre of **Montbonnet**. The alternative route from Le Bains meets the D589 here and rejoins the GR®65	Welcome sign ahead	SW	1106
51	16.7	Turn right onto track before Gîte La Grange	Signpost	NW	1110
52	16.7	Leave village of Montbonnet and continue straight on track	Pine hills visible ahead	NW	1110
53	17.0	Continue straight on track towards hills	Pass between two barns	NW	1126
54	17.2	Continue straight on tracks towards pine hills	Pass under power lines	NW	1122
55	17.6	Turn right and cross over brook	Brook	N	1114
56	18.0	Continue straight on rocky track climbing hill	Pine forest ahead	NW	1135
57	18.4	Stay to the left at fork and continue climb	Fork	W	1170
58	18.6	Turn right into pine forest	Pine forest	NW	1202
59	18.7	Turn left in pine forest on track towards Lac de l'Œuf		W	1206
60	19.0	Continue straight on track	To the right is Lac de l'Œuf, a peat bog with a rich biodiversity	SW	1212
61	19.2	Turn left onto asphalt road	Signpost	SW	1209
62	19.3	Turn right descending onto track	Signpost	SW	1212
63	20.7	Continue descent on road	Village of Le Chier visible below	SW	1101
64	21.1	Cross road D589 and stay to the right towards village of Le Chier	Village of Le Chier visible to the right. Sign post "Le Chier"	SW	1067
65	21.4	Enter village of Le Chier	Stone farmhouse to the right	SW	1044
66	21.5	Continue straight passing through village of Le Chier	Cross on right and town hall (la Mairie) on the left	SW	1039
67	22.0	At fork stay to the right. Steep descent	Sign post	W	1014
68	22.2	Continue steep descent on foot path	Saint-Privat-d'Allier visible to the left in valley	NW	1005
69	22.5	Turn left onto narrow foot path. Steep and rocky descent into ravine. Slippery when wet; recommend alternative route.	Sign post	N	954
70	22.9	Continue straight on path crossing stream (Ruisseau Rouchoux) on wooden foot bridge.	Pass mill on right and Cross of Piquermeule (16th century)	W	907
71	23.3	Merge left onto D589 and continue straight into Saint-Privat-d'Allier	Sign post	SW	881
72	23.5	Arrive at **Saint-Privat-d'Allier**	Village centre (Le Kompost'l cafe ahead)		877

stage 1

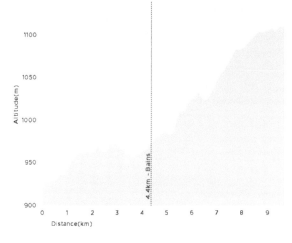

LENGTH **9.7km**

STAGE ASCENT **260m**

STAGE DESCENT **77m**

Route - the historic alternative route through Bains, which uses the same white-red way markings as the main GR®65, adds approximately 2.5 kilometres to Stage 1. The route is relatively flat, but is less-frequented and not as well way-marked as the main route. Particular attention should be paid when entering and exiting villages. The route is shrouded in history. Notably, the village of Fay was closely associated in the 13th century with the Knights Templar (a powerful medieval Christian military order that played a decisive role in the crusades). The Romanesque church of Saint Foy in Bains was placed under the domain of the powerful Conques Abbey, of which it bears certain artistic traits.

CULTURAL DISCOVERIES

Bains

The 12th century Romanesque Church of Saint Faith (*Eglise Sainte-Foy*) in the village of Bains (popl. 1,400, alt. 975m) is classified as a historic monument. In 1105, the church fell under the authority of the Conques Abbey, whose patron saint is also Saint Faith. It is remarkable for its ornate Roman-esque façade, including vaulted arched entrance and a stone baptismal font depicting the Virgin and the Baptism of Christ.

ROUTE INSTRUCTIONS

Waypoint	Total(km)	Directions	Verification	Compass	Altitude(m)
1	0.0	After **Tallode**, leave main road and turn right on track	Sign posts	N	928
2	0.1	Stay on track which veers to the left		W	928
3	0.5	Continue straight on track	Ignore track to the left which heads to Liac. Power lines to the right.	NW	929
4	1.4	Turn right		SW	958
5	2.0	At fork, turn left towards village	Village of Augeac to the left	W	965

6	2.1	Take first right on asphalt road towards village centre.	Red house.	NW	962
7	2.2	At end of street, turn left	Augeac village centre	W	968
8	2.4	After crossing village turn right	Pass lavoir to the right	NW	968
9	2.5	Turn right onto main road, toward Bains	Former school house on the left	NW	966
10	2.8	Leave main Champ Richard road, and keep right on the small country road. Continue straight.		NE	971
11	3.7	Turn left onto route de Jales	Bains visible to the left	W	958
12	4.4	Continue straight and cross route de Saugues/D589 and enter **Bains**	**Church of Saint Faith** straight ahead	NW	967
13	4.6	Pass church on left. Take second left onto chemin de la Garde de Moutet.	Signpost	SW	975
14	4.7	Continue straight on chemin de la Garde de Moutet, which becomes track.	Pass cemetery on the right	W	979
15	5.6	Continue straight on track	Pass red barn on the right and pine tree grove to the left	SW	1002
16	6.3	At end of road turn right	Pine grove directly behind	N	1027
17	6.5	Take sharp left towards hamlet of Fay	Pine grove visible again	SW	1030
18	7.2	Continue straight on track	Leave pastures behind	W	1025
19	7.8	Turn right onto asphalt road	Hamlet of **Fay** to the right.	W	1060
20	7.8	At fork stay to the left.	Leave village of Fay to the right. Pass Gîte du Velay on the right.	SW	1077
21	7.9	Turn left in the direction of Montbonnet (south)		S	1083
22	8.5	Continue straight on road until reaching the village of Montbonnet	Fay behind you and village of Montbonnet visible ahead.	S	1092
23	9.1	At intersection continue straight towards village of **Montbonnet**	Montbonnet visible ahead	S	1104
24	9.7	Turn right onto route de Saugues/D589 to rejoin main GR®65			1108

ACCOMODATION & TOURIST INFORMATION

Le Puy-en-Velay

Relais du Pèlerin de Saint Jacques, 28 rue Cardinal de Polignac, 43000 Le Puy-en-Velay, Haute Loire, France; +33(0)4 71 09 43 92; +33(0)6 37 08 65 83; Donation (breakfast included); Located in the old town, near the Cathedral, this hostel is run by volunteers (mostly former pilgrims). There are 27 places in dormitories and is a jump straight into the pilgrim experience.

Grand Seminaire Saint-George, 4 rue Saint Georges, 43000 Le Puy-en-Velay, Haute Loire, France; +33(0)4 71 09 93 10; grandseminaire43@live.fr; €23/1 bed, €40/2 beds, €54/3 beds, €72/4 beds. €12 breakfast and dinner (wine and coffee included); A former seminary located in the old town, a few steps from the Cathedral, it is now a catholic run institution. While in need of updating, it offers various sized rooms. Rough English spoken. Nearby park where donkeys can be kept.

Maison Saint François, 6 rue Saint-Mayol, 43000 Le Puy-en-Velay, Haute Loire, France; +33(0)4 71 05 98 86; gite.stfrancois@wanadoo.fr; €19/single room (shared WC, breakfast included), €10.50/dinner (except Thurs. and Sun.); Great location in the old town between the Cathedral and Notre Dame de France, accommodation is in a historic building run by Franciscan nuns. 19 places in single or shared rooms.

Gîte d'Étape - l'Appart Hôtel des Capucins, (Paul-Emilie and Klaus), 29 rue des Capucins, 43000 Le Puy-en-Velay, Haute Loire, France; +33(0)4 71 04 28 74; contact@lescapucins.net; www.lescapucins.net; Hostel: starting at €22.50/1 pers. (breakfast included); hotel: starting at €67/room; Commercial establishment, with 19 places in hostel and 31 rooms. English spoken.

Auberge de Jeunesse, Centre Pierre Cardinal, 9 rue Jules Vallès, 43000 Le Puy-en-Velay, Haute Loire, France; +33(0)4 71 05 52 40; auberge.jeunesse@mairie-le-puy-en-velay.fr; €15/pers. (sheets included), €4.50/ breakfast.; Entirely renovated in 2013, this modern hostel is conveniently located in the old town, below the Cathedral, and offers 50 places in various sized rooms for 2 to more than 7 persons.

Office de Tourisme, 2 place du Clauzel, 43000 Le Puy-en-Velay, Haute Loire, France; +33(0)4 71 09 38 41; info@ot-lepuyenvelay.fr; www.ot-lepuyenvelay.fr

Saint-Christophe-sur-Dolaison

Chambre d'Hôtes-Gîte de Groupe Allègre, (Family Allègre), Tallode, 43370 Saint-Christophe-sur-Dolaison, Haute Loire, France; +33(0)4 71 03 17 78; +33(0)6 18 11 38 06; Michel.allegre38@sfr.fr; B&B: €26/single room, €45/double room, Dormitory: €24/pers. (breakfast included), €14/dinner (upon reservation).; Located on a working farm, 1/2 km after Saint-Christophe-sur-Dolaison, offering 2 rooms in B&B and 14 places in dormitory. Meals are served using farm and local products. Horses welcome.

Chambre d'Hôtes le Champ de l'Oustau, (Family Chamard), Eycenac, 43370 Saint-Christophe-sur-Dolaison, Haute Loire, France; +33(0)4 71 01 51 55; +33(0)6 50 58 60 27; www.lechampdeloustau.com; €39/1 pers. €49/2 pers., €59/3 pers., €10/additional person, €18/dinner (local and farm produce); 5km from Le Puy, a B&B with 5 rooms on a working farm. Horses welcome.

Bains

Gîte du Velay, (Sylvette Piq and Laurent Debeaux), Fay, 43370 Bains, Haute Loire, France; +33(0)4 71 02 71 60; +33(0)6 47 75 96 42; sylvetteetlaurent@grand-gite.fr ; www.grand-gite.fr; Dormitory: €12.50/pers. €5/breakfast, €13/ dinner; in rooms with bedding: €28/pers., €36/2 pers., €46/3 pers., 57€/4pers., 67€/5pers., 77€/6pers.; In the charming hamlet of Fay, 38 places in rooms of 1 to 6 and dormitory (12 places). Very welcoming hosts. Laurent speaks English. Horses welcome.

Montbonnet

Gîte d'Étape Privé, (Family Gentes), La Grange-Bar le Saint-Jacques, 43370 Montbonnet, Haute Loire, France; +33(0)4 71 57 54 44; +33(0)6 20 74 47 43; christiangentes@orange.fr; www.christian.gentes.pagesperso-orange.fr/; €14/pers. €5/breakfast, €12/dinner; 15 places in 4 rooms of 3 to 4 pers. In modern and entirely renovated farmhouse.

Gîte d'Étape Privé l'Escole, (Marie-Annick Blanc), Le Bourg, 43370 Montbonnet, Haute Loire, France; +33(0)4 71 57 51 03; +33(0)6 22 71 90 09; gite@lescole.om; www.lescole.com; €13/pers. €5.50/breakfast, €31/half board; 15 places in 4 rooms of 3 or 6 pers. Kitchen. Horses welcome. English spoken.

Chambre d'Hôtes, (Géraldine Felce), La Barbelotte, 43370 Montbonnet, Haute Loire, France; +33(0)6 50 93 54 07; labarbelotte@gmail.com; www.labarbelotte.fr; €59/half board, €88/half board 2 pers. €132/half board for 3 pers., €10/horse.; 3 double and triple rooms. Horses welcome. English spoken.

Saint-Privat-d'Allier

Gîte la Cabourne, (Hélène and Christophe), Le Bourg, 43580 Saint-Privat-d'Allier, Haute Loire, France; +33(0)4 71 57 25 50; +33(0)6 23 46 03 06; jereserve@sfr.fr; www.lacabourne.fr; €40-€51/half board; Located in the village , 50 metres from the GR®65, gîte designed for pilgrims offering modern accommodation, 53 beds in rooms of 2, 4, 5, 6 pers. English spoken. Donkeys welcome.

Gîte le Kompost'l, (Mr. and Mrs. Fel.), Le Bourg, 43580 Saint-Privat-d'Allier, Haute Loire, France; +33(0)4 71 57 24 78; julien.fel1@orange.fr; www.lekompostl.fr; €13-€15/pers. €5.50/breakfast, €13/ dinner; 2 4-pers rooms.

Gîte l'Estaou, (Elfed Caradog and Pascale Pothée), Combriaux, 43580 Saint-Privat-d'Allier, Haute Loire, France; +33(0)4 71 09 58 91; +33(0)6 48 12 63 80; estaou7@gmail.com; €20/pers. (breakfast included), €10/ dinner; Located in Combriaux, 1.5km after Saint-Privat-d'Allier on the GR®65 (last house on the left). Charming house with 12 places in dormitory. English spoken (Madam Pothée is an English teacher in Le Puy). Horses welcome.

Saugues © Alexia Adamski

MARGERIDE

Margeride is a 60km mountain chain in the south-eastern part of the Massif Central. The deep gorges of the Allier river act as its natural boundary with the volcanic region of Velay to the east.

Like the Alps, Margeride is only 10 million years old, yet the granite rock from which it was formed is Hercynian, dating to the collision of the African and North-American-North European continents some 350 million years ago. Today, its landscape includes granite highlands with meadows, slopes with recent pine growth and lowland peat bogs.

The generally high elevation of Margeride (1000m) renders the climate cool, and the mountains are covered with snow during the winter months. In mid-May, the highland meadows blossom with wild white narcissus which is used in French perfumes.

The Margeride highlands, specifically Mont Mouchet (1497m), were an important centre of French resistance during the Second World War. In 1944, French resistance fighters, known as the Maquis du Mont Mouchet, fought to forestall Nazi troops in the south from converging with those in Normandy, to the north, in aid of the Allied invasion of France. Today the Mont Mouchet Resistance Museum pays tribute to this period.

Escluzels Madonna © Alexandra Huddleston

DISTANCE	**24km**
ASCENT	**882m**
DESCENT	**787m**
FROM LE PUY	**24km**
TO RONCEVAUX	**751km**

Route - The route is well marked and consists of asphalt roads, tracks and footpaths. Nevertheless this is one of the most challenging stages. The descent by footpath and road to the Allier river is steep, as is the long climb, mostly on roads, into the Margeride chain and the village of Saugues. Villages such as Roziers, Vernet and Rognac, before Saugues are typical of the region, reflecting the emphasis on agriculture and the use of porphyroid granite (granite with white felspar).

Pointers - Use caution when descending the steep footpath from Rochegude to Pratclaux, which can be muddy and slippery when wet. In case of rain, consider taking the longer (but safer) track that descends to the D301 from the village of Rochegude. **Views:** There are lovely views of the Allier river valley from Rochegude (Chapel of Saint Jacques) and when climbing to Montaure from Monistrol-d'Allier. **Advance planning:** After

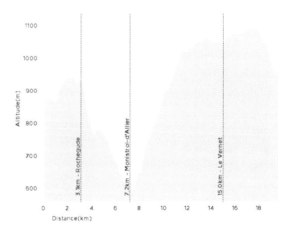

Monistrol-d'Allier, there are no cafés/restaurants/grocers until Saugues; consider buying lunch in Monistrol or ensuring provisions in Saint-Privat. **Festival:** Each August (11-13 August 2016), Saugues hosts a large Celtic festival, featuring Celtic music, crafts and foods. www.festivalengevaudan.com

Rochegude

Rochegude, Chapel of Saint James

Perched on the volcanic Déves mountains opposite Margeride, Rochegude, meaning sharp rock, dominates the Allier valley. The fortress of Rochegude, today in ruins but for an impressive 6 metre tower, was once used as a watchtower to control the trade routes that passed through the valley. Next to the fortress is the **Chapel of Saint James** (*Chapelle de Saint-Jacques*), which was built into the rock. Note also the beautiful views of the river valley and the Margeride mountain chain.

Eiffel Bridge (*Pont Eiffel*)

The Eiffel bridge is named after engineer Gustave Eiffel whose company designed and built the bridge in the late 19th century. At the time, Monistrol was growing rapidly thanks to the railway that was being built through the Allier gorge, and which is still in operation. The bridge was completed one year before the 1889 World's Fair at which the Eiffel Tower in Paris was unveiled.

Magdalene Chapel
(*Chapelle de la Madeleine*)
Built in the 17th century in a grotto below the village of Escluzels, the chapel was dedicated to Mary Magdalene, a follower of Jesus. In 1872, the tombs of several children and adults were discovered nearby. Of note is the wooden 18th century statue of Mary Magdalene and two wooden statues of Jesus and Mary Magdalene in niches built into the rock.

Saugues

Saugues (popl. 2000, alt. 960m) was an important stronghold in the historic Gévaudan, a territory of the Gabali, a Celtic people. In the 12th century, the village grew wealthy under the rule of the bishops of the city of Mende. However, all that remains of the village's medieval fortifications is the English Tower (*Tour des Anglais*), which was part of a 13th century fortress. The name "English Tower" dates to the Hundred Years' War, when in 1362 English mercenaries captured Saugues. A fire in 1788 destroyed most of the town's historic centre. The town, which was once known for its wooden carved clogs, holds a popular Celtic festival in the second week of August. A market is held on Monday and Friday mornings.

From 1764 to 1767, the famous **Beast of Gévaudan** (*Bête du Gévaudan*) terrorized the region. It was responsible for the deaths of over 100 people, mostly women and children. According to witnesses, it resembled a wolf and had enormous teeth and a sweeping tail. With public hysteria mounting, nobles, the army, civilians and even King Louis XV's huntsmen tried to hunt the animal down. But it was only after three years of terror that the beast was finally killed by Jean Chastel, a local. An animated museum, *Le Musée Fantastique de la Bête du Gévaudan,* recounts the story (in French only).

The 13th century Romanesque **Church of Saint Médard** (*Eglise Saint-Médard*) is registered as a historic monument. Of note are two wooden polychrome statues - an early 13th century statute of the Christ Child seated in the Virgin's lap, a position known as the Throne of Wisdom (*sedes sapientie*), and a 16th century pieta (a representation of Mary mourning over the dead body of Christ) in polychrome wood. There is also a shrine and statue of the patron saint of Saugues, Saint Bénilde, who dedicated his life to education and who is prayed to for healing cancer. See also the magnificent alter depicting Mary's Ascension by sculptor Pierre Vaneau (1653-1694) in the **White Penitents Chapel** (*Chapelle des Pénitents blancs*).

Waypoint	Total(km)	Directions	Verification	Compass	Altitude(m)
1	0.0	From **Saint-Privat** village centre, turn right off the road D589, with Cafe/Gîte Kompost'l to the left and continue uphill towards Garage Jobert	Le Kompost'l and Garage Jobert	N	876
2	0.1	Stay to the left around corner	Sign post	NW	875
3	0.3	Turn left onto Le Marchat path	The village of Saint-Privat is below on the left	SW	889
4	0.6	Turn right onto D301 road, leaving village of Saint-Privat behind		SW	889
5	0.7	Turn left onto foot path. Descend into the valley and cross the stream (Ruisseau de la Planchette)	After crossing under power lines. Sign posts.	W	884
6	1.0	Emerge from valley and cross road D301 road, continue straight	Sign post	SW	868
7	1.1	Turn right onto asphalt road	Head towards a brown stone house	NW	867
8	1.1	Turn left and continue straight on cobblestone road	Pass house with terrace on left	W	868
9	1.3	Turn left onto asphalt road and cross through the hamlet of **Combriaux**		SW	896
10	1.5	Leave road and turn right onto track through woods	Sign post	S	921
11	1.8	Cross road and continue straight on track		NW	928
12	2.1	Turn left onto road		SW	941
13	2.3	Turn right onto footpath	Track runs parallel to road	W	942
14	2.5	Turn right onto road	Pass under power lines	W	949
15	2.6	Turn left off road onto track		NW	943
16	3.1	Merge left onto road	Village of Rochegude visible ahead	W	932
17	3.1	In **Rochegude** centre, at château ruins and chapel, turn left	Sign post	S	939
18	3.2	Continue straight on footpath. Very steep and rocky descent.		SW	939
19	4.1	Turn left onto D301 road		NE	792
20	4.2	Turn left onto track towards hamlet of Pratclaux	Hamlet visible	E	774
21	4.3	Turn left onto asphalt road and then immediately right and cross hamlet		NE	768
22	4.6	Leave asphalt road turning right onto track	Pratclaux directly behind	S	791
23	4.7	Cross D301 road and continue straight on track		S	788
24	4.9	Turn right onto road		S	775
25	5.0	After passing brown stone house turn left onto track	Stone house to the left	S	773
26	5.3	Turn right at fork	Head towards the valley	SW	759
27	5.6	Turn left onto road and descend into Monistrol-d'Allier	Monistrol visible in valley	E	731

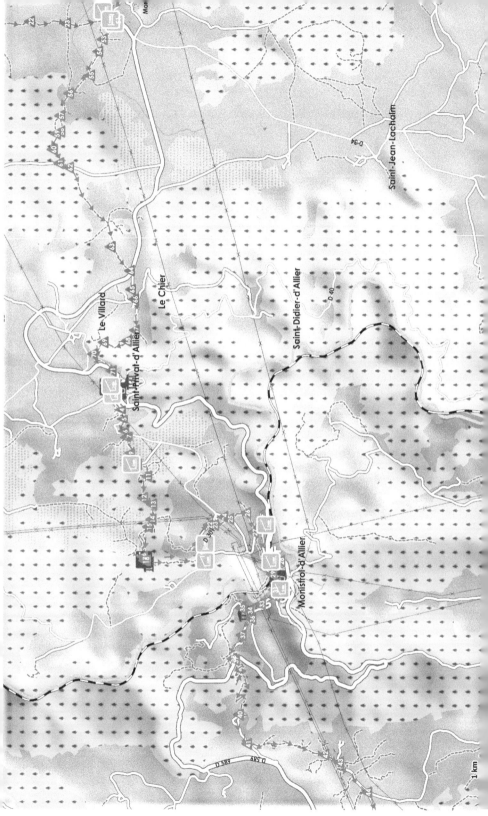

28	6.8	Take sharp right onto rue des Jacquets	Pass town hall (la Mairie) on the left	W	627
29	7.0	Cross **Eiffel Bridge** built by the Eiffel Company in 1888 over the Allier river towards village centre		SW	615
30	7.2	In the centre of **Monistrol-d'Allier** turn left onto and stay on rue des Lombards	Immediately after cafe, Le Repos du Pèlerin, on the left	SW	592
31	7.4	Turn left onto rue des Jacquets	River on right side	W	606
32	7.5	Turn right onto Montée de la Madeleine which descends towards mill. From here the main climb to the Margeride plateau begins.	Mill and stream (L'Ance)	NW	608
33	7.7	Leave road and turn right onto track, continue straight	Pass shed on the left. Beautiful river views of Monistrol to the right.	NW	605
34	8.2	Turn right rejoining asphalt road		N	663
35	8.3	Turn left onto track and climb staircase	After passing iron cross with beautiful figure of Mary on the left and the **Chapel Magdalene** on the right	W	672
36	8.6	Turn right into village of **Escluzels**, followed by another immediate right		NW	717
37	8.9	Continue ascent on road		W	738
38	9.4	Turn right off asphalt road, take short-cut and cross D589 road.	Pine forest ahead	SW	775
39	9.5	Turn right onto the serpentine path that climbs	Pine forest	SW	785
40	11.2	Enter hamlet of Montaure and continue straight on road	Village cluster to the right	W	986
41	11.7	Turn left onto track leading to Roziers.		S	1021
42	12.9	Continue straight on track	Pass under power lines	SW	1055
43	13.1	In Roziers village turn right on road and continue straight	Pass fountain	SW	1051
44	13.8	Turn right at fork in the direction of Le Vernet	Sign post	W	1065
45	15.0	Turn left in the village of **Le Vernet** and continue straight through village	Fountain	NW	1046
46	15.1	After the last houses, turn left onto track that becomes a path passing under power lines	Sign post	W	1052
47	16.7	Turn right onto road and continue straight through village of Rognac. Continue on road	Rognac visible to the right	W	1076
48	17.6	At fork stay to the left on path and continue straight to departmental road D589	Farm to the left and sign post	NW	1094
49	18.8	Cross D589 and continue straight on rue des Cimes to descend into Saugues	Wooden sculptures to the left	NW	1027
50	19.3	Stay to the left on rue des Cimes followed by immediate right onto route du Puy to enter village of Saugues	Sign Post	W	968
51	19.7	Arrive at **Saugues** centre	Office of Tourism		957

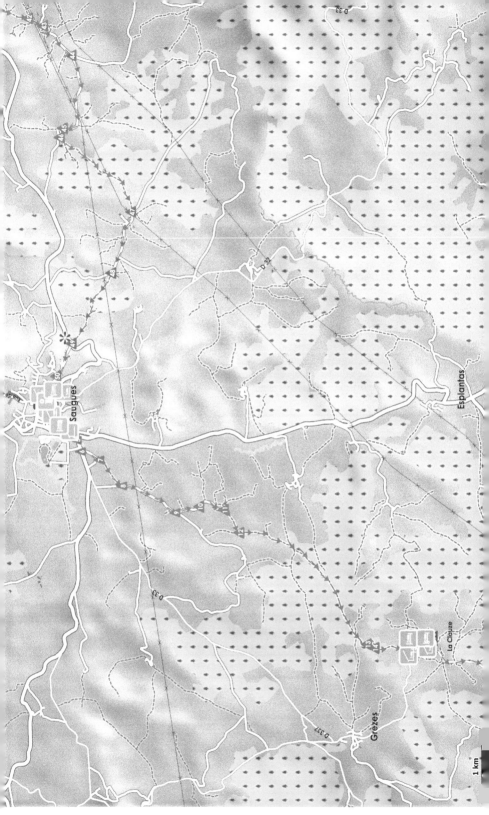

Saugues

Esplantas

La Clouze

Grèzes

D 33

D 32

D 337

D 33

1 km

Monistrol-d'Allier

Gite d'Étape au Ricochet, (Magail Peronny), Route du Gévaudan, 43580 Monistrol-d'Allier, Haute Loire, France; +33(0)4 71 57 20 97; +33(0)6 59 07 70 66; auricochet@gmail.com; www.auricochet-monistrol. com; €14/pers. €5/breakfast, €13/dinner (reservations required); 15 beds in rooms of 2 to 5 pers. The hostel underwent a recent and high quality renovation.

Gite d'Étape la Tsabone, (Patrick and Myriam Fourquet), Montée des Deux Chiens, 43580 Monistrol-d'Allier, Haute Loire, France; +33(0)4 71 06 17 23; +33(0)6 15 15 38 39; latsabone@yahoo.fr; www.latsabone.fr; €33/ half board; 12 beds. English spoken. Very welcoming. Behind the gîte is a pasture reserved for horses. Dinner is prepared using organic and local produce. Near the church.

Centre d'Accueil de Monistrol d'Allier, Route du Gévaudan, 43580 Monistrol-d'Allier, Haute Loire, France; +33(0)4 71 57 24 14; +33(0)4 71 57 21 21; www.monistroldallier.fr/gite-d-etape.php; €12/pers. €6/breakfast, €13/dinner; Comfortable, well equipped gîte, located about 200m from the GR®65. Kitchen. Horses welcome.

Gîte de la Ribeyre, (Christelle and Stéphane Robert), Pratclaux, 43580 Monistrol-d'Allier, Haute Loire, France; +33(0)6 63 46 37 09; stephane.robert.4@cegetel.net; www.gitedelaribeyre.com; €34/half board; A former barn (grange) tastefully converted with modern facilities. 13 beds in 3 rooms. Kitchen.

Saugues

Gîte a la Croisée des Chemins, (Patrick and Catherine Edon), 33 rue Alexandre Borde, 43170 Saugues, Haute Loire, France; +33(0)4 71 76 96 61; +33(0)6 42 03 53 91; patrick.edon@wanadoo.fr; Donation (breakfast and dinner included); Welcoming hosts (former pilgrims). 7 beds in rooms of 3 to 4 persons. Closed Sundays in July and August. Located upon leaving the village, approximately 200m off the GR. Large kitchen.

Gîte À la Ferme Itier-Martins, (Brigitte and Jacky Martins), Rue des Roches, 43170 Saugues, Haute Loire, France; +33(0)4 71 77 83 45; €37/half board; The gîte with 6 rooms is set apart from a working farm and main house. Beautiful views of the countryside, family atmosphere and meals made from farm products. Horses welcome.

Gîte d'Étape Communal de Saugues, 8 rue de la Margeride, 43170 Saugues, Haute Loire, France; +33(0)4 71 77 80 62; +33(0)6 65 15 04 32; campingsaugues@saugues.fr; €12/pers.; 15 beds in shared rooms of 5 maximum. Comfortable and recently renovated. Kitchen. English spoken.

La Margeride, Centre d'Hébergement et d'Activités, 8 rue des Tours Neuves, 43170 Saugues, Haute Loire, France; +33(0)4 71 77 60 97; info.lamargeride@wanadoo.fr; www.lamargeride.com; €15/pers. €6/breakfast, €12/dinner, €33/half board; 40 places in rooms of 2 to 5. Take first right after the post office. Kitchen. English spoken. Accommodation for horses can be arranged.

Chambre d'Hôtes l'Arc en Ciel, (Boris and Sandrine Dubourg), 1 rue du Mont Mouchet, 43170 Saugues, Haute Loire, France; +33(0)4 71 77 68 60; +33(0)6 19 19 29 45; san1@orange.fr; www. chambredhotearcenciel.jimdo.com; €28/pers. (breakfast included), €45/half board; Very welcoming. English spoken. 3 rooms (1 double and 2 triple). Dinner prepared using local products. Horses welcome.

Chambre d'Hôtes les Gabales, (Patricia and Maurice Gonneaud), 70 avenue Lucien Gires, 43170 Saugues, Haute Loire, France; +33(0)4 71 77 86 92; info@lesgabales.com; www.lesgabales.com; €79/pers. €104/2 pers., €150/3 pers., €200/4 pers. (with breakfast and dinner included); A charming B&B in a 1930s manor house with a lovely French garden, and 5 guest rooms of various sizes. Dinner recommended.

Office de Tourisme, Cours Gervais, 43170 Saugues, Haute Loire, France; +33(0)4 71 77 71 38; ot.saugues@ haut-allier.com; www.paysdesaugues.com/tourisme.php

stage 3

DISTANCE **19.5km**

ASCENT **719m**

DESCENT **396m**

FROM LE PUY **43km**

TO RONCEVAUX **731km**

Saugues © Alexandra Huddleston

Route - The route, which is well marked, consists mostly of rocky tracks and asphalt roads that climb and descend the largely barren landscape of the Margeride, crossing cattle pastures and pine forests until arriving at the monumental farm of Le Sauvage.

Pointers - **Reservations:** Accommodation at Domaine du Sauvage should be booked in advance, as space is limited.

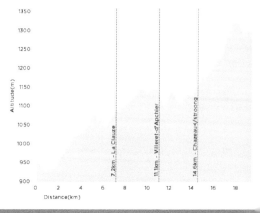

CULTURAL DISCOVERIES

La Clauze

The tower of La Clauze, which is registered as a historical monument, is a rare octagonal tower perched on a granite block (without foundation). It is the remains of a fortress from the 14th century and an excellent example of regional medieval military architecture.

Villeret-d'Apchier

In the lower village is a natural spring (*Source Saint-Pierre*) dedicated to Saint Peter (one of Jesus' 12 disciples and the leader of the early Christian church), which was famous for its miraculous ability to heal eyes.

Domaine du Sauvage

The Domaine du Sauvage, with its imposing granite buildings, was used as a farm throughout the Middle Ages. Today, the Domaine is owned by the Department of Haute-Loire and operates as a farm, hostel and store/restaurant run by a cooperative of 40 farmers from the Margeride.

Forest before Le Sauvage © Alexandra Huddleston

ROUTE INSTRUCTIONS

Waypoint	Total(km)	Directions	Verification	Compass	Altitude(m)
1	0.0	In **Saugues**, with the Office of Tourism to the right continue straight on departmental road D589	Fountain and Office of Tourism on the right	W	958
2	0.1	Stay to left on D589 through village		SW	959
3	0.4	At fork stay to right on D589	Carved wooden mushroom sculptures on the left	SW	963
4	0.7	At roundabout continue straight on D589	Roundabout	SW	936
5	0.8	Cross bridge over La Seuge river and continue straight	Bridge	W	934
6	0.9	Take first left on chemin de Saint Jacques also known as chemin du Pinet	Opposite large wooden pilgrim statue	S	928
7	1.2	Continue straight on track	Leave houses on the right behind you	S	932
8	1.7	At the end of the track turn left onto asphalt road leading towards hamlet of Pinet		S	936
9	2.6	At fork with iron cross bear left towards Le Pinet	Sign post and cross	S	980

10	3.0	Enter Le Pinet		SE	992
11	3.4	Stay to the right, leaving village behind, and continue straight on track	Village behind	SW	1017
12	3.8	Follow road to the left heading towards pine grove	Pine grove	S	1022
13	6.5	Leave main track and turn right on footpath climbing hill		S	1046
14	6.6	Rejoin track and continue straight		SW	1055
15	7.2	Enter village of **La Clauze** and continue straight on the road towards the tower of La CLauze	Sign post	S	1090
16	7.4	Merge onto main road D335 and continue straight to leave village	**Tower of La Clauze** visible on the left	SE	1094
17	9.3	At fork stay left on the smaller road, direction Le Falzet	Sign post	S	1150
18	9.9	Enter village of Le Falzet, continuing straight on road		S	1144
19	10.2	Continue straight on road leaving behind Le Falzet		S	1139
20	10.3	At road's end turn left onto departmental road D335	Sign post	SE	1136
21	10.4	After a short climb, take first right onto track and continue straight		SE	1141
22	11.1	Enter village of **Villeret-d'Apchier** and continue straight on road		S	1147
23	11.3	At end of road in village centre turn right and immediately left crossing the D587 and continue straight through village	Sign post. Pass Auberge des 2 Pèlerins on the right	S	1134
24	11.3	At bottom of steep hill and end of road turn left		E	1131
25	11.4	Turn right, staying on road and continue straight	Sign post	S	1126
26	12.1	After steep climb reach intersection of roads and turn right	Sign post	W	1136
27	12.9	At end of track turn left and continue straight, climbing	Road passes between 2 houses. Hamlet of La Virlange	S	1112
28	13.8	At end of track turn right	Pass farm	S	1133
29	14.0	Leave road, staying to the left on track	Power lines to the right	S	1129
30	14.6	Enter hamlet of **Chazeau**		S	1152
31	14.7	Turn left in village centre and continue straight (climb)	Pass Chez Jerome	NE	1156
32	14.8	Stay right leaving village behind		SE	1160
33	15.1	Cross department road D34 and continue straight on track	Sign post	S	1176
34	15.6	Leave larger track and turn left to ascend hill		SE	1182
35	17.5	Pass through cattle gate turn left and continue ascent	Cattle gate	E	1293
36	17.6	Turn right on track through pine grove		SE	1306
37	18.2	Pass through the second gate and continue on the track. Turn right towards Le Sauvage.	Monumental farm of Le Sauvage visible	S	1323
38	19.4	Enter grounds of Farm Le Sauvage.		W	1298
39	19.5	Arrive at **Le Sauvage**			1297

La Clauze

Gîte d'Étape le Refuge des Pèlerins de Margeride, (Michèle and Michel Estrade), La Clauze, 43170 Grèzes, Haute Loire, France; +33(0)6 81 20 66 08; www.chemindecompostelle.com/estrade/index.html; €12/pers. €5/breakfast, €12/dinner, €26/half board; 6 places in two dormitories in a lovely old stone house typical of the Margeride region.

Gîte et Chambres d'Hôtes À la Ferme au Repos d'Antan, (Sonia and Michel Vidal), La Clauze, 43170 Grèzes, Haute Loire, France; +33(0)4 71 77 66 56; +33(0)6 66 47 67 18; sonia.vidal@orange.fr; www.au-repos-d-antan.sitew.com; €37/half board; A former farm, with 4 guest rooms and a Finish pine hut for 2. Relaxed atmosphere. Dinner prepared with farm products, which may include *truffade* (a local dish made with potatoes and cheese).

Chambre d'Hôtes À la Coustette de La Clauze, (Brigitte and Bernard Guinand), La Clauze, 43170 Grèzes, Haute Loire, France; +33(0)9 82 57 45 88; +33(0)6 78 17 18 27; brigitte@autour-de-la-clauze.fr; www.autour-de-la-clauze.fr; €74/pers. €79/2 pers., €102/3 pers., €24/dinner.; 5 rooms. Remarkable for its location at the foot of the famous 14th century octagonal tower.

Chanaleilles

Accueil À la Ferme Delcros, (Marinette and Germain Delcros), Le Falzet, 43170 Chanaleilles, Haute Loire, France; +33(0)4 71 74 42 28; €15/pers. €5/breakfast, €32/half board; A separate building on a working farm has 7 places in 3 shared rooms. English spoken. Kitchen. Dinner, made with farm products. Horses welcome.

Gîte d'Etape l'Auberge des 2 Pèlerins, (Lucette and Jean-Louis Bouffar-Roupé), Le Villeret-d'Apcher, 43170 Chanaleilles, Haute Loire, France; +33(0)6 07 28 06 44; jean-louis.bouffar-roupe@wanadoo.fr; www.aubergedes2pelerins.com; €15/pers. €6/breakfast, €32/half board, €3/horse; A welcoming hostel run by two former pilgrims who are members of a choral group and love singing. Kitchen. Accommodation for horses.

Domaine du Sauvage - Ferme Auberge, (Mrs. Eliane Chausse), Domaine du Sauvage, 43170 Chanaleilles, Haute Loire, France; +33(0)4 71 74 40 30; +33(0)6 66 12 92 25; domainedusauvage@orange.fr; www.sauvage-en-gevaudan.fr/; €16/pers. €34/half board, €7.50/breakfast, €14.50/dinner; Operated by a collective of farmers who have revived this historical site. Once a Templar farm, it was later bought by the Hotel Dieu of Puy-en-Velay to accommodate pilgrims. Farm products are featured. English spoken. Accommodation for horses. Kitchen.

Breakfast Domaine du Sauvage © Alexandra Huddleston

DISTANCE **21.0km**

ASCENT **478m**

DESCENT **829m**

FROM LE PUY **63km**

TO RONCEVAUX **712km**

Leaving Le Sauvage © Alexandra Huddleston

Route - The route, which is well marked, consists mostly of asphalt roads and tracks, as it continues to cross the Margeride. Shortly after the farm of Le Sauvage, the route reaches one of its highest altitudes, the Hospitalet ridge (1,304 metres). The Chapel of Saint Roch, with its magnificent views, marks the boundary between the Haute-Loire and Lozère departments.

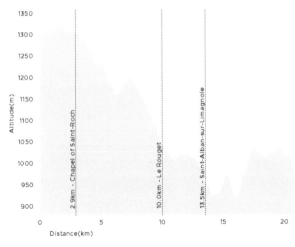

Pointers - Between Le Sauvage and Le Rouget, be careful to stay on the GR®65, as opposed to the GR®4 (Tour of Margeride), which uses the same red/white way markings and which intersects twice with the GR®65. **Caution:** There are two steep descents: into Le Rouget, which can be slippery when wet, and in the forest before Estrets. Use caution. **Advance planning:** Do any necessary food shopping in Saint-Alban-sur-Limagnole, as the next grocers are in Aumont-Aubrac. Accordingly, there are no grocers or restaurants in Les Estrets, though meals can be reserved with accommodation.

Col de l'Hospitalet and the Saint Roch Chapel (*Chapelle de Saint-Roch*)

Saint Roch Chapel © Alexandra Huddleston

In 1198, a hospital for pilgrims and travellers crossing the barren highlands was founded on the hill, Col de l'Hospitalet. The hospital and chapel, dedicated to Saint James, were under the protection of the Knights Templar (a Christian military order that came to prominence in the Middle Ages). While there is no vestige of the hospital, both a natural spring, purported to have healing properties, and a chapel that was constructed at the end of the 19th century, are dedicated to Saint Roch and bear remembrance to the former hospital. The current chapel was reconstructed in 1901.

Le Rouget

The name "Rouget" is derived from *rouge,* or red in French, which is the colour of the sandstone that was used to build the houses, walls and crosses of the village. In this region, including in St-Alban-sur-Limagnole, it is the most commonly used stone.

Church of Saint Alban (*Eglise paroissiale Saint-Alban*)

Saint-Alban-sur-Limagnole (popl. 1450, alt. 950m) was the site of a medieval fortress in the Middle Ages and was one of eight fiefdoms of the Gévaudan. The village's 12th century red sandstone and granite church, which was likely part of a former monastery, is dedicated to Saint Alban, the first English Christian martyr. The oldest part of the church is the choir, which has lovely Romanesque sculpted capitals.

Les Estrets

During the Middle Ages, Les Estrets was a command post for the Knights of Malta (a medieval Christian military order), whose presence in the village is mentioned as early as 1266. The command post was strategically located on the Truyère river at the edge of the Aubrac plateau. The current church, which was built in the second half of the 19th century, is made out of granite and incorporated certain elements of the original medieval priory of the Knights of Malta.

Saint Roch Fountain © Alexandra Huddleston

Waypoint	Total(km)	Directions	Verification	Compass	Altitude(m)
1	0.0	From the entrance of **Le Sauvage** turn right and regain the track to leave the Domaine		SE	1296
2	0.1	At fork turn right and continue straight on track	Turn into forest grove	W	1292
3	0.7	Stay to the right on principal road and continue straight	Forest grove will be to your left	W	1305
4	1.5	Merge left onto track and continue straight through forest	Cross hill Col de l'Hospitalet (1304m)	NW	1312
5	2.9	Turn left onto departmental road D587 and continue straight until the **Chapel of Saint-Roch**		W	1312
6	3.5	Enter department of Lozere	Sign post	SW	1297
7	3.7	Keep on the D587/D987 and continue straight in the direction of Lajo	Sign post	SW	1297
8	3.8	At bend in the road, turn left off the D987 onto a track that descends	Track runs largely parallel to the D987 which is to the right	SW	1284
9	5.4	Cross the D987 and continue straight on track	Sign post	SW	1216
10	6.1	At intersection of tracks continue straight	Head towards pine forest and cross stream (Ruisseau de Gazamas)	W	1174
11	6.8	At intersection of tracks continue straight		SW	1186
12	7.5	Keep left/straight as the track merges with another track		S	1204
13	8.0	At fork keep right	Pass through pine forest	SW	1180
14	9.1	At end of track turn right	Sign post	NW	1120
15	9.7	Enter village of Le Rouget		W	1081
16	9.8	Turn left to cross the D987 and then keep right	Watering point on the right	SW	1061
17	10.0	At end of road in **Le Rouget** turn left	Sign post	SW	1054
18	10.2	Turn right onto asphalt road	Pass wooden barn and pass under power lines ahead	S	1044
19	10.8	At fork keep right towards road D987	Pass stone cross	SW	1018
20	11.6	Turn left onto D987	Head towards village of Saint-Alban-sur-Limagnole	S	1025
21	11.7	At fork turn left off D987 onto smaller road - rue des Quatre Vents	Sign post "Hôpital" and pass stone cross on the right	S	1023
22	12.4	Turn right	Signposts for village centre and Office of Tourism	SW	1018
23	12.6	Turn left on rue Beau Soleil	Cross through hospital complex, Centre Hospitalier François-Tosquelles	S	1012
24	12.8	Turn right onto rue de l'Hôpital and descend to village centre	End of hospital complex	S	1012
25	13.3	At end of the road turn left onto main street - Grand Rue	Café de la Paix on right	SW	980
26	13.4	Continue straight on Grand Rue	Towards village centre	S	975
27	13.5	In **Saint-Alban-sur-Limagnole** turn right off Grand Rue into square in front of the church	Place de l'Eglise	NW	968

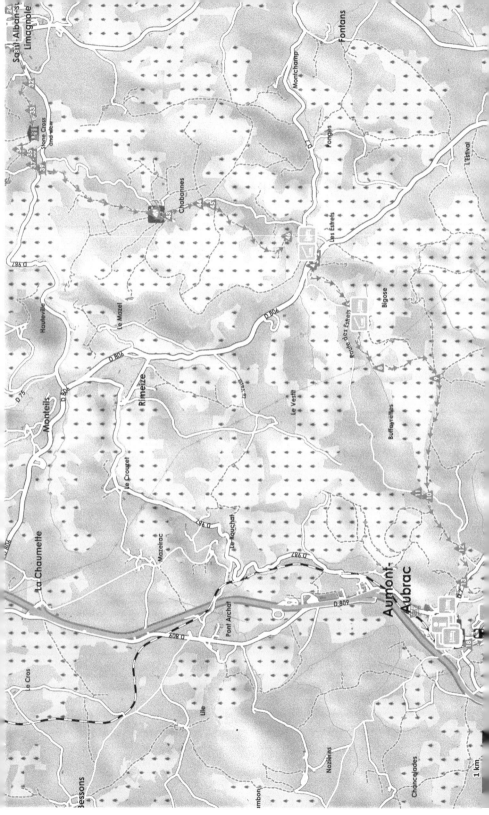

28	13.5	In Place de l'Eglise turn right to pass church on right	**Church of Saint Alban**	NW	968
29	13.6	After church, turn left onto rue de la Tournelle	School ahead and iron cross to the right	W	964
30	13.6	Turn left into Place du Breuil	Pass Auberge Saint-Jacques on left. Town hall (*Mairie*) ahead.	SW	960
31	13.9	At end of road turn right onto D987/ avenue de Saint-Chèly-d'Apcher		SW	949
32	14.4	Turn right off D987 onto track	Sports complex to the right	N	928
33	14.9	At fork keep right, climbing towards hill top	Stone cross to the right	W	946
34	15.6	Follow road taking a sharp left and de-scend into hamlet of Grazières-Mages		S	963
35	15.8	After descent, and at road's end turn left		SW	950
36	15.8	Turn right and leave hamlet	Iron cross	W	943
37	16.0	Turn left and cross the La Limagnole stream	Stream	SW	925
38	16.1	Cross the D987 and continue straight on path (steep climb)	Sign post	W	918
39	16.1	Stay on path which veers right direc-tion Les Estrets	Signposts	NW	917
40	18.1	Enter hamlet of Chabanes-Planes		S	1024
41	18.1	Turn right onto road	Head in direction of village centre	SW	1023
42	18.1	Continue straight on road which goes around the village	Picnic area and watering point on left	W	1024
43	18.4	Leave hamlet of Chabanes-Planes and continue straight on road	Cross on right	SE	1017
44	18.9	Turn right off road onto track	Sign post	S	1029
45	19.1	Turn right onto second track and con-tinue straight		SW	1030
46	20.6	Keep to left on forest path and use caution in steep and rocky descent into Les Estrets		E	1021
47	20.9	At end of path, turn right into the vil-lage of Les Estrets, and then turn left.	Church	S	973
48	20.9	Turn right onto D7 road and continue straight to village centre	Head in direction of church	W	956
49	21.0	Arrive at **Les Estrets** village centre	Church		948

ACCOMODATION & TOURIST INFORMATION

Saint-Alban-sur-Limagnole

Accueil Bénévole Familial la Maison du Pèlerin, (Françoise and Jean-Marc Connan), 37 Grand rue, 48120 Saint-Alban-sur-Limagnole, Lozère, France; +33(0)4 66 45 74 33; rai.connan@orange.fr (reservations not taken by e-mail); www.lamaisondupelerin.over-blog.com; Half board with donation.; A couple, both former pilgrims, welcome you in their home with garden (and a dog and cat) offering 12 places in 3 rooms. English spoken. Shared family meal.
Gîte de l'Europe-Snack-Bar, (Philippe Parent), 30 Grand rue, 48120 Saint-Alban-sur-Limagnole, Lozère, France; +33(0)4 66 31 15 82; +33(0)6 81 14 81 78; philippeparent48@orange.fr; www.gite-leurope-margeride.com; €15-€20/pers. €7/breakfast; Centrally located commercial establishment. 22 places in 6 rooms.

Gîte d'Étape À la Ferme la Croix du Plô, (Valérie and Maurice Pic), Le Rouget, 48120 Saint-Alban-sur-Limagnole, Lozère, France; +33(0)4 66 31 53 51; +33(0)6 33 55 61 03; €15/pers. €5/breakfast, €30/half board. The welcome is warm on this working dairy farm. Accommodation is on the first floor of a converted barn, 12 places in 3 rooms, with beautiful views of the wooded landscape. Local produce is on the menu. Accommodation for horses. English spoken.

Chambre d'Hôtes les Drailles de la Margeride, (Véronique and Alain Trauchessec), 1 Grand rue, 48120 Saint-Alban-sur-Limagnole, Lozère, France; +33(0)6 70 11 20 54; drailles.margeride@gmail.com; www. lesdraillesmargeride.wix.com/site; €55/half board, €90/half board 2. pers.; Former presbytery recently renovated and converted into an excellent B&B with a peaceful garden. Dinner consists of regional specialities 5 bedrooms, accommodating 13 people. English spoken.

Chambres d'Hôtes-Gîte sur le Chemin-Lou Carreirou, (Marie-Hélène Soubiran), Route de Mende, 48120 Saint-Alban-sur-Limagnole, Lozère, France; +33(0)4 66 31 53 03; +33(0)6 37 10 96 18; marieh48@orange.fr; www.cybevasion.fr/go_annonce.php?id_annonce=7579&from_source=chambres-hotes.fr; €25.50/pers. €48.40/2 pers., €60.60/3 pers. (breakfast included).; Located about 250m from the GR (opposite the post office). A spacious and comfortable B&B, with a welcoming host willing to share her local knowledge of the region. 10 beds in 5 rooms. English spoken. Horses welcome.

Hôtel Relais Saint-Roch, (Marie-Thérèse and Christian Chavignon), Château de la Chastre, Chemin du Carreirou, 48120 Saint-Alban-sur-Limagnole, Lozère, France; +33(0)4 66 31 55 48; rsr@relais-saint-roch.fr; www.relais-saint-roch.fr/; €106-€144/1-2 pers. 20% discount available to pilgrims. €25-€78/dinner served at the restaurant opposite the hotel, La Petite Maison.; 9 rooms in a 19th century pink granite castle with gardens and heated swimming pool. A three-star hotel, which welcomes guests with a glass of champagne. English spoken. Accommodation for horses possible.

Office de Tourisme, Rue de l Hôpital, 48120 Saint-Alban-sur-Limagnole, Lozère, France; +33(0)4 66 31 57 01; ot.stalban@gmail.com; www.ot-saint-alban-sur-limagnole.fr

Les Estrets

Le Gévaudan, (Pascal Rousset), Les Estrets, 48700 Fontans, Lozère, France; +33(0)4 66 45 61 90; +33(0)6 88 90 97 89; pas.rousset@orange.fr; www.legevaudan-gite-chambre.com; Hostel: €35/half board; B&B: €96/half board and double room; A recently renovated, welcoming and calm gîte in the historic granite village of Estrets. The B&B includes 3 2-3 pers. rooms and the hostel includes 3 4-pers. rooms and a dormitory for 8. Accommodation for horses. English spoken.

Bigose

Les Granges de, Bigose (Benoit Castarède), Bigose, 48200 Rimeize, Lozère, France; +33(0)4 66 47 12 65; contact@grangesbigose.com; www.grangesbigose.com; B&B: €114/half board and double room, Hostel: €39/half board; 1.5 km after Estrets on the GR®65, 30 places in a restored farmhouse bordering pastures and a creek. English spoken. Horses welcome. Aligot, a typical potato and cheese dish, is served at dinner.

Buron © Alexandra Huddleston

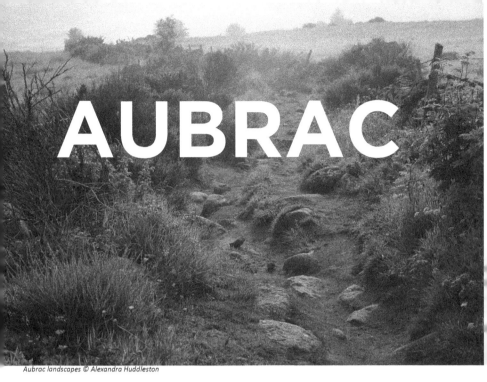

AUBRAC

Aubrac landscapes © Alexandra Huddleston

Aubrac is a sparsely populated high volcanic and granite plateau (average elevation 1200 metres) that is about 40km long and 20km wide, extending from the Truyère river in the north to the Lot river in the south. Like the Margeride, its rock base is granite, however, it was covered by fluid volcanic lava several metres deep some 6 to 9 million years ago.

This high plateau, which is covered with pastures, leads into thick beech and oak forests as it descends into the Lot river valley. The plateau boasts some 50,000 head of cattle. The beige long-horned Aubrac is the most common breed, and its sure-footedness makes it well-adapted to the terrain. While today the Aubrac breed is considered foremost for its highly prized meat, it was originally bred for dairy, which was traditionally prepared into cheese in *burons,* the shale and basalt huts

that can be seen in some pastures. Certain cheeses are still produced in Aubrac, the most famous being *Laguiole.* The region is also known for its knife industry, notably the *Forge de Laguiole* (the main factory was designed by Philippe Starck) where local craftsmen use traditional techniques to make knives. The climate in Aubrac is mountainous, with snow covering the plateau in winter, and Spring bringing an explosion of native flowers, including wild narcissus and orchids.

On 25 May, the feast day of Saint Urbain, cattle are driven from the valleys onto the plateau, where they stay through the feast day of Saint Géraud on 13 October. The spring cattle drive, known as the *transhumance,* is the occasion of a popular and colourful celebration, in which cattle are decorated with flowers.

Aubrac landscapes © Alexandra Huddleston

The Via Podiensis crosses Aubrac for approximately 45 kilometres; the section between Nasbinals and Saint-Chély-d'Aubrac is listed as a UNESCO world heritage site.

LES ESTRETS TO FINIEYROLS

DISTANCE	24km
ASCENT	679m
DESCENT	417m
FROM LE PUY	84km
TO RONCEVAUX	691km

Cross in Aubrac © Alexandra Huddleston

Route - The route, which is well marked, consists mostly of tracks and asphalt roads and footpaths. After Aumont-Aubrac, the route climbs and descends pastures and pine forests before entering the solitary and exposed Aubrac plateau, after Les Quatre Chemins.

Pointers - **Advance planning:** Do any necessary food shopping in Aumont-Aubrac, as there are no grocers until Nasbinals. Accordingly, there are also no grocers or restaurants in Finieyrols, though meals can be reserved with accommodation. **Caution:** Ensure that you stay on the GR®65, as the GR®, Tour of the Aubrac Hills, which uses the red/yellow way markings intersects with the GR®65 in Aumont-Aubrac. **Reservations:** The Fête de la Transhumance, the celebration that marks the driving of cattle from the valleys to the Aubrac plateau for the summer, occurs each year at the end of May

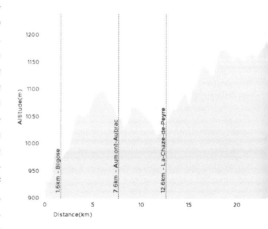

(22 May 2016) and attracts almost 15,000 visitors a year. During this long weekend, accommodation between Aumont-Aubrac and Saint-Chely-d'Aubrac may be scarce. Best to reserve in advance.

Aumont-Aubrac

Aumont-Aubrac church

The village of Aumont-Aubrac (popl. 1100, alt. 1000m) developed around a fortified priory founded by the Barons of Peyre (one of eight fiefdoms in Gévaudan). The Church of Saint Stephen (*Eglise Saint-Étienne*) was built around the 12th century, and was thereafter extensively renovated. Certain Romanesque elements can be seen on the eastern side of the church. The village holds a market every Friday morning (Place du Foirail).

La Chaze-de-Peyre

La Chaze-de-Peyre (popl. 300, alt. 1040), which means house of stone, has a church dating from the 12th century with an impressive granite bell tower. One kilometre after the village, is the lovely **Bastide Chapel** (*Chapelle de Bastide*), named after the Bastide de Grandvialia family who contributed to the chapel's renovation in the 18th century. The original structure, built in 1522, was remodelled over the centuries and is now dedicated to the Our Lady of La Salette (commemorating Mary's apparition to two children at La Salette-Fallavaux, France in 1846).

Bastide Chapel © Alexandra Huddleston

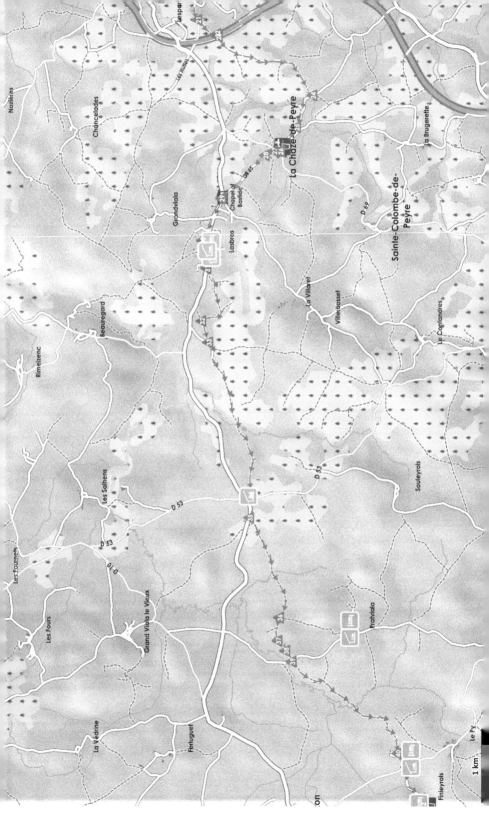

Waypoint	Total(km)	Directions	Verification	Compass	Altitude(m)
1	0.0	In **Les Estrets**, with the church on the right, continue straight on D7 road.	Church on the right and iron cross on the left.	W	947
2	0.3	Cross the D806 road and turn right at end of the road	Signpost	SW	933
3	0.4	Continue straight and cross bridge over the La Truyère river	Bridge and signpost	NW	931
4	0.5	Turn left onto track, the historic road to Aubrac, and climb	Pass between two large stone buildings	W	930
5	1.4	Turn left onto the road towards the village of Bigose	Iron cross	SW	996
6	1.6	Enter village of **Bigose** and keep right on the road		W	985
7	1.6	Before Grange de Bigose, turn right onto track	Café	W	981
8	2.6	Continue straight, climbing, on path passing along pine grove.		SE	988
9	3.6	Leave pine forest and continue straight on track	Track runs alongside forest to the right	SW	1055
10	5.3	At end of track turn right onto D7 road	Signpost	N	1091
11	5.5	Turn left onto track direction Aumont-Aubrac	Signpost	SW	1092
12	6.5	Keep right on track	D7 road to the left	W	1089
13	7.0	Turn right onto main road (D7) in the direction of the village centre		NW	1075
14	7.5	Turn right and descend small flight of stairs. Walk down rue du Barry Haut	Pass La Ferme du Barry B&B	NW	1059

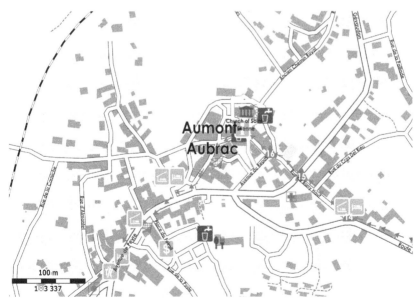

15	7.6	Cross D809 (avenue du Gévaudan) and continue straight	Iron cross on left	NW	1059
16	7.6	At fork in the centre of **Aumont-Au-brac** stay left on rue du Prieuré, climb. Reach the central square (Place du Portail) and turn right onto D809 road.	Church to the right. Pass office of tourism on the right	W	1055
17	7.9	Turn right onto D987 road	Pass fountain on the right. War monument to the left.	SW	1050
18	8.2	Pass under railway tracks and turn left onto chemin de la Gazelle	Railway tracks to the left	SW	1043
19	8.6	Turn right onto the track that ascends hill	Signpost	SW	1039
20	9.0	Turn right onto road chemin de Beau-regard	New housing development "Beauregard" on the left	W	1070
21	9.4	Leave Aumont-Aubrac and turn left onto track	Signpost and pass beige wall	SW	1069
22	9.7	Turn right and go through underpass beneath highway A75	Underpass	W	1063
23	9.8	Turn right after underpass, and then take first left and continue straight on track		NW	1063
24	11.6	Leave track and turn right onto asphalt road direction La Chaze-de-Peyre	Signpost	N	1023
25	12.1	At fork keep right to enter village of La Chaze-de-Peyre	Cemetery to the right	NW	1022
26	12.6	In **La-Chaze-de-Peyre** keep right on D69 road	Church on right and War Me-morial	N	1042
27	12.7	At fork keep left , direction of Lasbros	Iron cross	N	1043
28	12.8	Leave village of La Chaze-de-Peyre. Continue straight on road.	Signpost	NW	1046
29	13.7	Turn left onto D987 and continue straight	Pass the **Chapel of the Bastide** to the right	W	1066
30	14.4	Enter village of **Lasbros** and continue straight on D987	Signpost	W	1088
31	14.8	After leaving village of Lasbros, turn left onto road that descends	Small stone cross (right)	W	1091
32	15.8	At end of road turn left and climb hill		W	1111
33	16.1	Turn left onto asphalt road direc-tion **Quatre-Chemins** and continue straight.	Signpost. Thereafter cross the stream (Riou Frech)	SW	1128
34	18.4	Cross D53 road and continue straight past small iron cross to merge left onto the D987 road	Iron cross. Pass Chez Regine on left.	W	1174
35	18.7	Turn left onto path that passes through pine forest	Wooden gates	SW	1172
36	20.3	Continue straight on track		NW	1156
37	20.6	Pass through gate and continue straight on path	Gate	SW	1156
38	20.8	Pass through second gate and contin-ue straight on path	Gate	SW	1155
39	21.0	Cross road (La Bouge del Prat) and continue straight on path through cow pastures.	Stone Mill "Moulin de la Folle" to the right	SW	1158
40	23.2	Continue straight on the road		SW	1190
41	23.4	Cross D73/Vierge de Fineyrols and continue straight on road		W	1193
42	24.0	Arrive at **Finieyrols**	La Rose de l'Aubrac on the left		1198

Aumont-Aubrac

Gite Chemin Faisant, (Annie Lautard), 15 avenue du Peyre, 48130 Aumont-Aubrac, Lozère, France; +33(0)3 62 48 31 93 6; annie.lautard@live.fr; €15/pers. €5/breakfast; Recently renovated, 14 places in 5 rooms, fully equipped kitchen. English spoken. Good value. Possibility to accommodate horses.

La Ferme du Barry, (Vincent Boussuge), 9 rue du Barry, 48130 Aumont-Aubrac, Lozère, France; +33(0)4 66 42 90 25; +33(0)6 71 83 17 46; fermedubarry@yahoo.fr; www.ferme-du-barry.com; €15/pers. €16/ dinner, €34-€40/half board, B&B:€56/double room; Accommodation on a restored farm, famous for the meal prepared by host Vincent, namely the *aligot* (a cheese and potato dish). Opt for half board. Hostel has 24 places in rooms of 2 to 5 persons. B&B has one room. English spoken.

Les Sentiers Fleuris, (Christianne nd André Gibelin), 7 place du Portial, 48130 Aumont-Aubrac, Lozère, France; +33(0)4 66 42 94 70; +33(0)6 42 64 80 02; sentiersfleuris48@yahoo.fr; www.sentiers-fleuris. com; Hostel: €42/half board, B&B: €52/half board; Centrally located next to town hall, well known for its home-made *aligot* (a cheese and potato dish). 20 places located in rooms of 2 to 3. Accommodation for horses.

Hotel-Restaurant Chez Camillou, 10 route du Languedoc, 48130 Aumont-Aubrac, Lozère, France; +33(0)4 66 42 80 22; chezcamillou@wanadoo.fr; www.camillou.com; €92- €149/room (varying sizes), €11.50/breakfast buffet, €24-€36/dinner (in the bistro).; Lovely 3-star hotel located a walk from the city centre is reputed for its comfortable rooms, attentive staff and Michelin starred restaurant (reservations required). Outdoor swimming pool. English spoken.

Hotel-Restaurant Prunieres, Place du Relais, 48130 Aumont-Aubrac, Lozère, France; +33(0)4 66 42 85 52; hotelprunieres@gmail.com; www.hotelpruniers.free.fr/; €68-€70/double room, €9/breakfast, €15-€30/ dinner; Centrally located on the GR®65 with a welcoming staff. 40 rooms. English spoken.

Office de Tourisme, Rue du Prieuré, 48130 Aumont-Aubrac, Lozère, France; +33(0)4 66 42 88 70; www.ot-aumont-aubrac.fr

La-Chaze-de-Peyre

Bar Chez Régine, (Mrs. Régine Souliér), Les Quatre Chemins, 48130 La-Chaze-de-Peyre, Lozère, France; +33(0)4 66 42 83 36; €16/pers. (breakfast included); An iconic stop of the GR®65, known for the charismatic owner, Régine. 8 places in 2 or 4 person rooms.

Le Champ du Théron, (Mr. Roger Brochot), Lasbros, 48130 La-Chaze-de-Peyre, Lozère, France; +33(0)4 66 31 01 45; +33(0)6 61 55 92 17; lolaquentin_21@hotmail.fr; €17/pers.; €5/breakfast; €5/sheets; €35/half board.; Bungalow with 4 places in 2 rooms, plus sofa-bed, toilet, kitchen and terrace. Accommodation for horses. Very welcoming. English spoken.

Gite-Chambre d'Hôtes Hernandez, (Mr and Mrs Hernandez), Lasbros, 48130 La-Chaze-de-Peyre, Lozère, France; +33(0)4 66 47 08 94; +33(0)6 75 37 20 21; www.gite-aubrac-lasbros.e-monsite.com; Hostel: €15-€18/ pers. €5/breakfast; Cozy well maintained house in tiny hamlet of Lasbros, which has no commerce. If necessary, Mrs. Hernandez sells some simple ingredients/products that can be prepared in the kitchen.

Prinsuéjols

Les Gentianes, (Karine and Damien), Finieyrols, 48100 Prinsuéjols, Lozère, France; +33(0)4 66 32 52 77; auberge.gentianes@wanadoo.fr; B&B: €43/half board; Hostel: €38/half board.; B&B includes 5 rooms with 2-5 places; hostel includes 19 places in rooms of 4-6 pers. In need of updating. English spoken. *Aligot* (cheese and potato dish) is served at dinner.

La Borieta del Prat, (Pascal and Corrinne Bardin), Prat Viala, 48100 Prinsuéjols, Lozère, France; +33(0)4 30 43 43 45; +33(0)6 19 13 32 38; pascaletcorrine.bardin@sfr.fr; www.laborietadelprat.fr; B&B prices start at €25/pers. €40/half board ; Yourte €15/pers.; €35/half board; €5/breakfast; Approximately 900m off the GR®65. Basic accommodation in B&B (2 rooms) or yurt (6 places), an interesting experience. English spoken. Horses welcome.

La Rose de l'Aubrac, (Fabienne and Daniel Garcia), Finieyrols, 48100 Prinsuéjols, Lozère, France; +33(0)3 46 64 57 85 5; +33(0)6 08 31 55 61; larosedelaubrac@orange.fr; www.larosedelaubrac.wix.com; €48/ half board; Extremely welcoming lovely B&B, with excellent meals (the owner formerly had his own restaurant). 4 double rooms. Accommodation for horses.

DISTANCE **18.9km**

ASCENT **518m**

DESCENT **413m**

FROM LE PUY **108km**

TO RONCEVAUX **667km**

Hiker after Rieutort © Alexandra Huddleston

Route - The route, which is well marked, consists mostly of tracks and footpaths, as it continues to cross the sun and wind-exposed Aubrac plateau, in what is one of the loveliest stages of the GR®65. After Nasbinals, there are climbs through cattle fields, including opening various gates.

Pointers - **Culture:** The 17km section of the GR®65 from Nasbinals to Saint-Chély-d'Aubrac has been recognized as a UNESCO world heritage site. **Cows:** When crossing a field of cows, walk calmly at a normal pace and avoid getting between a cow and its calf. **Advance planning:** Best to do any food shopping in Aumont-Aubrac, as there are no grocers until Saint-Chély-d'Aubrac. However, Maison d'Aubrac does sell regional delicacies. Meals in Aubrac can be reserved with accommodation. **Reservations:** The Aubrac cross country race, which begins in Nasbinals takes place

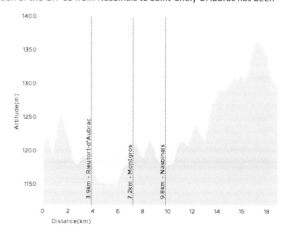

each June (19 June 2016), during which time it is difficult to find accommodation in Nasbinals. Best to reserve in advance, if this overlaps with your trip.

Rieutort-d'Aubrac

Note the communal oven and two impressive granite watering troughs.

Nasbinals

The economic centre of Aubrac, Nasbinals (popl. 500, alt. 1100) offers skiing in winter and hiking in summer. The 13th century church of Saint Mary (*Eglise Sainte-Marie*) is an example of regional Romanesque architecture and is built from brown basalt with a schist roof and a unique octagonal bell tower. The double vaulted entrance faces south and includes a remarkable sculpted capital showing a fight between Sagittarius (an archer that is half human and half horse) and a lancer.

Church of Nasbinals © Alexandra Huddleston

Aubrac

Aubrac village © Alexandra Huddleston

The village of Aubrac (alt. 1300m) houses the remains of a medieval monastery and hospital (*dômerie*) that was founded in the 12th century by the powerful Conques Abbey upon the initiative of Adalard, a Flemish noble. The village, which offered pilgrims and travellers medical care and respite from the elements, became a regional political and economic power in the Middle Ages. However, the monastery was abandoned during the French Revolution and left to ruin. Today what remains is the church and tower with its "bell for the lost" that once rang out to guide travellers crossing the Aubrac plateau.

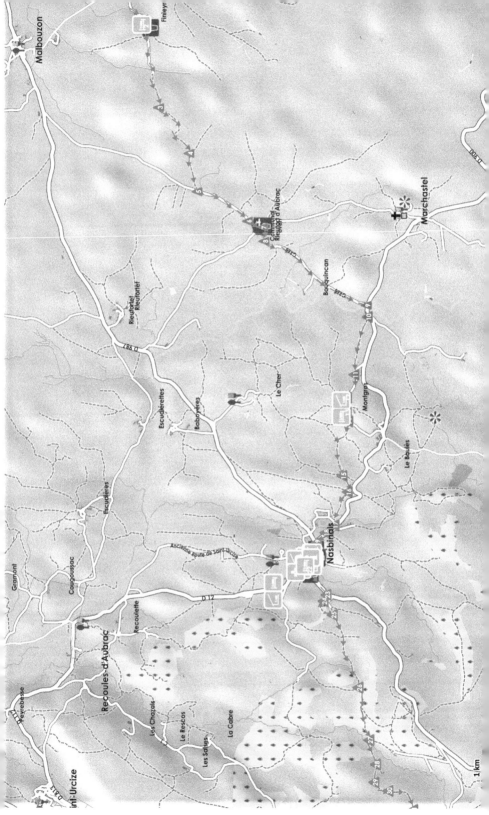

Waypoint	Total(km)	Directions	Verification	Compass	Altitude(m)
1	0.0	Follow road through **Finieyrols**	La Rose de l'Aubrac to the left	W	1200
2	0.1	At fork keep right and climb hill. Continue straight on road.		NW	1203
3	1.3	Continue straight on path climbing hill.	Rock formation called Roc des Loups (wolves) to the left	SW	1246
4	2.2	Turn right and continue descent.	Signpost	W	1218
5	2.8	Turn left onto road and cross bridge/stream. Continue straight climbing hill.	Stream (La Peyrade)	S	1181
6	3.6	Enter village of Rieutort-d'Aubrac	Signpost	SW	1193
7	3.9	Turn right to leave **Rieutort-d'Aubrac** (curved road to right)	**Communal oven** and two historical granite **watering troughs**	W	1196
8	4.1	Leave village continuing straight on road	Stone wall borders road. Lovely views of plateau	SW	1195
9	5.8	Turn right onto D900 road and cross bridge over Le Bès river.	Pass iron cross on the left side of the bridge	W	1151
10	6.0	Take first right on gravel road up hill and continue straight	Pass white and yellow road marker on the right	W	1155
11	6.9	Turn right onto the road Le Carrouquet		W	1153
12	7.2	Enter village of **Montgros** and continue straight towards village centre	Signpost	W	1166
13	7.4	Continue straight on road to leave Montgros	Pass cross on right	SW	1198
14	7.6	Continue straight on track	Stay to right of white iron cross	W	1214
15	8.4	Cross road and continue straight on gravel track (climb)		SW	1203

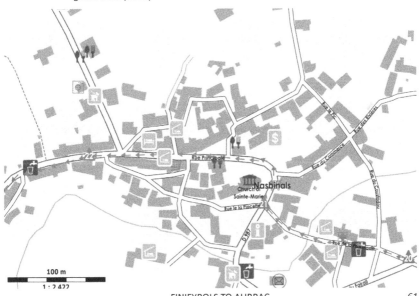

100 m
1 : 2 422

FINIEYROLS TO AUBRAC

16	8.7	Continue straight through intersection towards village	Nasbinals visible	NW	1219
17	9.2	Turn right onto D900 and continue straight towards village centre	Tractor and farm equipment garage to the right	NW	1192
18	9.4	After passing cemetery on the left turn left and then right to follow path running parallel to D900 road	Cemetery on left	NW	1185
19	9.6	Merge left onto D900 and continue straight		NW	1183
20	9.6	Continue straight on rue de la Pharmacie	Pass pharmacy on right	W	1179
21	9.8	In the centre of **Nasbinals** turn right in front of the church (place de l'Eglise) and continue straight on rue Principale	Church. Pass town hall on the right.	N	1173
22	10.0	Continue straight on rue Principale to leave village		SW	1177
23	10.5	Turn right at Le Coustat onto rue La Coustette	Turn right after house with pine hedges	W	1179
24	10.6	Continue straight climbing into wood grove	Wood grove	NW	1182
25	11.0	Keep right	Pass memorial to Pilgrim Patrick Coudert	SW	1210
26	12.1	Keep left at fork and head towards forest.		SW	1227
27	12.8	Keep right	Cross stream (Ruisseau de la Cabre ou Pascalet)	W	1222
28	13.2	Keep right and pass through gate (climb)	Gate and farm ahead	W	1231
29	13.5	After climbing hill pass through 2nd gate on left and continue straight following fence	Gate	SW	1255
30	13.7	Pass through 3rd gate climb right through field	Gate	S	1271
31	14.3	Pass through 4th gate and continue straight along fence	Gate and fence	SW	1292
32	14.7	Pass through 5th gate and continue straight following fence	Gate	W	1291
33	15.3	Pass through wood grove and then keep right	Follow stone wall	S	1308
34	16.2	Cross stream and pass through additional gate. Climb hill ahead	Gate	SE	1311
35	17.1	Pass through gate and continue straight toward wooden shed on hilltop	Gate	S	1355
36	17.2	Continue straight following stone wall	Pass shed on right	S	1365
37	18.0	Descend towards village of Aubrac	Follow stone wall. The enormous and austere Royal Aubrac, a former sanatorium, visible on hilltop to the right.	SW	1352
38	18.3	Cross the D987 road and continue straight on track towards village of Aubrac	Village visible and signposts	S	1326
39	18.6	Continue straight on path, passing around the back of the Church	Church	SE	1305
40	18.9	Turn right onto asphalt road and arrive at **Aubrac** village centre	Place des Fêtes		1298

Montgros

 La Maison de Rosalie, (Karine and Philippe), Montgros, 48260 Nasbinals, Lozère, France; +33(0)4 66 32 55 14; maisonderosalie@sfr.fr; www.hotel-aubrac.com; Double room + half board: €54/pers. single room + half board: €69/pers., hostel: bed + half board: €42-€46/pers.; Under new (and appreciated) ownership since 2015, this two-star hotel in a restored stone farmhouse has 9 rooms and a hostel with 2 3-pers. rooms and 2 4-pers. rooms. Meals are prepared with local produce. English spoken.

Nasbinals

Le Sorbier, (Mr. Hervé Rey), Route d'Aubrac, 48260 Nasbinals, Lozère, France; +33(0)4 66 32 56 79; chaletderoc.rey@free.fr; €12.50-15/pers. €6/breakfast (at Hotel de France across the street); 18 places in 5 rooms. Modern toilet. Kitchen.

Gîte la Grappière, (Marjori Buffière), Rue de la Pharmacie, 48260 Nasbinals, Lozère, France; +33(0)4 66 32 15 60; marjori.lagrappiere@laposte.net; €20/pers. (breakfast included).; Hostel in a house with 15 places in a dormitory, next to pharmacy and close walk to church. Kitchen.

Las Paros, (Mr and Mrs Bergounhon), Route de la Rosée du Matin, 48260 Nasbinals, Lozère, France; +33(0)6 80 78 63 96; +33(0)6 07 80 29 23; las-paros@orange.fr; www.lasparos.fr; €17/pers.; 2 fully equipped apartments for 4 to 6 persons on farm. Very welcoming. Meals can be taken in the village.

Gîte d'Étape Communal de la Maison Richard, Maison Richard, rue Principale, 48260 Nasbinals, Lozère, France; +33(0)4 66 32 59 47; mairie.nasbinals@laposte.net; €12-14/pers.; 19 places. Kitchen. Rudimentary.

Gîte Lô d'Ici, (Laurence Rieutort), Village, 48260 Nasbinals, Lozère, France; +33(0)4 66 32 92 69; +33(0)6 80 28 51 12; contact@lodici-aubrac.com; €30/pers.; €9/breakfast; 20 places in 4 rooms in tastefully decorated restored granary, with peaceful tea room serving world teas and a boutique with local arts and crafts. Kitchen. English spoken.

Centre d'Accueil Nada, Village, 48260 Nasbinals, Lozère, France; +33(0)4 66 32 50 42; +33(0)6 32 18 43 53; contact@nada-aubrac.com; www.nada-aubrac.com; €14/in room €12/pers. in dormitory; 38 places, including 2 dormitories of 6 to 8 beds, 13 rooms of 2 to 3 beds, 2 toilets. Kitchen.

Centre Équestre des Monts d'Aubrac, (Gérard and Marie-Claude Moisset), Route de Saint-Urcize, 48260 Nasbinals, Lozère, France; +33(0)4 66 32 50 65; +33(0)6 77 51 03 25; gerard.moisset0343@orange.fr; www.equitation-aubrac-lozere.fr; €38-€40/half board; 22 places in rooms of 2 to 4. Accommodation for horses in paddock and stall. Welcoming. English spoken - approximately 500m from track.

Hôtel de France, (Mr. Hervé Rey), Route d'Aubrac, 48260 Nasbinals, Lozère, France; +33(0)4 66 32 50 19; chaletderoc.rey@free.fr; €25-40/1-2 pers. €50/3-4 pers., €6/breakfast; 5 rooms in simple centrally located hotel. Welcoming staff.

Office de Tourism, Place du Foirail, 48260 Nasbinals, Lozère, France; +33(0)4 66 31 91 76; www.nasbinals.fr/tourisme

Aubrac

Les Gîtes du Royal Aubrac, (Mr. Cousty), Village d'Aubrac, 12470 Saint-Chely-d'Aubrac, Aveyron, France; +33(0)5 65 44 28 41; info@royal-aubrac.com; www.royal-aubrac.com; €30/pers. (sheets and breakfast included); 14 dormitories of 2 to 7 places. In need of refreshing. Large building on hill with beautiful views, just off GR®65, 500m before Aubrac. Small grocery store. Kitchen. Accommodation for horses.

La Tour des Anglais, Aubrac, 12470 Saint-Chély-d'Aubrac, Aveyron, France; +33(0)5 65 44 28 42; +33(0)5 65 44 21 15; accueil.stchelydaubrac@orange.fr; €10/pers.; €23/ for dinner and breakfast at La Domerie.; Hostel located in fortified tower dating to the 14th century. Simple accommodation but an interesting experience. 16 places in 3 dormitories. Kitchen.

La Colonie, (Cyril Lérisse), D987,, 12470 Aubrac, Aveyron, France; +33(0)5 65 51 64 79; contact@la-colonie. com; www.la-colonie.com/fr; €46/single, €66-€89/double, €109-€129/triple, €18/dinner; Located near the village centre on the GR®65. English spoken.

L'Annexe d'Aubrac, (Virginie and Darwin), Place des Fêtes, 12470 Aubrac, Aveyron, France; +33(0)5 65 48 78 84; +33(0)6 75 88 41 19; contact@lannexedaubrac.com; www.lannexedaubrac.com; €105-€180/double room, €200/suite 2-5 pers.; Upscale, elegant B&B, with 5 rooms located in village centre with private garden. English spoken.

Hôtel-Restaurant de la Domerie, Village d'Aubrac, 12470 Aubrac, Aveyron, France; +33(0)5 65 44 28 42; contact@hoteldomerie.com; www.hoteldomerie.com; €60-€100/1-2 pers. room, €12/breakfast, €25-€36/dinner, €86/pers. half board.; 23 rooms. English spoken.

Office de Tourisme, Place d'Aubrac, 12470 Aubrac, Aveyron, France

DISTANCE **23.9km**

ASCENT **536m**

DESCENT **1469m**

FROM LE PUY **127km**

TO RONCEVAUX **712km**

Leaving Aubrac

Route - The route is overall well-marked. From Aubrac, it descends on rocky tracks and footpaths through fields and forests to Saint-Chély-d'Aubrac. Thereafter it descends mostly on asphalt roads and tracks to the Lot River valley and Saint-Côme-d'Olt.

Pointers - **Advance planning:** Ensure sufficient provisions in Saint-Chély, as there are no grocers or restaurants until Saint-Côme-d'Olt. **Caution:** When leaving Saint-Chély-d'Aubrac, be careful not to follow the GR®6 in a north-east direction; it also uses the same red and white way markings.

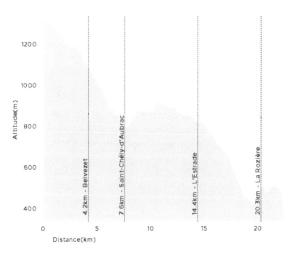

Saint-Chély-d'Aubrac

In Saint-Chély-d'Aubrac (popl. 540, alt. 650m), there is the church of Our Lady of the Poor (*Notre-Dame-des-Pauvres*), which has a lovely sundial and a 15th century bell tower that was once a defence tower. When leaving the village, note the small bridge across the *boralde* (mountain stream), with its 16th century stone cross and a stylized depiction of a pilgrim holding a stick in one hand and a rosary in the other.

Saint-Côme-d'Olt

With many well preserved medieval buildings, the village of Saint-Côme-d'Olt (popl. 1,330, alt. 450m), which sits on the Lot River, is classified as one of the most beautiful villages in France. The village church (*Eglise Saint-Côme*) was built between 1522-1532 in a flamboyant Gothic style and has a rare twisted spire, which the French describe as "flaming" (*flammé*). Also of note are the 30 beautifully carved oak panels on the main doors.

Waypoint	Total(km)	Directions	Verification	Compass	Altitude(m)
1	0.0	In **Aubrac**, from Place des Fêtes, turn left onto road D987, direction Espalion	Pass Hôtel Restaurant de la Dômerie on right	W	1299
2	0.2	Continue straight on D987 road		SW	1316
3	0.7	Turn left onto track and descend	Signpost	SW	1313
4	1.0	Continue straight	Pass cross on right	SW	1303
5	3.1	Continue straight, passing cross on the right. To the right is the turn off for the Alternative Route to Bonneval Abbey		SW	1196
6	3.2	Continue straight on track	Information panel to the right	S	1190
7	3.7	At fork keep left		SE	1156
8	4.0	Continue straight on path	On left pass volcanic neck of Belvezet with the ruins of a fortress	W	1121
9	4.2	Turn left onto asphalt road (Vierge de Belvezet) and pass through farm houses of the hamlet of **Belvezet**		SE	1108
10	4.3	Take first right	Pass picnic area on the left	W	1096
11	4.4	Continue straight on road which curves right at farm		W	1089
12	4.7	Turn right	Signpost	SW	1058
13	5.0	Cross stream (Ruisseau de l'Aude) and descend on path	Stream (Ruisseau de l'Aude)	SW	1043
14	5.6	Continue straight and pass through two gates	Gates	W	984
15	6.0	Continue straight	Abandoned farm house on left	W	947
16	6.0	Turn left onto footpath, direction Saint-Chély-d'Aubrac, followed by a steep descent into ravine.	Signpost	W	927
17	6.5	Turn left onto asphalt road, which leads to Saint-Chély-d'Aubrac	Village visible	W	884
18	7.1	Enter Saint-Chély-d'Aubrac	Cross and signpost	SW	850
19	7.3	Turn right onto D19/Route d'Aubrac and continue straight towards village centre		SW	826
20	7.5	Turn left onto rue de la Marie	Public toilets to the right	SW	818
21	7.6	In the centre of **Saint-Chély-d'Aubrac** cross Place de la Marie	Pass war monument	SW	820
22	7.6	Turn left and descend on rue du Pont des Pèlerins	Descent towards river (Boralde de Saint-Chély) and historic bridge	S	819
23	7.8	Cross Pont des Pèlerins	Note cross on bridge with depiction of pilgrim	SE	813
24	7.9	Turn right off asphalt road onto track that abuts cemetery.	Signpost. Pass along cemetery wall on the right	SW	795
25	8.3	Turn left onto D19 road and take immediate right onto track	Signpost	NE	840
26	8.5	Continue straight on track which runs parallel to D19 road	Pass cross on the left. D19 to the right.	SW	851
27	8.8	Merge onto the D19 road and take first right into the hamlet of Le Recours	Signpost	S	877

28	9.3	After passing through hamlet turn right onto footpath that passes through forest	Signpost	S	878
29	10.6	Turn right onto asphalt road and continue straight towards hamlet of Les Cambrassats	Toilet to the right	SW	902
30	10.9	At fork keep right	Head towards the farm house and hamlet of Les Cambrassats (signpost)	S	920
31	10.9	Take immediate left onto footpath	After first barn	S	919
32	11.4	In the hamlet of Foyt, turn left onto path	Farmhouse	SW	900
33	11.6	Turn right	Path cuts between pastures	SW	900
34	11.9	Turn right onto asphalt road, which was a former Roman road - Via Agrippa - in the direction of L'Estrade	Signpost	SW	898
35	13.1	Turn right onto footpath	Signpost	SW	858
36	14.3	Continue straight and enter hamlet of L'Estrade	Pass farm on right	S	837
37	14.4	At end of path in hamlet centre turn right and continue straight to leave **L'Estrade**		W	833
38	15.5	Continue straight on path through forest (chestnut trees) on descent towards river valley		SW	783
39	17.8	At intersection continue straight on path, descending		SW	598
40	18.8	Cross stream (Ruisseau de Cancels) and continue straight on path		S	461
41	18.9	Turn right onto asphalt road		W	461
42	19.0	At fork follow footpath to the left of a picnic area		SW	467
43	19.3	Turn left onto road D557 and cross bridge. Continue straight		W	441
44	19.7	Turn right off road. Steep climb on path in the direction of La Rozière	Signpost	SE	433
45	19.8	Turn right onto track and continue climb straight.		NW	443
46	20.3	Arrive in hamlet of **La Rozière**		W	498
47	20.4	Continue straight through hamlet	Pass shrine to Mary on the left	W	507
48	20.7	Turn right off track and descend.	Signpost	W	506
49	21.4	Turn left onto track and continue straight	Towards power lines	SW	515
50	22.3	Turn left onto asphalt road to enter hamlet of Cinqpeyres		SW	473
51	22.5	Turn left onto foot path	Pass behind barn	S	453
52	22.7	Turn right onto the road		W	425
53	22.8	Take first left onto rue de la Draille	Pass cross to the left	SW	423
54	23.4	Turn right onto gravel road D557		W	401
55	23.4	Cross the D987 road and continue straight towards Saint-Côme-d'Olt centre	Signpost	SW	395
56	23.7	At end of road turn right	Pass vegetable gardens	SW	375

57	23.7	Turn left through underpass, then immediate right on rue Mathat to reach village centre.	SW	370
58	23.8	Continue straight crossing Place de la Porte Neuve. Pass through gate (porte) and turn left onto rue du Greffe	W	366
59	23.9	Arrive at **Saint-Côme-d'Olt** in Place Church and Office of Tourism Château de Castelnau		368

ALTERNATE ROUTE VIA BONNEVAL ABBEY

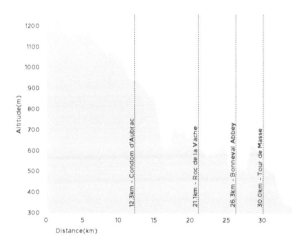

LENGTH **34.6km**

STAGE ASCENT **1518m**

STAGE DESCENT **2369m**

Route - From Aubrac it is possible to take a shorter alternative route to the Bonneval Abbey, a Cistercian abbey founded in 1147, and to re-join the GR®65 in Espalion, without adding extra time to the hike. The route, which is not very frequented, can be challenging, with some steep descents. It is marked by light blue way markings and crosses spectacular plateaus and forests before arriving at the abbey, which is hidden in a forest valley. The abbey is self-sufficient and today houses a Cistercian Convent and its craft chocolate factory. For the more adventurous, spiritually oriented or nature loving, this detour is recommended.

Pointers - The way markings can be unclear. Best to print out the detailed map of the route from the Abbey website before leaving or at the Maison d'Aubrac information point, in Aubrac www.abbaye-bonneval.com/frame_new/hotellerie/saint_jacques.php **Advance planning:** Ensure to have sufficient provisions/water before setting off from Aubrac. **Reservations:** Make reservations at the Abbey for the night/meals in advance. If you intend to spend the night in Condom d'Aubrac, call in advance. With advance notice, meals in Condom can also be organised at the local café.

Abbey of Bonneval

The impressive Abbey of Bonneval was founded in 1147 on the edge of the Aubrac plateau. By the 12th-13th century, it was rich from donations and one of the most important monasteries in the region with significant lands and several granaries. The abbey nevertheless suffered both during the Hundred Years' War (the intermittent struggle between England and France in the 14th-15th centuries), during which it fell under English control, and the Wars of Religion (16th century conflicts between French Protestants and Catholics), when it was pillaged. The abbey was abandoned during the French Revolution, and its lands were sold and its buildings left to ruin. It wasn't until 1875, that a small community of Cister-

cian nuns, seeking a place to settle, began restoration works. This same religious community today numbers approximately 35 nuns. The congregation is largely self-sufficient and operates a chocolate factory (delicious chocolate for sale in the gift-store) as well as provides accommodation for pilgrims and guests. Historical sources suggest that the abbey was a stop for pilgrims in the Middle Ages. Guests are invited to take part in religious services, including the beautiful Gregorian chants for which the congregation is renown. Above the entrance to the abbey is a lovely 12th century Virgin and Child relief.

ROUTE INSTRUCTIONS

Waypoint	Total(km)	Directions	Verification	Compass	Altitude(m)
1	0.0	Turn right at cross and follow signpost for Tour des Monts d'Aubrac Route.	Note that way markings are light blue for the Bonneval Route	NE	1192
2	1.3	Turn left onto D987 road		NW	1235
3	1.5	Turn right into picnic area and enter the forest	Picnic area and cross	N	1235
4	1.6	Immediately after passing through gate, keep left and head towards information board		NE	1231
5	1.6	Follow path behind information board	Information board	NE	1232
6	2.2	Cross gravel road and continue straight descending		N	1208
7	2.5	Cross stream using footbridge		NW	1172
8	2.6	Rejoin main path on left		W	1166
9	3.1	Cross stream and continue on path		W	1159
10	3.1	Enter Forêt Domaniale d'Aubrac	Signpost	W	1158
11	3.6	Cross stream and continue straight	Climb hill	SW	1139
12	3.7	Continue straight. Steep climb.		W	1154
13	4.5	Continue straight on track along forest	Forest to the left	W	1186

ALTERNATE ROUTE VIA BONNEVAL ABBEY

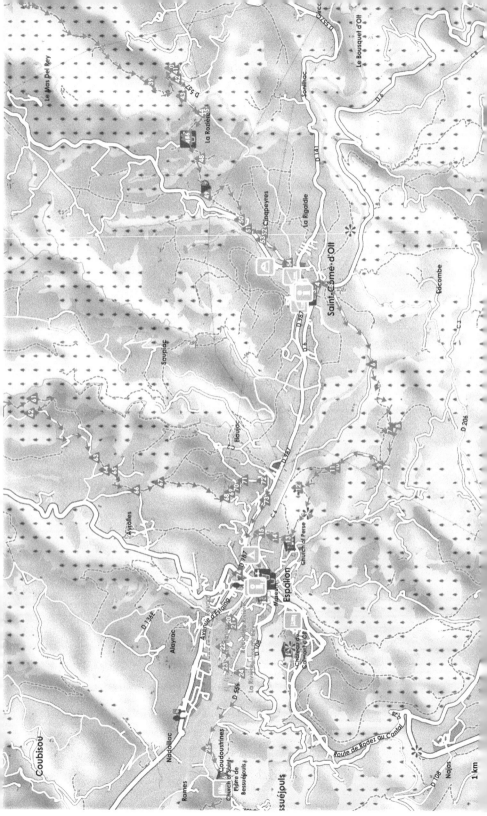

Le Mas Del Rey

Le Bousquet d'Olt

La Rivière

La Rigaldie

Cinqpeyres

Saint-Côme-d'Olt

Escombe

Souylac

Flaujac

Ayrolles

Church of Perse

Espalion

Alayrac

Château de
Calmont-d'Olt

Castelnau

Nadaillac

Coudoustrines
Church of Saint-
Pierre de
Bessuéjouls

Bessuéjouls

Rames

Route de Rodez au Cantal

Nafas

Coubisou

1 km

14	5.2	At end of road turn left, cross stream and take immediate left in the direction of Le Puech du Serre	Signpost	W	1174
15	7.2	Turn right and continue straight passing farm houses on the left		W	1122
16	7.7	Turn right onto road		NW	1109
17	8.0	Turn left onto track	Pass farm house (left)	W	1099
18	8.8	Turn left onto track	Signpost	SW	1082
19	8.8	Take immediate right onto track followed by immediate left	Path passes between narrow stone walls	N	1086
20	9.2	Cross track and continue straight		W	1085
21	9.3	Merge straight onto track (descent) and take immediate left	Wooden cross on right	W	1083
22	10.4	Turn right onto asphalt road	Descend in direction of farm house	S	1053
23	10.8	Turn left off asphalt road onto path	After first sharp corner	S	1018
24	11.1	Turn right onto the D900 road and then take immediate left (descend)	Turn before farmhouse	W	998
25	11.2	Turn right onto asphalt road and continue straight	Farm buildings	SW	978
26	11.6	Continue on narrow path between stone walls/fields	Pass farmhouse to the left	SW	954
27	11.7	Turn left onto asphalt road and head towards village of Condom d'Aubrac		SW	956
28	12.2	Enter village of Condom d'Aubrac	Signpost	S	926
29	12.3	Turn right in **Condom d'Aubrac** village centre	Pass church to the right	SW	929
30	12.4	At end of street turn right	Cow statue to the right	W	939
31	12.4	Take immediate left and follow track between stone walls	Turn after school	W	941
32	12.8	At end of track turn right and continue straight	Farm house	NW	948
33	13.0	At end of path turn right onto asphalt road	Farm	W	938
34	13.9	At fork keep right	Steel gate to the left	SW	902
35	15.1	Enter forest staying to the right on footpath. Steep descent.		SW	852
36	15.4	Keep right and proceed with caution down steep incline towards valley		N	830
37	16.2	Before bridge take sharp left following path along river (Boralde Flaujaguèse)	Do not cross this bridge. River to the right	SW	628
38	16.5	Cross river using concrete bridge		W	607
39	16.5	Follow path uphill along river		S	605
40	17.4	Follow path switch-backing up the hillside		NE	671
41	17.6	Turn sharp right and continue switch-backing up hillside		NW	689
42	17.8	Continue straight on track		SW	694
43	18.3	Follow road along ridge	River valley to the right	S	711
44	20.2	Continue straight on track	Chemin de Raymond on the left	E	657
45	20.6	Cross mountain brook and continue straight on track		SW	681

stage 7

#	km			Dir	Alt
46	21.1	Pass **Roc de la Vache** (cow rock) on right, with beautiful valley views		SW	672
47	24.2	Continue straight on track	Pass Roc del Cayre on right	SW	616
48	24.5	Continue straight on track	Abbey visible across valley	SE	620
49	24.6	Turn right onto narrow path and switchback towards valley bottom. Steep	Signpost for Bonneval	NW	630
50	25.5	Continue down steep path towards river	Pass ruins of farm house to the right	S	548
51	25.8	Reach valley bottom and cross bridge over river	Hydroelectric plant to the left	W	470
52	25.9	Turn left after crossing bridge and climb hill towards Abbey	Pass hydroelectric plant on the left	W	471
53	26.2	Continue straight on main path towards paved road and Abbey	Follow stone wall on right	SW	466
54	26.3	Cross over gate (on the left side) and continue climb towards main road		SW	467
55	26.3	Turn right onto a asphalt road and arrive beside the **Bonneval Abbey**	Entrance of Bonneval Abbey	SW	473
56	26.3	To leave Bonneval Abbey, from the entrance continue straight on the asphalt road. Then, turn left onto the track	Cross. Path eventually follows the stations of the cross (*chemin de la croix*)	SW	473
57	26.5	Pass through gate and cross pasture		SW	507
58	26.6	Pass through gate and continue on path	Path follows the Stations of the Cross (*chemin de la croix*)	S	543
59	26.8	Pass through gate and cross pasture	Gate	SE	552
60	27.0	Pass through gate and continue straight through forest	Gate	SE	532
61	27.7	At fork keep left climbing hill		S	541
62	28.3	After switchback turn left onto road D661 and continue straight		S	614
63	29.8	Turn left off road onto track in direction of La Grange (granary)	Signpost	SW	579
64	30.0	Turn left onto road beside **Tour de Masse**	Pass granary on left	S	559
65	30.1	Turn right onto narrow track between stone walls and fields	Pass entrance to Granary and cross on left	W	550
66	30.8	Keep left on track	Pass ruins of house on left	S	518
67	31.2	At fork keep right	Pass cross on right	S	507
68	32.2	Continue on track (descent)	Pass between private houses, garden and pool	SE	445
69	32.3	Descend left onto gravel road		SE	434
70	32.4	Turn right onto asphalt road and continue descent		SE	426
71	32.6	At end of road turn right		S	390
72	32.9	Turn right direction Espalion	Cross	SW	364
73	33.2	Turn right onto the D987 road towards Espalion centre	Signpost and Lot River to the left.	NW	355
74	34.3	Turn left onto rue du Dr Tremolières and continue straight towards city centre.	Before curve	SW	339
75	34.6	After crossing bridge, turn right to regain the GR®65	**Le Pont Vieux**		341

Saint-Chély-d'Aubrac

Gîte d'Étape le Chemin, (Mr and Mrs. Vaysset), Route d'Aubrac, 12470 Saint-Chély-d'Aubrac, Aveyron, France; +33(0)6 76 17 22 36; ferronnerie-aubrac@orange.fr; €15/pers.; Very welcoming hosts. 6 beds in 2 rooms in a lovely independent house with terrace and fully equipped kitchen. 80m from the GR®65, before entering village, and 300m from village. Basic English.

Gîte Saint André, (Roland and Sylvie Nicoli), Sibe Long, 12470 Saint-Chély-d'Aubrac, Aveyron, France; +33(0)5 65 44 26 87; randogitestandre@free.fr; www.randogitestandre.free.fr; €18/pers. €37/half board, €5.50/breakfast; 20 places in rooms of 2, 3 or 4 persons. Lovely terrace with view. English spoken. About 70 metres from GR®65, before entering village on left. 400 metres from village centre.

Gîte d'Étape la Tour des Chapelains, (Christine Brunier), Rue de la Tour, 12470 Saint-Chély-d'Aubrac, Aveyron, France; +33(0)5 65 51 64 80; +33(0)6 69 14 33 38; latour.j.c@gmail.com; www.tour-chapelains.fr; Hostel: €25/pers. (breakfast and sheets included), €36/half board; B&B: €65-76/2 pers. €93/ 3 pers., €118/4 pers, €12.50/dinner; Unique accommodation in charming medieval tower. In city centre next to office of tourism. 6 places in a dormitory and 3 B&B rooms.

Brasserie le Relais Saint-Jacques-Chambres d'Hôtes, (Karine Vidal), Avenue d'Aubrac, 12470 Saint-Chély-d'Aubrac, Aveyron, France; +33(0)5 65 44 79 83; +33(0)6 47 32 04 08; contact@le-relais-saint-jacques.fr; www.lchambre-hote-saint-chely.fr; €38/pers. €60/2 pers., €50/half board, €86/half board for 2 pers., starting from €13/dinner; A father daughter duo welcome guests. 6 rooms, recently renovated. Centrally located near office of tourism. English spoken.

Hotel-Restaurant de la Vallée les Coudercous, Avenue d'Aubrac, 12470 Saint-Chély-d'Aubrac, Aveyron, France; +33(0)5 65 44 27 40; lescoudercous@orange.fr; www.lescoudercous.fr; €47-85/room, €9/breakfast, €43-70/half board, €24.50/pilgrim dinner and breakfast; 21 rooms of 1 to 4 persons. Simple but welcoming hotel. English spoken.

Office de Tourisme, Rue de la Tour, 12470 Saint-Chély-d'Aubrac, Aveyron, France; +33(0)5 65 44 21 15; accueil.stchelydaubrac@orange.fr; www.stchelydaubrac.com

Condom-d'Aubrac

Municpal Hall, Mairie, le Bourg, 12470 Condom-d'Aubrac, Aveyron, France; +33(0)5 65 44 27 11; Donation; In case of need, this tiny welcoming village makes its municipal hall available to hikers. No beds (but mats are available) and no shower. Breakfast/dinner can be arranged in advance at the friendly Café Poujouly (+33 5 65 44 27 74). Call in advance.

Mairie, Le Bourg, 12470 Condom-d'Aubrac, Aveyron, France; +33(0)5 65 44 27 11

Castelnau-de-Mandailles

Gîte d'Étape de L'Estrade, (Betty and Hervé Brouzes), L'Estrade, 12500 Castelnau-de-Mandailles, Aveyron, France; +33(0)6 75 59 00 91; brouzes.herve@wanadoo.fr; www.gites-de-france-aveyron.com/fr/gites-de-groupes/castelnau-de-mandailles-GS36-fiche-produit.htm; €18.50/pers. €14.50/dinner, €5/breakfast, €36/halfboard; Modern recently renovated farmhouse/barn designed for pilgrims. 17 places in 5 rooms. Fully equipped kitchen. Owned and operated by welcoming local farming family. Accommodation for horses.

Le-Cayrol

Abbaye Cistercienne Notre-Dame de Bonneval, Route de l'Abbaye de Bonneval, 12500 Le-Cayrol, Aveyron, France; +33(0)5 65 44 48 83; www.abbaye-bonneval.com; Donation (breakfast, lunch and dinner can be provided); Beautiful working convent from the 12th century with chocolate factory. Simple comfortable single rooms in convent complex or dormitory with 6 places in the Tour St-Jacques. Possibility to participate in religious services. Reservations required. English spoken.

Saint-Côme-d'Olt

Espace Angèle Mérici & Gîte du Couvent de Malet, Route d'Aubrac, 12500 Saint-Côme-d'Olt, Aveyron, France; +33(0)5 65 51 03 20; accueil@espaceangelemerici.com; www.espaceangelemerici.fr; €16/pers. €6/breakfast, €33/half board, €11/dinner; An iconic stop of the GR®65. Beautiful and historic convent with 27 places in rooms of 3 to 6. English spoken. Free accommodation for horses and free wifi. Possibility to take part in religious services. Located north on the D987, 500m before village.

Gîte d'Étape Compagnon de Route, (Mrs. Rous), 4 Résidence de Brugière, 12500 Saint-Côme-d'Olt, Aveyron, France; +33(0)5 65 48 18 16; +33(0)6 70 61 83 22; jmgrous@orange.fr; €14/pers. €6/breakfast; Fair accommodation in home. 6-7 places in 3 rooms. Located 5 min outside village.

Gîte d'Étape del Romiou, (Sabien and Sylvain), 12 rue Crémade, 12500 Saint-Côme-d'Olt, Aveyron, France; +33(0)6 35 59 16 07; gitesaintcome@gmail.com; www.gite-delroumiou.jimdo.com; €13/pers. €6/breakfast, €14/dinner, €31/half board; Run by a welcoming French-Canadian couple, both former pilgrims. Space is a bit tight with 18 places (bunk beds) in 3 dormitories. English spoken. Accommodation for horses. Kitchen.

Chambres d'Hôtes les Jardins d'Eliane, (Jean-Raymond Lacan), 3 avenue d'Aubrac, 12500 Saint-Côme-d'Olt, Aveyron, France; +33(0)5 65 48 28 06; +33(0)6 82 64 04 49; les.jardins.d.eliane@wanadoo.fr; www.lesjardinsdeliane.com; B&B: €48/pers. €54-€60/2 pers., Hostel: €15/pers., €6/breakfast, €15/dinner; In an old house, centrally located, operated by a baker and his wife. 5 B&B rooms, and 2 dormitories with 6 beds. Pool and garden. Basic English. Accommodation for horses. Croissants at breakfast recommended.

Mairie, Place Château de Castelnau, 12500 Saint-Come-d'Olt, Aveyron, France

Condom d'Aubrac Café © Alexandra Huddleston

AUBRAC TO SAINT-CÔME-D'OLT AND ALTERNATE

LOT RIVER VALLEY

Espalion Vieux Pont

A verdant and forested valley is created by the Lot River, which starts at an elevation of 1,241 metres in the Cévénnes mountains and flows 480 km west before joining the Garonne river, after Cahors.

The Lot River is an important presence on the Via Podiensis - it flows through the mining basin of Decazeville, it separates Aubrac from the *Causses* (limestone plateaus), loops around the city of Cahors (the historic capital of Quercy), and widens with the waters of many tributaries like the Célé river (followed on the alternative route through the Célé Valley) and the Dourdou river (crossed in Conques).

The stage between Saint-Côme-d'Olt and Estaing, largely follows the Lot, and is known as the *Pays d'Olt* (*Olt* being the Lot's name in Occitan). This stage is considered a world heritage site.

DISTANCE **20.3km**

ASCENT **710m**

DESCENT **769m**

FROM LE PUY **151km**

TO RONCEVAUX **624km**

Lot River Valley landscape

Route -The route is well-marked, even in the city of Espalion, as it follows footpaths, tracks and asphalt roads through the lush Lot River valley. After crossing the Lot River in Saint-Côme d'Olt there is a steep and rocky climb to the statue of Notre-Dame-de-Vermus, with panoramic views of Espalion and the river valley. Apart from a short but steep climb out of Saint-Pierre-de-Bessuéjols, the route is thereafter mostly flat as it follows the southern bank of the Lot river to Estaing.

Pointers - **Culture:** The 20km section of the GR®65 from Saint-Côme-d'Olt to Estaing has been recognized on the UNESCO world heritage list. **Choice of routes:** There is an unmarked variant to Espalion after Saint-Côme-d'Olt, which is flat and borders the Lot River, thus avoiding the steep climb to the statue of Notre-Dame-de-Vermus. **Note:** The GR®65 does not enter Estaing, but rather continues along the Lot River. To visit Estaing, turn right off the GR®65 and cross the bridge into Estaing. To rejoin the GR®65, backtrack and pick up where you left off, continuing west along the river.

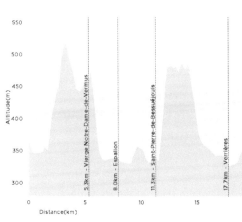

Espalion

Espalion (popl. 4,400, alt. 380m) is a dynamic and picturesque town on the Lot River, with a welcome bustle of shops, cafes and restaurants, as well as a lively market on Friday and Sunday mornings.

The town is dominated by the **Castle of Calmont-d'Olt** (*Château de Calmont d'Olt*), which in the Middle Ages served as a military fortress for the Barons of Calmont (the noble family that ruled the region until 1300), and which today houses an interactive museum dedicated to medieval warfare and offers spectacular valley views. The town also boasts the lovely **Old Bridge** (*Pont-vieux*), which was mentioned as early as the 11th century, and was once a toll bridge that had several towers and shops. The present red sand-stone bridge, dating from the 14th century, is a designated world heritage site and offers views of the historic river-side tanneries. Finally, the red-sandstone **Church of Saint Hilary of Persia** (*Eglise Saint-Hilarian-de-Perse*), built around the 12th century, was once part of a monastery complex that did not survive the 16th century Wars of Religion. The southern portal has an extraordinary tympanum depicting the Last Judgment, which bears some resemblance to the tympanum of the Church of Saint Faith in Conques. Inside, the church's vaults are covered with lovely 15th-16th century frescoes.

Saint-Pierre de Bessuéjouls

Except for its bell tower, the Church of Saint Peter (*Eglise Saint-Pierre*) was entirely rebuilt in the 16th century. However, the upper floor of the 11th century bell tower has an impressive chapel dedicated to Saint Michael with a carved alter, capitals and panels. To access the chapel, climb a steep staircase at the back of the church.

Estaing

Estaing (popl. 607, alt. 300m) is considered one of the most beautiful villages in France. The village is dominated by Estaing castle, a 15th century Gothic castle that was built on the site of a previous castle from 850. The Estaing family was one of the oldest noble families in France and had produced several famous knights and crusaders. Nevertheless, the name expired when the last male heir was guillotined in 1794, after which the castle passed to the order of Saint Joseph. In the early 20th century, the Giscard family took the d'Estaing name (e.g., Valery Giscard d'Estaing (former president of France)). The castle was purchased from the commune in 2005 by the Giscard d'Estaing family with the aim of renovating it and opening certain parts to the public. The 15th century Gothic bridge over the Lot is considered a world heritage site. In July and August, a market is held each Friday morning.

Saint-Pierre de Bessuéjouls © Alexandra Huddleston

Estaing © Alexandra Huddleston

SAINT-CÔME-D'OLT TO ESTAING

Waypoint	Total(km)	Directions	Verification	Compass	Altitude(m)
1	0.0	In **Saint-Côme**, from Place de l'Eglise head south	Church will be to the left	S	376
2	0.0	Take a right at Place Malimane and pass through former gate (porte)		SE	377
3	0.1	Cross place de la Barrieyre and continue straight on rue du Terral		SE	377
4	0.2	Turn right onto the D6 road and cross bridge over Lot River	Cross and river	S	373
5	0.4	Turn right onto asphalt road and continue straight	First road after crossing Lot	SW	348
6	1.7	After crossing bridge turn left onto footpath, which climbs steeply	An unmarked alternative route is to continue straight on the flat road to Espalion, thus avoiding the climb to the Notre-Dame statue	W	352
7	2.9	Keep left and continue climb	Signpost	SE	482
8	3.2	Turn right on track	Top of climb	NW	507
9	3.8	Turn right onto road		NE	490
10	4.6	Turn right in the direction of the Vierge Notre-Dame-de-Vermus	Signpost	W	448
11	4.7	Turn left and continue straight on track	Cross through gravel pit	NW	442
12	5.3	Arrive beside **Vierge Notre-Dame-de-Vermus**. Continue on path to left, steep descent.	Statue and panoramic views of Lot River valley	SW	477
13	6.5	Turn right	Follow stream (Ruisseau de Perse) on the right. **Church of Saint Hilary** ahead	NE	349
14	6.7	Continue straight through sports complex and cross street (avenue Pierre Monteil)		N	339
15	6.9	Continue straight and follow path next to the Lot River		N	336
16	7.7	Turn right onto rue Saint-Joseph	Sculpture (bust) on the right	W	339
17	7.8	Turn right at Place du Plo onto rue Arthur Canel	Pass Office of Tourism on the right	NW	338
18	7.9	Turn right onto rue Droite towards the old bridge (*le Pont Vieux*), and then immediate left on Quai Henri Affre. Here, the alternative route from the Abbey of Bonneval crosses le Pont Vieux to rejoin the GR®65.	Keep river to the right	NW	340
19	8.0	In the centre of **Espalion** cross D920/ Boulevard Joseph Poulenc and follow Quai du 19 mars 1962 along the Lot River	Pont Neuf and Lot River to the right	NW	344
20	8.5	Turn left, away from river, onto rue Dr Jean Capoulade	Cross	SW	333
21	8.6	Turn right onto rue Eugène Salettes		NW	334
22	9.0	Continue straight on gravel road		W	332

23	9.3	After short climb continue straight on asphalt road (Lotissement de la Crouzette)	Pass through residential area Les Hauts de Reversac	SW	343
24	9.6	At end of road turn right onto avenue de Saint-Pierre/D556	Cross on right	W	354
25	10.8	Turn left onto small road	Cross and signpost for "Eglise Romaine" (Romanesque church)	SW	333
26	11.3	Continue straight and enter hamlet of **Saint-Pierre-de-Bessuéjouls**	**Church of Saint Peter** on right	W	343
27	11.5	After crossing bridge turn right	Town hall (**Mairie**) and gardens to the right	NE	336
28	11.5	Turn left direction Estaing	Pass town hall	N	336
29	11.5	Turn right onto footpath, pass gate and climb very steep incline to reach plateau		N	336
30	12.4	Turn left onto asphalt road to reach hamlet of Briffoul	Signpost	SW	481
31	13.4	Turn left	Leave behind hamlet of Le Briffoul	W	475
32	13.6	Turn right onto path through fields	Pass farm hanger on left	N	482
33	14.7	Continue descent on footpath	Pass through forest. Village of Beauregard becomes visible.	NW	460
34	15.0	Enter village of Beauregard. Keep right on asphalt road.	Pass castle on left	NW	419
35	15.1	Keep left and continue descent straight	Towards church of Sainte-Madeleine (Trédou)	W	399
36	15.3	Turn left and continue straight descending hill	Cemetery	S	378
37	15.7	Turn right after crossing hamlet of Les Camps and continue straight	Head in direction of power lines	W	360
38	16.2	At intersection continue straight on track	Away from power lines	W	351
39	16.5	At end of road turn left. Direction Verrières.	Signpost	SW	348
40	16.9	At end of road turn right onto D100 (Route d'Estaing) and continue straight	Pass through hamlets of Les Acacias and Les Lilas.	NW	344
41	17.4	Enter village of Verrières. Continue straight through intersection and old village centre.	Signpost	NW	344
42	17.7	In the centre of **Verrières** turn left at end of road	Iron cross on the left	NW	336
43	17.9	Keep right	Pass stone cross and Chapelle de Verrières on left	W	335
44	18.0	Turn right onto the D556 road after crossing the bridge (pont des Pèlerins)	Bridge and stream (Ruisseau de Magrane)	N	329
45	18.2	Turn left onto the D100 road	Signpost	N	323
46	18.7	Turn left off the D100 road and follow footpath. Climb.	Path follows the D100 to the right	NE	325
47	19.5	Rejoin the D100 road turning left in the direction of Estaing		NW	351
48	20.3	Arrive at **Estaing**	Note: The GR®65 does not enter Estaing. After crossing the bridge to visit the village, backtrack to rejoin the GR®65		326

Espalion

Gîte d'Étape Obrador, 7 rue Arthur Canel, 12500 Espalion, Aveyron, France; +33(0)5 65 48 71 52; gite. obrador@orange.fr; www.gite.obrador.free.fr; €17-25/pers. €56/2 pers. (breakfast included); Located in the city in an entirely renovated building on the Lot river.12 places in 3 rooms each with toilet.

Gîte d'Étape au Fil de l'Eau, 5 rue Saint Joseph, 12500 Espalion, Aveyron, France; +33(0)6 24 83 19 36; +33(0)6 77 58 53 08; annie.lautard@live.fr; €15/pers. €5/breakfast; Close to the Vieux Palais (old palace) and on the banks of the Lot river. 20-28 places in 5-7 rooms (bunk beds). Kitchen. English spoken.

Chambre d'Hôtes la Fontaine, (Mr. and Mrs. Regis), 15 Chemin de Calmont, 12500 Espalion, Aveyron, France; +33(0)5 65 48 45 91; +33(0)6 07 22 72 95; christian.regis3@wanadoo.fr; €45-€54/pers. €50-€60/2 pers.; 3 rooms for 6 persons. A few minutes' walk from the city centre. Beautiful views of the château de Calmont d'Olt. Terrace with garden and pool.

Camping le Roc de l'Arche, Le Foirail, 12500 Espalion, Aveyron, France; +33(0)5 65 44 06 79; info@ rocdelarche.com; www.rocdelarche.com; €72-87/4 pers.(€48-€58 if 2 consecutive nights) mobile home with 2 bedrooms (price varies based on size of home and season); Centrally located camping ground next to the Lot river. Possibility to rent mobile homes, a fun and unique experience. English spoken. Free access to nearby municipal pool.

Office de Tourisme, 23 place du Plô, 12500 Espalion, Aveyron, France; +33(0)5 65 44 10 63; infos@tourisme-espalion.fr; www.tourisme-espalion.fr

Bessuéjouls

Chambres d'Hôtes Domaine d'Armagnac, (Gille Sanglier et Françoise Gadelin), Saint Pierre de Besuéjouls, 12500 Bessuéjouls, Aveyron, France; +33(0)5 65 48 20 71; sanglier.gilles@wanadoo.fr; www.domaine-armagnac.com; B&B: €100/double, €93/single; A beautiful estate in a lovely village just after Espalion. 3 rooms in upscale B&B. Accommodation for horses. Kitchen.

Estaing

Hospitalité Saint-Jacques, 8 rue du Collège, 12190 Estaing, Aveyron, France; +33(0)5 65 44 19 00; www. hospitalite-saint-jacques.fr; Donation (breakfast and dinner); Located in the heart of the village. Operated by volunteers and reserved for pilgrims. Possibility to participate in religious ceremonies. Possible accommodation for horses with prior notice.

Gîte d'Étape Chez Anne, (Anne Le Bloas), 3 rue François d'Estaing, 12190 Estaing, Aveyron, France; +33(0)7 87 96 68 75; anne.b12@hotmail.fr; www.gite-etape-anne-estaing12.fr; €15/pers. €6/breakfast; 14 places in 4 rooms and 2 flats. Kitchen, washing machine/dryer. Basic English. Possible accommodation for horses in a nearby field.

Gîte d'Etape Communal d'Estaing, Place du Foirail, 12190 Estaing, Aveyron, France; +33(0)6 44 95 52 14; gitecommunalestaing@gmail.com; www.estaingdouze.fr/heberge/gite_etape.php; €17/pers.; Recently renovated, clean and well equipped hostel housed in the former chapel of Saint Fleuret. Garden, terrace and kitchen. 22 places in 5 rooms. English spoken.

Chambres d'Hôtes Dijols, (Mr. Urbain Dijols), Les Chenevières, 12190 Estaing, Aveyron, France; +33(0)5 65 44 71 51; +33(0)6 70 38 42 81; jean.dijols12@orange.fr; €37/pers. €41-€44/2 pers.; 4 rooms in cute B&B located on the GR®65/Lot, as leaving Estaing. Garden and terrace. Accommodation for horses possible.

Chambres d'Hôtes la Marelle, 11 rue Basse, 12190 Estaing, Aveyron, France; +33(0)5 65 44 66 78; +33(0)6 70 88 16 61; lamarelle12@orange.fr; www.lamarelle12.fr; €53-€55/pers. €58-75/2 pers., €95/3 pers., €115/4 pers.; Charming B&B with very welcoming hosts, situated in the heart of the village at the foot of the castle. 6 places in 3 bedrooms.

Hotel Aux Armes d'Estaing, (Mr. and Mrs. Catusse), 1 Quai du Lot, 12190 Estaing, Aveyron, France; +33(0)5 65 44 70 02; remi.catusse@estaing.net; www.estaing.net; €55-€70/room, €9.50/breakfast, €56.50/half board; Centrally located, simple hotel with 32 rooms of various sizes and restaurant operated by the owner-chef. (Avoid rooms in the annex to the hotel).

Office de Tourisme, 24 rue François d'Estaing, 12190 Estaing, Aveyron, France; +33(0)5 65 44 03 22; www. tourisme-aveyron.com/fr/decouvrir/incontournables/estaing.php

DISTANCE **22.8km**

ASCENT **971m**

DESCENT **898m**

FROM LE PUY **171km**

TO RONCEVAUX **603km**

Landscape leaving Estaing

Route - The route is well-marked and follows mostly asphalt roads. After a breezy walk along the Lot River, the route turns south-west and steadily but steeply climbs through pine forests and exposed pastures to Golinhac, before descending into Espeyrac.

Pointers - When leaving Estaing, pay attention to follow the GR®65 along the Lot River, as opposed to the GR®6, which uses the same red and white way markings. **Advance planning:** Be certain to leave Estaing with sufficient water and provisions. While there is a watering point before Golinhac, there are no restaurants or grocers, and the climb is long and hot in summer.

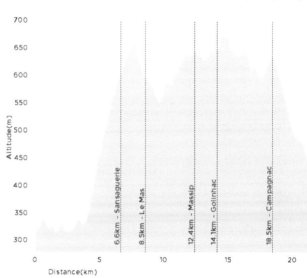

Golinhac

The Church of Saint Martin (*Eglise Saint-Martin*) in Golinhac (popl. 380, alt. 500m) has some Romanesque features that date to an original 11th century Benedictine priory, which was affiliated with Conques Abbey. The present 14th century structure was modelled on the Church of the Holy Sepulchre in Jerusalem (built on the spot where Jesus was said to have been crucified).

Shaver-Crandell, A., Gerson, P. L., & Stones, A, p. 199 (1995). *The pilgrim's guide to Santiago de Compostela: A gazetteer*. London: Harvey Miller Publishers.

Espeyrac

According to the 11th century *Book of Miracles of Saint Faith*, in 960, a pilgrim in Espeyrac (popl. 240, alt. 250m) was attacked and blinded by bandits. He miraculously recovered after praying to Saint Faith, patron saint of Conques. Espeyrac was formerly the seat of a priory that was connected to the Conques Abbey. The present church of Saint Peter was built on the site of a feudal castle.

Shaver-Crandell, A., Gerson, P. L., & Stones, A, p. 186 (1995). *The pilgrim's guide to Santiago de Compostela: A gazetteer*. London: Harvey Miller Publishers.

ROUTE INSTRUCTIONS

Waypoint	Total(km)	Directions	Verification	Compass	Altitude(m)
1	0.0	In **Estaing**, from bridge head south, and take first right on rue Le Pont d'Estaing	Keep right of chapel. River to your right. Follow signpost for GR®65 and La Rouquette. Lot River to the right.	S	326
2	3.1	Keep left on road and continue straight	Lot River to the right and La Rouquette hamlet to the right.	SW	321
3	3.9	Cross bridge over the stream (Ruisseau de Luzane) and continue to right on the road. Climb until Montegut.	Route changes intermittently from road to forest paths as it climbs to Montegut.	N	332
4	4.0	Turn left off road. Climb		W	335
5	4.1	Turn left rejoining road. Climb.		W	336
6	4.5	Turn left onto footpath. Continue switchback climb up hill.		NE	392
7	4.7	Turn right onto asphalt road.		NE	403
8	4.8	Turn left onto footpath. Continue switchback climb.		NE	423
9	5.0	Turn left and continue straight on road. Climb.		W	458
10	6.6	At **Sansaguerie** continue on the road, climbing	Water point and toilets on the right	W	595
11	7.6	At intersection continue straight, direction Golinhac		NW	657
12	8.4	Continue straight. Direction Le Mas.	Signpost.	NW	621
13	8.5	Pass through farming hamlet of **Le Mas**. Continue straight.		N	598
14	9.2	At end of road turn left	Wooden cross	W	580
15	9.4	Continue straight	Castaillac to the right	NW	574
16	9.8	Turn left onto footpath and climb	Signpost	NW	563

17	10.1	Cross stream and continue on path		NW 583
18	10.4	Cross road and continue descent on footpath		NW 589
19	11.6	Turn left	Follow fencing	NW 638
20	12.2	Continue on track and enter village of Massip	Signpost	W 641
21	12.4	In the centre of **Massip** turn left up footpath. Climb.	Road to the right	NW 643
22	12.6	Cross road and continue straight on footpath		NW 652
23	12.7	Turn left onto road.		SW 663
24	12.8	Turn right onto track and continue straight		N 636
25	13.5	At end of road turn left	Cross	NW 635
26	13.6	Turn right on asphalt road and continue climb		N 633
27	13.9	Turn right on main road (D519) and continue straight towards village centre.	Keep stone wall and houses to the left.	N 645
28	14.1	At place du village in **Golinhac** turn left.	Keep church to the right. Pass war monument to the left.	NW 646
29	14.2	Turn left, then take first right. Climb.	Wrought iron cross on the left	S 645
30	14.4	At road's end, turn right onto asphalt road and continue straight		W 665
31	14.7	Cross road and continue straight on path passing between fields.		W 672
32	15.2	Keep left and continue straight	Pass farm on the right	SW 666
33	15.4	Pass through hamlet of Le Poteau and cross D904 road. Continue straight on D42 road		W 653
34	15.9	Turn right onto track heading into pine forest and continue straight	Signpost	NW 638
35	16.4	Turn right onto D42 road. Enter hamlet of Albusquiès.	Farm to the right	N 655
36	16.5	Turn left following road between stone houses. Descend.	Stone cross and signpost	SW 646
37	16.6	At fork, keep to the right on path		W 642
38	17.6	Turn left onto road	Pass public toilet	SW 596
39	18.5	At road's end, turn right and continue straight on road through hamlet of **Campagnac**		NW 631
40	19.9	Continue on main road and pass through hamlet of **Le Soulié**	La Condamine to the left	NW 524
41	21.4	After Carboniés, turn right off road onto track	Signpost	NW 449
42	21.8	Turn right to rejoin road and continue descent into Espeyrac		NW 457
43	21.9	Turn left onto footpath. Continue descent		NW 451
44	22.3	Cross bridge and continue straight on track		NW 407
45	22.7	Turn left towards centre of Espeyrac.	Signpost	W 399
46	22.8	Arrive at **Espeyrac**, turn left in front of the church for the village centre	Pass fountain on left	396

Sébrazac

Accueil Pèlerin Votre Petit Chez Nous, (Saint-Geniez-des-Ers), Saint-Geniez-des-Ers, 12190 Sébrazac, Aveyron, France; +33(0)5 65 44 29 69; +33(0)6 60 25 50 64; votrepetitcheznous@hotmail.fr; Donation (breakfast and dinner included); Located outside of Estaing in the village of Saint-Geniez-des-Ers. 8 places, 6 in dormitory and 2 in cabin. Accommodation for horses.

Golinhac

Gîte d'Étape l'Orée du Chemin, (Mr. Stephan Dissac), Massip, 12140 Golinhac, Aveyron, France; +33(0)5 65 48 61 10; +33(0)6 71 38 07 57; stephan.dissac@wanadoo.fr; www.loreeduchemin.fr; €14.50/pers. €33/half board, , €13.50/dinner, €5/breakfast, €5/ horses; In hamlet of Massip (before Golinhac), 20 places in 6 rooms in a restored barn. Run by the Dissac family, a much appreciated stop on the route. English spoken. Accommodation for Horses. Kitchen.

Pôle Touristique Bellevue, Camping -Gîte d'Etape- Bar-Snack, D 20 / Bozouls, 12140 Golinhac, Aveyron, France; +33(0)5 65 44 50 73; +33(0)6 89 55 46 32; pole-bellevue12@orange.fr; www.golinhac-hebergements.com; Hostel: €15-€17.50/pers.€60/2-pers cabin, €75/3-pers. cabin, €85/4-pers. cabin, €5.10/breakfast.; Hostel: 18 places in 4 rooms and 15 cabins with 2-6 places. The hostel is cramped and basic, while the cabins offer more luxury. The welcome is warm and there is a heated pool. Kitchen. English spoken. Free accommodation for horses.

Chambre d'Hôtes les Rochers, (Régine Bolis), Le Bourg, 12140 Golinhac, Aveyron, France; +33(0)5 65 48 18 85; +33(0)6 81 86 44 05; bis@infonie.fr; www.hebergement-golinhac.com; €65/double, €86/triple, €105/4 pers.; 4 places in 2 rooms in historic home in Golinhac village centre. Welcoming hosts. English spoken.

Le Petit Saint Jacques, (Mr. Paul Reniers and Maria Heitkamp), Les Hauts de Golinhac, 12140 Golinhac, Aveyron, France; +33(0)5 65 44 59 12; paul.reniers@orange.fr; www.petitsaintjacques.fr; €58/2 pers.€56/3 pers., €55/4 pers., €15/dinner; Located 200 metres above Golhinac village on the GR®65, comfortable B&B with private toilet. English spoken.

Gîte d'Étape du Radal, Pôle Touristique, Bellevue, 12140 Golinhac, Aveyron, France; +33(0)5 65 44 50 73; +33(0)6 89 55 46 32; pole-bellevue12@orange.fr; www.tourisme-aveyron.com/diffusio/fr/dormir/hebergements-collectifs/golinhac/gite-d-etape-du-radal; €14.90/pers. €4/horse.; Charming equestrian centre located 700 metres before the village centre offers accommodation for horses. 13 places in 1 dormitory and 1 room. Kitchen.

Espeyrac

Gîte d'Étape Chrétien-Accueil au Soulié de Saint Jacques, Hameau le Soulié, 12140 Espeyrac, Aveyron, France; +33(0)5 65 72 90 18; +33(0)6 42 35 69 01; mroudil@yahoo.fr; www.gite-soulier-saint-jacques.com; Donation (breakfast and dinner included); 2 km before Espeyrac. Created by former pilgrims that found faith on the Route. Run by volunteers. Simple accommodation 11 places in 2 dormitories and 2 double rooms. Accommodation for horses. Garden. Access to the Chapel of Saint Fleur.

Gîte d'Étape Communal, Le Bourg, 12140 Espeyrac, Aveyron, France; +33(0)5 65 72 09 84; +33(0)6 89 08 72 29; audrey.combres@yahoo.fr; €12.80/pers. €5/breakfast; Simple hostel located in the village centre. 12 places in 2 dormitories. Accommodation for donkeys. Kitchen and Terrace. Basic English.

Hôtel-Restaurant de la Vallée d'Espeyrac, (Martine and Jan-Yves Garcia), Le Bourg, 12140 Espeyrac, Aveyron, France; +33(0)5 65 69 87 61; sarl.lavallee@orange.fr; www.espeyrac-hotel.com; €40/simple, €50/double, €55/triple, €7/breakfast; 12 simple rooms in village centre. English spoken.

DISTANCE **12.5km**

ASCENT **419m**

DESCENT **513m**

FROM LE PUY **194km**

TO RONCEVAUX **580km**

Conques Village © Alexandra Huddleston

Route - The route is well-marked and varies between paths, tracks and country roads that cross fields and forests with generally moderate climbs and descents. Nevertheless, use caution on the steep rocky descent into Conques, which can be slippery when wet. This stage is short in order to arrive early and have time to explore the historic village of Conques.

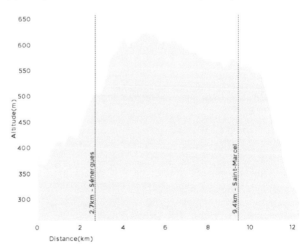

Conques church tympanum © Alexandra Huddleston

Conques (popl. 225, alt. 260m) is classified as one of the most beautiful villages in France and is on UNESCO's world heritage list. At the heart of the village is the abbey church of Sainte-Foy, which was once part of a monastery, though there are few remains. The church is dedicated to Saint Faith (*Sainte-Foy*), a 12 year old girl from Agen (about 220 km south-west) who was martyred by the Romans in 303 for refusing to sacrifice to pagan gods. In 866 her relics were brought to Conques.

The current church dates mostly from the 11th century, which was a time of significant prosperity for the Abbey. This prosperity stemmed in part from pilgrimage, as Saint Faith became famous for miracles, including curing blindness and releasing captives from their chains.

Above the main entrance is a tympanum that dates from the mid-12th century and which depicts the Last Judgment. Christ sits in a mandorla (almond-shaped ring) with his hand raised in blessing. To his left are the damned with scenes from hell and to the right, the saved, including Saint Faith, with scenes from heaven.

From 1987 to 1994, Pierre Soulages (1919-), a native of nearby Rodez and a major artist in the post-war abstract movement, designed the church's 100 plus modern stained-glass windows.

The **Treasury Museum** holds the abbey's *trésor*, or treasury, which includes several medieval reliquaries (containers used to hold holy objects (relics)) and the extraordinary Majesty of Saint Faith, or the Saint Faith reliquary, a gold and jewel-encrusted statue that symbolised the Saint's glory.

From April to October, each evening at 9 p.m. a priest from the abbey provides a commentary on the tympanum (in French). This is followed by an organ recital, including the opportunity to visit the church's upper ambulatory (recommended).

See Shaver-Crandell, A., Gerson, P. L., & Stones, A, pp. 179-181 (1995). The pilgrim's guide to Santiago de Compostela: A gazetteer. London: Harvey Miller Publishers.

stage 10

Waypoint	Total(km)	Directions	Verification	Compass	Altitude(m)
1	0.0	From the church in **Espeyrac,** continue descent through village and take first right	Church to the left.	SE	394
2	0.2	Cross the D42 road, continuing descent towards cemetery. Direction Sénergues	Pass Hôtel de la Vallée on left and cemetery on right.	SW	388
3	0.3	Cross bridge over the stream (La Daze) and continue on the track		SE	375
4	0.7	Keep left on road and continue straight.	Farmhouse to the right	W	395
5	1.0	Turn left onto path	Signpost	S	413
6	1.2	Cross stream (Ruisseau du Tayrac) and continue straight. At the end of the track, turn right onto road (D42)	Stone house and Signpost Sénergues	SW	414
7	1.8	Cross stone bridge to enter Célis. Turn left followed by immediate right.	Iron cross on left and signpost.	W	425
8	2.5	Continue straight on path to reach village of Sénergues.	Pass cemetery on right and cross on left.	W	484
9	2.7	In **Sénergues** turn right and continue straight	Pass church on right	NW	500
10	2.8	Turn left onto road (D42) to leave village	Cross	W	506
11	2.9	Keep left at fork and continue straight on road (D242)	Keep cafe to the right	SW	506
12	3.0	Turn right off road (D242). Climb.	After passing Q8 garage on left. Signpost.	NW	505
13	3.1	Cross street and continue straight on footpath. Climb.	Keep right of house	NW	509
14	3.3	Turn right off road onto footpath that crosses forest.		NW	548
15	3.9	Continue straight on track	Forest to the left	W	593
16	4.3	Keep left on track	Pass under power lines	W	603
17	4.8	Turn left onto D42 road		W	613
18	4.9	Turn right and continue straight. Direction Garbuech	Wooden cross and signpost	N	621
19	5.3	Turn left onto track running between wooden/barbed wire fencing		W	623
20	5.8	Turn left	Signpost	SW	613
21	6.6	Turn right onto D42 road and continue straight		W	611
22	7.7	Turn right onto track running parallel to road D42	Road D42 to the left	NW	578
23	8.6	Merge onto D42 road and continue straight on road	Pass through hamlets of Vernhe and Saint-Marcel	W	571
24	9.4	In **Saint-Marcel** keep left	Toilet and watering point	SW	576
25	10.5	In hamlet of La Croix Torte, turn left onto the track that descends into Conques.		SW	546
26	11.5	At intersection, continue descent straight on footpath towards village of Conques		SW	423

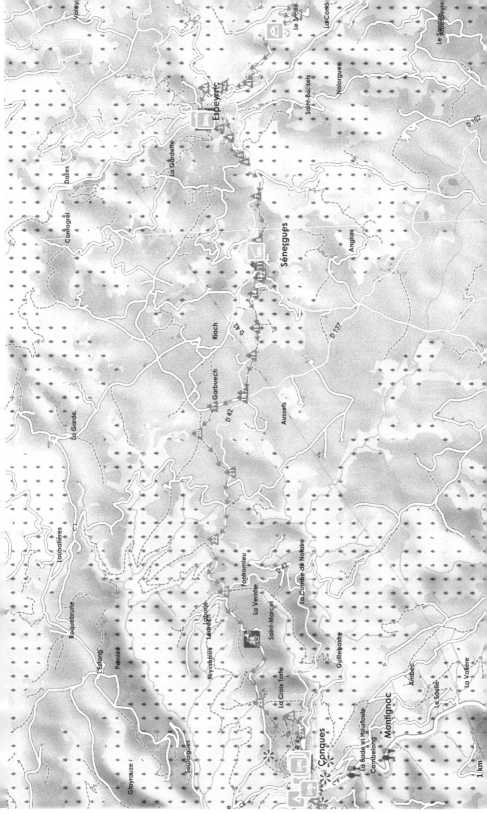

27	11.8	Cross road D42R and continue straight on rue Emilie Roudier to enter Conques	Pass police station (*Gendarmerie Nationale*) on left	W	359
28	12.1	Keep left. Steep descent, direction church of Sainte-Foy		W	324
29	12.2	Turn right on rue Gonzagues Florens. Continue descent towards church of Sainte-Foy		W	317
30	12.3	Arrive at **Conques** centre	Turn left to Place de l'Eglise		314

ACCOMODATION & TOURIST INFORMATION

Senergues

Gîte d'Étape Domaine de Senos, (Isabelle and Benoit), Chemin-de-Compostelle, 12320 Senergues, Aveyron, France; +33(0)5 65 72 91 56; www.gite-aveyron.com; €17/pers. €39/half board, €49/full board, €17.50/dinner, €5.50/breakfast; Hostel in a former convent, hosts are welcoming. 33 places in 12 rooms. English spoken.

Conques

Centre d'Accueil, Abbaye, 12320 Conques, Aveyron, France; saintefoy@abbaye-conques.org; www.abbaye-conques.org; €11/pers. in dormitory, €23-30/single room, €33-42/double room; €39-48/triple room; €60/4-pers. room, €12/dinner, €6/breakfast.; The traditional place that pilgrims stay on arriving in Conques. 96 places in 20 rooms or 4 dormitories in monastery complex. Accommodation for donkeys. English spoken. Recommended to take dinner elsewhere.

Gîte d'Étape Communal, Rue Emilie Roudié, 12320 Conques, Aveyron, France; +33(0)5 65 72 82 98; +33(0)5 65 72 85 00; gite-etape-conques@orange.fr; €14/pers. (reservation required); 30 places in two dormitories. Basic and cramped. Kitchen. English spoken.

Auberge Saint-Jacques, Rue Gonzague Florens, 12320 Conques, Aveyron, France; +33(0)5 65 72 86 36; info@aubergestjacques.fr; www.aubergestjacques.fr/; €59-€72/double room, €9/breakfast, €20-€42/dinner, €56-€69/half board; Hotel/restaurant located in the village centre. 13 basic rooms. English spoken. Restaurant serves traditional regional cuisine.

Chambre d'Hôtes au Nid d'Angèle, (Véronique Mary), Rue Charlemagne, 12320 Conques, Aveyron, France; +33(0)6 60 87 28 61; Veronique-mary@bbox.fr; www.aunidangele.com; €45-€65/1 pers. €65-€80/2 pers., €108/3 pers.; Lovely B&B that opened in 2015 with charming and welcoming host, cool decor. 3 rooms. English spoken. On the GR®65 descending from the Cathedral.

Chambre d'Hôtes Chez Alice et Charles, (Alice and Charles Gaillac), Rue du Chanoine André Bénazech, 12320 Conques, Aveyron, France; +33(0)5 65 72 82 10; +33(0)7 87 19 17 59; €60/single, €68-€79/double, €105/triple; Charming B&B in village centre with views on Abbey. 4 rooms.

Hôtel Sainte Foy, Rue Gonzague Florens, 12320 Conques, Aveyron, France; +33(0)5 65 69 84 03; hotelsaintefoy@hotelsaintefoy.fr; www.hotelsaintefoy.com; €97-€175/double, €13/breakfast; Fancier hotel with terrace. Certain rooms have lovely views on the Abbey. English spoken.

Camping Beau Rivage (Conques), Faubourg de Conques, 12320 Conques, Aveyron, France; +33(0)5 65 69 82 23; +33(0)6 61 17 47 73; camping.conques@wanadoo.fr; www.campingconques.com; €48/1-2 pers. €62/3-4 pers., €68/5 pers.; half board: €35/pers. (tent), €38-67/ pers. (mobile home), €7/breakfast.; Located in river valley after descending from village centre. Next to the GR®65, possibility to rent one of 12 modern mobile homes in camp-ground that borders the Dourdou river. Swimming pool. English spoken. Good restaurant on site.

Office de Tourisme, Le Bourg, 12320 Conques, Aveyron, France; +33(0)5 65 72 85 00; tourisme@conques.fr; www.tourisme-conques.fr

DISTANCE **25.8km**

ASCENT **1139m**

DESCENT **1212m**

FROM LE PUY **206km**

TO RONCEVAUX **568km**

Conques Romanesque Bridge © Alexandra Huddleston

Route - The route is well-marked. The first part includes a long steep climb out of Conques through forests and fields, followed by a long descent into the post-industrial city of Decazeville. Thereafter, the route follows mostly asphalt roads to Livinhac-le-Haut.

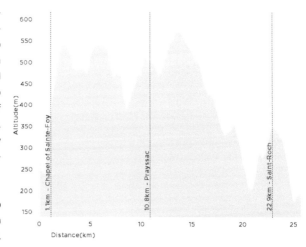

Pointers - Be sure to keep to the GR®65 between Conques and Decazville. There are two moments of possible confusion: (1) after the Chapel of Saint Foy, at a junction with the variant through Noailhac, and (2) where the GR®62B descends into Firmi, well before Decazeville, and which also uses the red and white way markings of the GR®.

Romanesque Bridge (*Pont Romain*)

The *Pont Romain* allowed pilgrims to Conques to cross the potentially dangerous Dourdou river. The 5 arched bridge made from red sandstone was originally medieval (14th century), though was largely rebuilt in the 16th-17th centuries.

Decazeville

Decazeville (popl. 6000, alt. 163m) was founded in the 19th century by Duc Decazes as an industrial centre. By the mid-19th century, the city was one of the most important and productive coal and steel producers in the country. To ac-commodate a growing population, the **Church of Our Lady** (*Eglise Notre-Dame*) was completed in 1861. Notably, the church has 14 paintings of the Way of the Cross (1862-1863) by Gustave Moreau, an important 19th century French painter and an early leader of Symbolism (an artistic movement that used non-naturalistic or dream-like images). Moreau was particularly inspired by Italian Renaissance painting, biblical themes and mythology. His former villa and studio in Paris houses a museum dedicated to his works.

The city holds a market each Tuesday morning (Place Cabrol).

ROUTE INSTRUCTIONS

Waypoint	Total(km)	Directions	Verification	Compass	Altitude(m)
1	0.0	In **Conques**, from place de l'Eglise (church)/rue du Trésor turn left onto rue Charlemagne. Steep descent.		W	313
2	0.3	Take staircase to the left and continue descent.		W	253
3	0.4	Cross the D901 road and cross **Romanesque bridge (*pont romain*)**	Pass Auberge du Pont Romain on the right	W	249
4	0.6	Take left onto footpath. Steep climb, switch backing up hill.	Signpost	N	225
5	0.8	Cross road D232 and continue climb on footpath to Chapel of Sainte-Foy.		SW	274
6	1.1	Beside the **Chapel of Sainte-Foy**, continue climb on track which heads left		SE	367
7	2.4	Turn right	Signpost	NW	539
8	2.7	Cross road and continue straight, descending.	Signpost	W	546
9	5.3	Turn right onto road D606		NW	530
10	5.6	Turn left. Direction Les Clémenties	Signpost	W	541
11	6.6	After passing through hamlet of Les Clémenties, turn left onto path and pass through hamlet of Les Bréfinies.	Signpost	SW	538
12	7.8	Turn left and pass through hamlet of Eyniès	Village	NW	474
13	7.9	After watering point turn left onto footpath	Watering point	N	474
14	10.4	Cross road D183 and continue straight to village of Prayssac	Cross	S	505
15	10.8	Cross the village of **Prayssac** and continue straight on road		SE	507
16	12.9	Enter village of Roumégous and turn left	Signpost. Farm to the right.	W	545

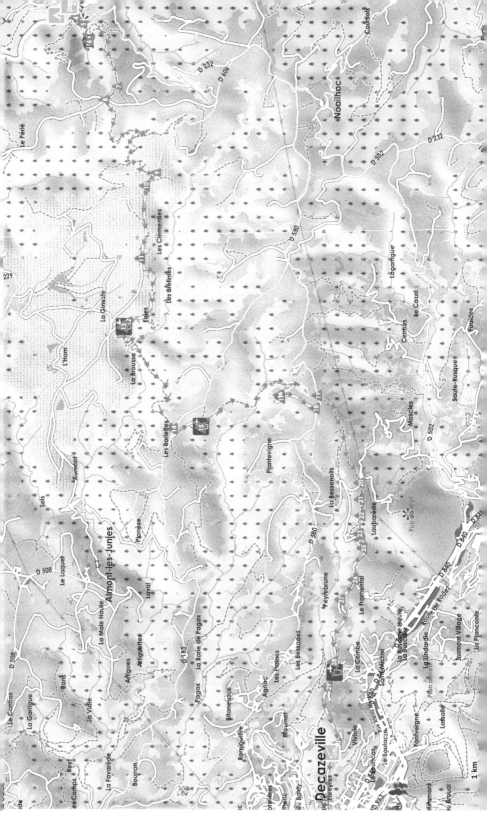

17	13.0	Continue straight on road through village centre.		SE	545
18	13.5	Turn left onto D580 road	Signpost	SE	573
19	13.7	Turn right onto track and continue straight	Signpost.	SW	574
20	15.2	Cross street and follow path straight through fields	Signpost	W	521
21	15.4	Merge right onto footpath. Continue straight through fields		W	501
22	15.7	Merge right onto track. Continue straight through fields		NW	507
23	15.9	Merge left onto track	Greenhouse	W	500
24	16.0	Turn left onto footpath	Farm to the right	W	483
25	16.1	Turn left onto the road that descends towards Decazeville		W	471
26	16.6	Enter village of Plegat and keep right on main road.	Signpost	NW	436
27	17.0	At the farm keep left. Enter the hamlet of Le Fromental.	Pass farm to the right.	W	427
28	18.0	Enter hamlet of La Combe and continue straight on road around sharp corner.	Pass farm on right	W	350
29	18.4	At fork keep right, direction Decazeville	Signpost	NW	333
30	19.2	Turn right on route de Viviole.	Keep to right of wooden information sign	W	357
31	20.1	Continue descent straight on route de Montarnal	Pass tourist information map on the left	SW	275
32	20.4	Turn left staying on route de Montarnal		SW	245
33	20.6	Merge left onto the D580 road and take immediate right at fork onto D615 road in **Decazville**	Head away from **Church of Our Lady**	S	222
34	20.9	Turn right at end of street onto avenue Laromiguière/D963. Take immediate left at picnic area onto route de Nantuech and continue straight.	Rest area to the left with watering point	N	207
35	22.2	Turn left onto chemin du Boutigou	Signpost	W	278
36	22.7	Cross route du Puech and continue straight	Pass cemetery ahead to the left	W	338
37	22.9	Keep left on route de **Saint-Roch**/D157	Pass church on the right	NW	349
38	23.9	Turn right onto path that leads towards forest and descends to the Lot River valley.	Pass farmhouse on left	NW	329
39	24.9	Cross the D21 road and the Pont de Livinhac bridge over the Lot River	Signpost	N	212
40	25.3	Turn left onto rue Camille Couderc towards centre of Livinhac-le-Haut	Stay left of wooden tourist information sign	N	185
41	25.5	Cross avenue Paul Ramadier and continue straight on rue de la République. Towards village centre.		NE	189
42	25.8	Arrive at **Livinhac-le-Haut**	Place de l'Eglise		202

Decazeville

Gîte d'Étape Sentinelle, (Brigitte d'Halluin), Place Saint Roch, 12300 Decazeville, Aveyron, France; +33(0)3 56 54 34 95 2; Donation (breakfast and dinner included, made with produce from garden); 7-10 places in 2 dormitories. English spoken. Possibility to participate in morning/evening prayers. Very welcoming and provide useful services (including shoe repair, accommodation for horses, etc.).

Ecogîte le Mineur Paysan, (Christian Lacombe), 765 route de Viviole, 12300 Decazeville, Aveyron, France; +33(0)5 65 43 33 44; +33(0)6 23 20 29 97; lemineurpaysan@laposte.net; lemineurpaysan.free.fr; €19/pers. in 6-pers. dormitory, €23/pers. in 4-pers. room, €24/pers. in double room), €11/tent (breakfast included), €6/horse; On the GR about 2km before Decazeville, 14 places in 1 dormitory and 3 rooms. An eco-friendly hostel that is welcoming, comfortable and well equipped. Serves organic foods (including take-away).

Office de Tourisme, Square Jean Ségalat, 12300 Decazeville, Aveyron, France; +33(0)5 65 43 18 36; www. decazeville-tourisme.com

Livinhac-le-Haut

Accueil Pèlerin la Vita É Bella, (Andrea and Jani), 90 place du 14 Juin, 12300 Livinhac-le-Haut, Aveyron, France; +33(0)6 77 55 78 33; maisonrigolo@yahoo.com; etapelavitaebella.blogspot.fr; €23/pers. in double room; €20/pers. in triple room; €18/pers. in four-pers. room; €16/pers. in six-person room; €5/breakfast; donation/dinner.; Located next to the church on the main square. 12 places in various sized rooms. Very welcoming couple who met on the Chemin. Organic food. English spoken.

Gîte d'Étape 'la Magnanerie', (Marie and Alain Simond), 170 rue du Faubourg, 12300 Livinhac-le-Haut, Aveyron, France; +33(0)5 65 43 25 56; +33(0)6 16 70 61 38; therese.wiart@wanadoo.fr; €13-€17/pers.; €6/breakfast (upon request); 15 places in rooms and dormitory. On the left upon entering Livinhac-Le-Haut, gîte housed on a charming historic property with garden. Cozy rooms. Accommodation for horses.

Gîte Communal, 85 place du 14 Juin, 12300 Livinhac-le-Haut, Aveyron, France; +33(0)5 65 80 84 82; +33(0)6 76 86 94 77; gitelivinhac@orange.fr; albums-gho.b2f-concept.net/12/GS26.html; €14.70/pers. €34.70/ half board (Dinner available upon reservation at the Bar-Restaurant de la Mairie (+33 5 65 63 80 22)); 29 places in 8 rooms. English spoken.

Chambre d'Hôtes sur le Chemin, (Stéphan Gleyal), Place du 14 Juillet, 12300 Livinhac-le-Haut, Aveyron, France; +33(0)6 89 55 55 32; +33(0)6 16 98 54 77; surlechemin@orange.fr or m.gleyal@laposte.net; www. surlechemin.net; €25-35/1 pers.; €49-€55/2 pers.; €70/3 pers.; €90/4 pers. (breakfast included); 5 rooms, renovated in 2012. Basic English. Free accommodation for horses with reservations. Kitchen.

Landscape towards Decazeville

QUERCY

Quercy gariotte © Alexandra Huddleston

Quercy, which extends from Figeac to Moissac, was the ancient home of the *Cadourques* or *Cadurci,* a Celtic people that inhabited the region before the Roman invasions of the first century. Quercy was subsequently occupied by the Visigoths (5th century) and Franks (6th century). It fell largely under English control from the 14th century until the end of the Hundred Years' War (1433) and was also a battleground in the 16th century Wars of Religion, which pitted French Roman Catholics against Huguenots (French Protestants).

Quercy is made up of a dry limestone plateau, called the *Causses,* which is covered with small oak trees. *Pigeonniers* (dovecotes or pigeon lofts) that were built in the 18th-19th centuries also dot the landscape. At the time, pigeons were raised for their droppings, or *guano*, an important fertilizer that was later replaced by chemical fertilizers. The region is also marked by *cayrous* (stone walls) and *caselles* or *gariottes*, small circular stone huts built by shepherds. Sheep farming remains an important business, and the region boasts its own race of sheep which is white with black ears and rims around the eyes.

The traditional capital of Quercy is Cahors. The region is famous for its cuisine, notably duck dishes, black truffles, and the red wines of Cahors. The Occitan language continues to be spoken by a dwindling minority (mostly the elderly).

DISTANCE **24.4km**
ASCENT **707m**
DESCENT **731m**
FROM LE PUY **232m**
TO RONCEVAUX **542km**

Figeac centre

Route - The route is well-marked, and consists mostly of tracks and asphalt roads through farmland, forests and villages. Proximity to the Lot and Célé Rivers makes this area agriculturally rich.

Pointers - **Culture:** The 18km section of the GR®65 from Montredon to Figeac is on UNESCO world heritage list. **Advance planning:** Ensure sufficient provisions in Livinhac-le-Haut, as there are no grocers until Figeac, and limited opportunities for meals in between. **Market:** There is a lively and colourful market in Figeac on Saturday mornings, selling local produce and goods.

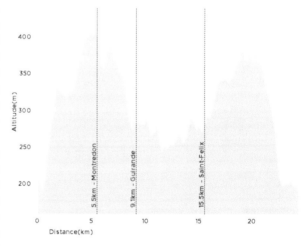

Chapel of Mary Magdalene (*Chapelle Sainte-Marie-Madeleine*)

Built in the 12th-13th century, the chapel is remarkable for the late 15th century frescoes that decorate its vaults. These depict the tetramorph (animal representations of the four evangelists - Matthew, Mark, Luke and John), as well as a scene from the Martyrdom of Saint Namphaise (a 9th century hermit from Quercy) and Mary Magdalene.

Note as well the late 12th century masks that decorate the base of the arches.

Figeac

The vibrant city of Figeac (popl. 9,775, alt. 200m) was founded in 830 and developed around the Benedictine **Abbey of Saint Saviour** (*Abbaye Saint-Sauveur*), built in the 11th century.

Positioned on the Célé river, Figeac became a dynamic trading and religious centre. The houses and market places that make up the old town are remarkable testaments of medieval architecture.

The Hundred Years' War, however, brought an end to Figeac's prosperity. The city later became a Huguenot (French Protestant) stronghold in the Wars of Religion, when its Catholic churches were destroyed. Figeac is also famous for Jean-François Champollion (1790-1832), the historian and linguist who founded Egyptology (the study of Egyptian antiquities) and who played a major role in deciphering the Rosetta Stone and Egyptian hieroglyphs. Both Egyptology and the history of world writing are on display at the **Champollion Museum.**

The city hosts a colourful market each Saturday morning.

ROUTE INSTRUCTIONS

Waypoint	Total(km)	Directions	Verification	Compass	Altitude(m)
1	0.0	From Place de l'Eglise in **Livinhac** take rue du Couderc to leave village.	Pass town hall (*Mairie*) and pharmacy on the left	W	206
2	0.3	Cross avenue de Paul Ramadier/D21 and keep right on road D627	Signpost	NW	212
3	0.6	Turn right onto the small road that climbs to Pérols	Cross on the left	N	192
4	1.1	Cross road and continue straight on Puech del Soyt in the direction of Le Thabor	Pass Gîte de Pérols on the left	N	248
5	1.9	Turn right onto track and continue straight	Leave behind houses of Le Thabor	N	328
6	3.2	Turn left onto road D21 and continue straight		NW	320
7	3.4	Turn left onto road. Direction Le Feydel (farm) and take immediate right on path	Pass barn in the distance to the right. Signpost.	S	327
8	3.7	Continue straight on path as it passes through Feydel-Haut and Cagnac before reaching Montredon	Signpost	NW	347
9	5.2	Merge left onto the D2 road and enter the village of Montredon.		W	405
10	5.3	Turn right and head towards the village centre, in the direction of the church (visible)	Chapel of Notre-Dame de Pitié behind	NW	404
11	5.5	Turn left in **Montredon** centre	Pass church on the left	SW	408

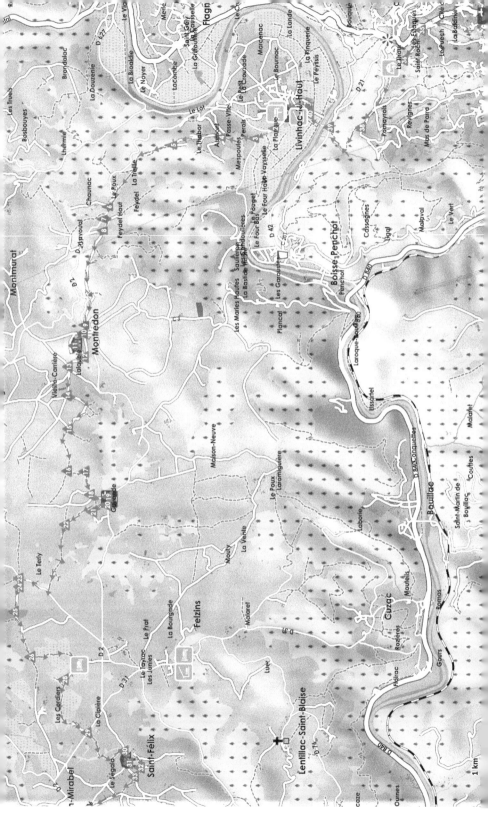

12	5.7	At road's end turn right and continue straight direction Lalaubie	Signpost	NW	407
13	6.0	Continue straight through farms of La-laubie		W	374
14	6.4	Turn left towards Tournié and pass through village	Signpost	SW	373
15	7.2	Continue straight on track	After last farm on the left	NW	375
16	7.9	Keep left into farm of Lacoste	Signpost	S	348
17	8.1	At fork keep right		W	342
18	8.5	Turn left onto the road, followed by an immediate left leading to the chapel of Guirande	Signpost	SW	315
19	8.8	Turn right at the chapel of Guirande	**Chapel of Mary Magdalene**	W	286
20	8.9	Turn right and climb to village of Guirande	After stone house on right. Signpost	N	279
21	9.1	After last houses in village of **Guirande**, turn right	Path lined with oaks	NE	285
22	9.7	Turn left	Pass hanger to the right	NW	285
23	11.1	Turn left and descend towards reser-voir.	Cross	NW	278
24	11.3	Turn right onto road D41 and continue straight towards hamlet of Terly	Signpost	NW	279
25	11.6	Cross reservoir (ruisseau de Guiande) and continue straight past the farm of Gévaudan (on the right)	Signpost	W	252
26	12.3	Turn left towards the hamlet of Bord	Signpost	S	246
27	13.1	Turn right onto road and continue straight.		NW	265
28	13.4	Before last barn turn right on track and rejoin to the left a path leading to the farm of La Cipière	Signpost	N	269
29	14.5	Cross the D2 road and continue straight on footpath		SW	284
30	15.4	Turn right onto road towards village of Saint-Felix	Signpost. Pass church and pic-nic area on right.	SW	271
31	15.5	In the centre of **Saint-Felix** turn left onto street	After passing church on right	S	275
32	15.8	Turn right onto asphalt road and con-tinue straight towards the farm Croix de Jordy		NW	292
33	16.0	At fork (farm) turn left and then right onto footpath, which leads to the D206	Signpost	W	288
34	16.9	Turn left onto road D206 and then right onto footpath.		NW	338
35	17.2	Cross D2 and continue straight on road in the direction of the church of Saint-Jean-Mirabel	Signpost and iron cross to the right	N	341
36	17.3	Turn left before the fork and entrance to the village (on the right). Continue straight to rejoin the D2 road	Picnic area to the left	SW	342
37	18.4	Continue straight on D2 road	Pass stone cross on left	SW	351
38	19.1	Turn left onto narrow footpath	Immediately after stone ga-rage on left	SW	379
39	19.2	Turn left onto road and take first right and pass through hamlet of l'Hôpital		S	381

40	19.5	Turn right onto footpath		NW	381
41	20.1	Turn right onto road then turn left onto footpath (after passing cross on the left)	Pass cross on the left	N	373
42	22.0	Continue straight on road (Roussilhe) to descend into Figeac.		W	301
43	22.7	Turn left onto Le Terrie	Railway tracks to the right	S	227
44	22.8	Pass through underpass and keep left on Le Terrie Road, which becomes Allée Victor Hugo	Célé River to the right	W	210
45	24.0	Turn right onto small road - rue du Griffoul - that runs along river		NW	201
46	24.2	Turn right over bridge and cross the Célé River to enter Figeac city centre		N	198
47	24.2	Turn left onto Quai Albert Bessières		W	199
48	24.4	Arrive at **Figeac** city centre			198

ACCOMODATION & TOURIST INFORMATION

Felzins

Le Pentadou, (Nanou and Laurent Fillot), Le Bourg, 46270 Felzins, Lot, France; +33(0)5 65 40 48 12; info@lepentadou.com; www.lepentadou.com; B&B: €60/1 pers. €66/2 pers., €93/3 pers., €116/4 pers., Hostel: €25/pers. (breakfast included), €20/dinner (reservations requested); Located off the GR®65, 10 places in dormitory and at least 9 places in 4 bedrooms. Belgium family completely restored a lovely home with garden and pool. English spoken. Accommodation for horses.

La Grange de Bord, (Christiane and Jean Bontemps), Bord, 46270 Felzins, Lot, France; +33(0)5 65 10 66 71; +33(0)6 18 62 25 24; lagrangedebord@orange.fr; www.lagrangedebord.net; €60/double room (breakfast included), €19/dinner (upon reservation); 2 rooms in lovely restored farmhouse. A generous breakfast and dinner feature products from garden and local specialities.

Figeac

Gîte Antoine le Pelerin, (Martha and Antoine), Chemin de Roussilhes, 46100 Figeac, Lot, France; +33(0)3 65 27 26 14 6; infos@antoinelepelerin.fr; www.antoinelepelerin.fr; Donation/dormitory; €35/half board ; €35/4 pers. room ; €35/3 pers. room; 1km before Figeac centre on the GR®65. 15 places in 3 rooms and a 6-pers. dormitory in a lovely home in typical Quercy style. The hosts, who are both former pilgrims, are famous for their hospitality. Organic food and vegetables from the garden are served.

Gîte du Carmel, 9 avenue Jean Jaurés, 46100 Figeac, Lot, France; +33(0)6 14 32 05 51; carmel.figeac@wanadoo.fr; www.paroissedefigeac.fr/Le-Carmel-de-Figeac; Donation (dinner and breakfast included); 8 places in 2 dormitories. Simple accommodation in Carmelite convent in city centre. Run by volunteers. Possibility to participate in religious ceremonies. English spoken.

Gîte d'Étape du Gua, (Frédérique Latrace), 14 Bis avenue du Maréchal Joffre, 46100 Figeac, Lot, France; +33(0)5 81 71 50 28; +33(0)6 74 73 22 69; gitedugua.figeac@gmail.com; www.figeac-gite-compostelle.fr/index.html; €14.50/pers.; €4.50/breakfast; €32/half board; 15 places in 6-pers. dormitories in old renovated house with garden and kitchen. English spoken.

Gîte Passiflore, 10 Chemin du Moulin de Laporte, 46100 Figeac, Lot, France; +33(0)5 65 40 56 93; +33(0)7 87 46 66 74; gitepassiflore@gmail.com; https://gitepassiflore.wordpress.com; €16/pers. (breakfast included), €15/dinner; €30/half board; 4 places in dormitory and 1 studio. English spoken.

Le Soleilho, (Martine Garsi and Jean-Louis Royer), 8 rue Prat, 46100 Figeac, Lot, France; +33(0)5 65 38 42 62; +33(0)6 75 89 96 53; jeanlouisroyer@yahoo.fr; www.chambres-hotes-figeac.com/chambres-hotes-figeac-lot.html; Hostel: €19/pers. (breakfast included); €75-120/2-4 pers. rooms.; 6 places in hostel and 4 bedrooms in B&B. A top-ranked hostel and B&B in Figeac with generous and welcoming hosts. Located in the old town with fully equipped kitchen. English spoken.

Le Chemin des Anges, (Lydie and Pierre), 30 Allée Victor Hugo, 46100 Figeac, Lot, France; +33(0)6 10 30 55 90; +33(0)6 07 12 35 63; gite.chemindesanges@gmail.com; www.chemindesanges.fr; € |5/2 pers. €5/breakfast, €16/dinner (upon reservation); 12 places. Located close to historic centre, run by former pilgrims, welcoming with garden.

Le Quatorze, 14 place de l'Estang, 46100 Figeac, Lot, France; +33(0)5 65 14 08 92; infos@le-quatorze.fr; www.le-quatorze.fr; €77-€98/double room. €7-€12/breakfast; Considered one of the nicest hotels in Figeac, 14 stylish rooms. Located in city-centre next to the Church of Saint-Saveur. English spoken.

Hôtel des Bains, 1 rue du Griffoul, 46100 Figeac, Lot, France; +33(0)5 65 34 10 89; figeac@hoteldesbains.fr; www.hoteldesbains.fr; €54-€80/double rooms; €9/breakfast; Cute and welcoming two-star hotel that was formerly a bathhouse with 19 rooms located on the Célé River. English spoken.

Le Club Figeacois du Poney et du Cheval, Avenue de Nayrac, 46100 Figeac, Lot, France; +33(0)5 65 34 70 57; +33(0)6 46 48 47 64; centre.equestre.figeac@gmail.com; www.cfpc.ffe.com; €10/horse stall (reservations required); Accommodation for horses. Possibility to camp on grounds, access to showers.

Apartment Cassagnes, (Isabelle Cassagnes), 14 rue Roquefort, 46100 Figeac, Lot, France; +33(0)5 65 34 77 27; +33(0)6 23 53 14 08; icassagnes@free.fr; www.tourisme-figeac.com/web/FR/154-detail-d-un-point-d-etape.php?id=HLOMIP046FS0039I ; €55-€85/2-5 pers. (sheets included); €7/breakfast; 1 apartment for 2-5 persons. Centrally located with view of Church of Saint-Sauveur. Kitchen. English spoken.

Office de Tourisme, Hôtel de la Monnaie - place Vival, 46100 Figeac, Lot, France; +33(0)5 65 34 06 25; info@tourisme-figeac.com; www.tourisme-figeac.com

stage 13

DISTANCE **19km**

ASCENT **648m**

DESCENT **453m**

FROM LE PUY **256km**

TO RONCEVAUX **518km**

Faycelles

Route - The route is well-marked and consists mostly of asphalt roads through pastures, as one enters the sparsely populated Causses region, which is composed of several dry limestone plateaus that form part of the Massif Central. There is a long climb on small country roads out of Figeac to Mas de la Croix, followed by paths through dry oak forests towards Gréalou.

Pointers - **Culture:** The 22.5 km section of the GR®65 from Faycelles to Cajarc is on the UNESCO world heritage list. **Caution:** Pay attention to stay on the GR®65, particularly in Figeac, where there is an intersection with the GR®6/GR®6A, as well as in Mas de la Croix, where the variant through the Célé Valley, the GR®651, forks to the right. These GR® also use the same red and white way markings as the GR®65

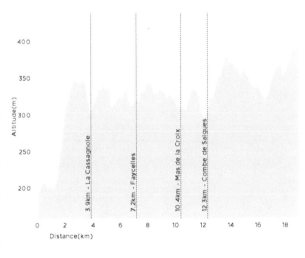

Figeac

Boulevard du Colonel Teulié

Abbatiale Saint Sauveur

Rue du Chapitre

Avenue du Maréchal Foch

Rue de la Gare

Avenue George

Avenue En

Rue Albert Bessières

Avenue Fernand Pezet

Avenue Maréchal Joffre

Avenue Jean Jaurès

Rue des Frères

Rue de la République

Rue de Clermont

Boulevard Georges Juskiewenski

Rue Gambetta

Rue des Courtaliers

Rue des Courtaliers

Rue Prat André

Rue Malleville

Rue Séguier

Rue Victor Delb

100 m

D 662

Faycelles

The picturesque village of Faycelles (popl. 640, alt. 170m), with its beautiful valley views, developed around a feudal castle in the Middle Ages, though excavations suggest prior Neolithic and Roman occupation nearby. During the Hundred Years' War the village was captured by the English, and in the 15th century the castle became a summer residence of the Abbot of Figeac. In an effort to centralize power, the castle was demolished under the reign of King Louis XIII (1610-1643), and a church was later built in its place (1886-1888).

Gréalou

At the centre of the tiny village of Gréalou (popl. 270, alt. 200m) is the 12th century Romanesque church of Our Lady of Assumption (*Notre-Dame-de-l'Assomption*), which was largely rebuilt in subsequent centuries, including important additions in the 15th century after the Hundred Years' War. The church has a lovely wooden sculpted pieta from the first half of the 16th century.

ROUTE INSTRUCTIONS

Waypoint	Total(km)	Directions	Verification	Compass	Altitude(m)
1	0.0	In **Figeac**, at intersection of boulevard Georges Juskiewenski and Le Célé River turn left over footbridge to cross river. The alternative route to Rocamadour - the GR®6 - also departs from this intersection, but instead heads north on the boulveard away from the river.		S	196
2	0.0	After crossing foot bridge turn left into parking lot and immediately right on avenue Jean-Jaurés	Follow wall on the left	SE	195
3	0.1	At fork stay left on high road		SW	192
4	0.3	Turn left though underpass and then right onto Le Cinglé Bas. Continue straight along tracks	Train tracks should be to the right	SW	197
5	1.2	Turn left onto avenue Président Georges Pompidou, then take first left.	Pass through underpass	S	201
6	1.4	Turn right onto road, direction Bois de Palhasse. Steep climb	Signpost	S	197
7	1.7	Turn left onto footpath and continue steep climb through forest.		SE	237
8	2.1	Turn right onto the road and cross highway D802. Continue straight		SW	309
9	2.3	Enter Balajou and continue straight on road, which continues to climb south	Signpost	SW	316
10	2.8	At road's end, turn right direction La Cassagnole	Signpost	SW	348
11	3.7	Cross road and continue straight in the direction of La Cassagnole	Signpost	SW	326
12	3.9	At **La Cassagnole** keep right at the fork and climb. Continue straight on road.	Signpost	SW	313
13	6.2	Keep left at fork. Direction Faycelles		S	325

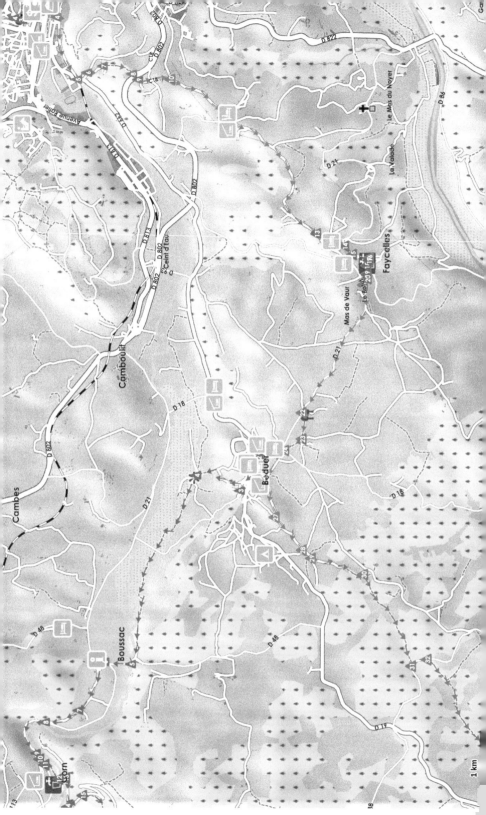

14	6.6	Merge right onto road and continue straight towards Faycelles		SW	330
15	6.8	Cross the D662 road and continue straight on Voie Romaine	Beautiful valley views on the left	SW	316
16	7.0	Turn right and climb staircase on rue de la Forge		W	314
17	7.1	Continue straight on road through village	Pass church on left.	NW	315
18	7.2	In **Faycelles** enter place Gallarde, pass church and turn left before cross. Then take immediate right	Church, cross and signpost.	SW	326
19	7.3	Continue straight on chemin de Saint Jacques	Signpost	W	326
20	7.4	Turn left onto footpath	Before road curves sharply to the right	W	320
21	7.5	Turn left onto the D21 road and continue straight	Head towards cross	SW	326
22	9.6	Turn left onto track and continue straight	Pass Bar de l'Eté on the left	SW	327
23	10.0	Turn right onto the road and then take immediate right onto footpath. Direction Gréalou	Signpost	NW	323
24	10.3	Turn right onto road and cross stone bridge. At end of road turn left onto D21 to arrive in Mas-de-la-Croix	Signpost	N	312
25	10.4	At **Mas de la Croix** intersection, turn left on GR®65. Direction Cajarc. The alternative route through the Célé Valley - GR®651 - continues straight on road D21 towards Béduer	Signpost	W	310
26	10.9	Leave the road and turn left onto the track	Before a bend in the road	SW	311
27	11.5	Turn onto track to the left and continue straight	Ahead pass fountain to the right	W	333
28	12.1	Turn left onto the road. Then take first right. Direction Mas de Surgues.	Signpost.	S	296
29	12.3	At fork keep left, Direction Cajarc, and pass through hamlet of **Combe de Salgues**	Signpost	S	307
30	13.1	At fork turn right and continue straight	Path follows stone wall	SW	351
31	14.6	Turn left onto the D38 road		SE	361
32	14.9	Turn right onto track and continue straight	Signpost	SW	358
33	16.7	At fork keep right on path. Climb towards hamlet of Le Puy Clavel.		SW	326
34	17.3	Turn right onto the road in the hamlet of le Puy Clavel	Signpost	W	362
35	17.4	Turn left onto track. Direction Gréalou.	Signpost	SW	365
36	18.2	Turn right onto the road and continue straight and cross the D19 road		SW	368
37	18.7	Turn left and then right to descend to village centre		S	399
38	19.0	Arrive at **Gréalou** centre	Church		388

Faycelles

Le Relais Saint-Jacques, (Marie-Claude and Jésus Gomez), La Cassagnole, 46100 Faycelles, Lot, France; +33(0)6 84 10 97 73; jesus.gomez.46@orange.fr or marieclaude.gomez@wanadoo.fr; www.cassagnole.com; Hostel: €13-€15/pers. €6/breakfast, €13/dinner (upon reservation) ; €37-€56/double or triple rooms; Located 5 km after Figeac on the GR®65. 33 places in dormitories and B&B rooms in a restored Quercy-style farmhouse with gardens and views. Accommodation for horses.

Bleu Lumière, (Anne Arbus), Mas du Rou, 46100 Faycelles, Lot, France; +33(0)3 97 55 15 95 5; +33(0)6 86 71 13 14; anne.arbus@gmail.com; www.chambredhotes-bleuslumiere.com; €50/pers. €70/2 pers., €12/dinner (upon reservation); Before Faycelles. 1 room in artist's home. Accommodation for horses. English spoken.

La Casellle, (Caroline and Christian Weidmann), La Croix Blanche, 46100 Faycelles, Lot, France; +33(0)5 65 34 05 68; +33(0)6 31 83 20 98; lacaselledhotes@gmail.com; www.lacaselledhotes.com; €56/2 pers. in caselle (breakfast included); €50-€72/2-3 persons in studio (breakfast included).; On the GR®65, 800 metres before Faycelles centre, lovely accommodation with garden and terrace in either the studio or caselle (small shepherd's house). Famous for its welcome. English spoken.

Béduer

Gîte Transhumance 46, (Sylvie Masbou), Mas de Bédorgues, 46100 Béduer, Lot, France; +33(0)6 80 60 01 90; transhumance46@orange.fr; www.transhumance46.sitew.com; €17/pers.; €6/breakfast, €15/dinner.; Located off the GR 65. 2 colourful rooms in a gypsy inspired gîte. Accommodation for horses.

Gîte le Bédigas, (Nadia Naegelen and Philippe Sandré), Le Bédigas Haut, 46100 Béduer, Lot, France; +33(0)5 65 33 49 85; +33(0)6 74 46 17 17; gite.bedigas@gmail.com; Dormitory €21/pers. (breakfast included), B&B: €40-€50/pers. €52-€65/2 pers., €74-€85/3 pers., €16/dinner; Located 1.5km from the GR®65 with access to the GR®651. 8 places in 2 dormitories and 5 B&B rooms in lovely 17th century stone house. English spoken. Horses welcome.

La Soursounette, (Nadia and Jean-Pierre Masson), Pech Rougié, 46100 Béduer, Lot, France; +33(0)5 65 38 12 60; +33(0)6 87 24 24 34; njp.masson@gmail.com; www.lasoursounette.fr/; Hostel: €17/pers.; €65/2-pers double room; €4.50/breakfast; €15/dinner (organic); Accommodation in a 19th century Quercy styled house that was renovated in 2013. Located on the GR 65 between Mas de la Croix and Fontaine de Fontieu, hostel with 4 places and B&B with one 2-pers. room.

Chambres d'Hôte la Coquille, (Jacqueline and Claude Ledoux), Le Bourg, 46100 Béduer, Lot, France; +33(0)5 65 11 40 18; +33(0)6 88 16 66 15; lacoquillebeduer@jimdo.com; €40/pers. €55-€60/2 pers.; Just below château Béduer, B&B in 12th century home. 8 places in 3 rooms. English spoken.

Chambres d'Hôtes Germier, (Jeanne and Christian Germier), Mas de la Croix, 46100 Béduer, Lot, France; +33(0)5 65 11 40 86; +33(0)6 38 94 10 47; lot.germier@gmail.com; www.chambresbeduerfigeac.com; €35/single, €55-€80/2 -3 pers. €20/dinner; 2 rooms in renovated farm house. English spoken.

La Mythié, (Myriam et Thierry Frugnac), Chemin du Château, 46100 Béduer, Lot, France; +33(0)5 65 34 22 25; +33(0)6 42 27 92 93; thierry.frugnac@wanadoo.fr; €45-€55/pers. €60-€70/2 pers., €80/3 pers., €22/dinner; Just below château Béduer, B&B with beautiful valley views, 3 rooms.

Camping du Pech-Ibert, (Jean-Paul Chassain), Mas de Vergnes, 46100 Béduer, Lot, France; +33(0)5 65 40 05 85; +33(0)6 71 15 42 72; camping.pech.ibert@orange.fr; www.camping-pech-ibert.com; 4-pers. cabin €20/pers. 4-6 pers. mobile home €17/pers., €5.50/breakfast, €15/dinner, €5-€10/horse; Located 500m from the GR®65, welcoming and familial camp ground with cabins and mobile homes for rent. Pool (15 June to 15 September). English spoken. Horses welcome.

Gréalou

Ecoasis, (Audrey et Emmanuel Sailly), Puy Clavel, 46160 Gréalou, Lot, France; +33(0)6 71 00 48 30; bonjour@ecoasis.fr; www.ecoasis.fr; €15-€21/pers.; €6/breakfast; €15/dinner; 30 places in 10 rooms of 2-5 pers. Beautiful views of Quercy. English spoken. Accommodation for horses.

Gîte des Volets Bleus, (Esther Marcoux), Place de l'Eglise, 46160 Gréalou, Lot, France; +33(0)5 65 40 69 86; +33(0)6 84 37 64 73; esther.marcoux@gmail.com; www.atelierdesvoletsbleus.sup.fr; €28/pers. (sheets and breakfast included); €14/dinner (garden and local produce); Converted Swiss artist's studio located across from Romanesque church. 8 places in dormitory and 2 bedrooms. English spoken. Accommodation for horses possible.

LENGTH	**129km**
STAGE ASCENT	**3806m**
STAGE DESCENT	**3877m**

Rocamadour Sanctuary © Alexandra Huddleston

Route - The alternative route through Rocamadour takes six days (as opposed to four on the main GR®65) and uses the red and white way markings typical of the GR®.

Rocamadour, revered for its miraculous black Madonna, has been an important Christian pilgrimage destination since the middle ages. Today, this stunning village built into the cliffs is the second most visited site in France.

The variant, which is less popular than the GR®65, is well marked. It departs from Figeac, following the GR®6 north through the villages of Cardaillac, with its lovely medieval centre, and Gramat. The arrival at Rocamdour through the valley of Alzou is particularly beautiful. From Rocamdour, the path then descends south on the GR®46 through the Natural Park of the Causse of Quercy, before rejoining the Lot River in the village of Vers. There, the route takes the GR®36, which runs alongside the

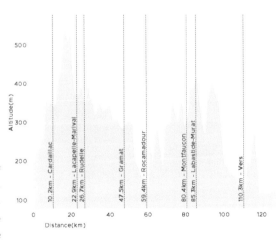

Lot to the city of Cahors, to reconnect with the main Way of Saint James (GR®65). Recommended intermediate resting places: Lacapelle-Marival; Gramat ; Rocamadour; Labastide -Murat and Vers.

Cardaillac

Cardaillac (popl. 600, alt. 375m) takes its name from the powerful family that ruled Quercy in the Middle Ages. Today, classified as one of the most beautiful villages in France, it has an impressive medieval quarter, parts of which date from the 11th century. It is possible to climb one of three medieval towers, each of which offers stunning views of the countryside. A market is held on Sunday mornings.

Lacapelle-Marival

Located at an important crossroads, the village of Lacapelle-Marival (popl. 1340, alt. 360m) developed at the end of the 13th century when Géraud de Cardillac, who was from a powerful Quercy family, built an imposing castle to defend the site. The castle was entirely renovated in the 15th century, but was abandoned during the French Revolution. Restoration of the castle began in 1992. Today, it houses the town hall (*Mairie*) and exhibitions. A market is held on Tuesday afternoons.

Fortified Church of St Martial (Rudelle)

Originally a 13th century hospital chapel, it was transformed into a defensive keep in the 14th century. An additional floor was added to provide shelter for villagers during the Hundred Years' War.

Rudelle fortified church of St Martial

Gramat

A picturesque town founded before the Roman period, Gramat (popl. 3,600, alt. 310m) became an important Roman town due to its position at the crossroads on the routes to Cahors and Rodez. In the Middle Ages, it was the seat of a powerful barony and an important market town. However, with the Hundred Years' War (14th-15th century), including repeated attacks by the English, and the Wars of Religion (16th century), Gramat's prosperity declined. It wasn't until the 19th century, and the arrival of the railway that the city's fortunes rebounded. It was also in the 19th century that the Congregation of Notre-Dame du Calvaire was founded by Pierre Bonhomme, the village priest who was beatified by Pope John-Paul II in 2003. The order is dedicated to teaching and helping the poor, and occupies an impressive convent (seen when entering the city) that provides accommodation for pilgrims. A market is held on Tuesday and Friday mornings.

Rocamadour

The Catholic sanctuary and village of Rocamadour (popl. 650, alt. 280m), which is built into the yellow cliffs that rise out of the Alzou river valley, is one of the most visited sites in France. A 216 step climb leads to the sanctuary with its seven Romanesque chapels. These include the Basilica of Saint Saviour (*Basilique Saint-Sauveur*) and the 12th century crypt of Saint Amadour, the hermit who according to legend founded Rocamadour. There is also the Chapel of Our Lady (*Chapelle Notre-Dame*), which houses the venerated 12th century Black Madonna whose miracles have drawn pilgrims from across Europe since the Middle Ages, including Henry II of England and several French kings. A bell that hangs in the chapel is said to ring by itself each time the Madonna performs a miracle. The lower village consists of a long street with fortified gates, tourist stores and cafes. Rocamadour is also the name of the local goat cheese made from raw milk.

Rocamadour Fortified Gate

Labastide -Murat

A former *bastide* (fortified village), Labastide-Murat (popl. 670, alt. 270m) takes its name from the famed Marshal of France and Napoleon Bonaparte's brother-in-law, Joachim Murat (1767-1815), who was born in the village. The son of an innkeeper, Murat's parents encouraged him to become a priest. However, he abandoned his studies at the seminary to enlist in a cavalry regiment and won rapid promotion. Murat was renowned for his daring cavalry charges and was one of Napoleon's most celebrated officers. He was later promoted to King of Naples and married Napoleon's youngest sister, Caroline Bonaparte. His childhood home and a former inn was made into a museum which is open from 15 July to 15 September.

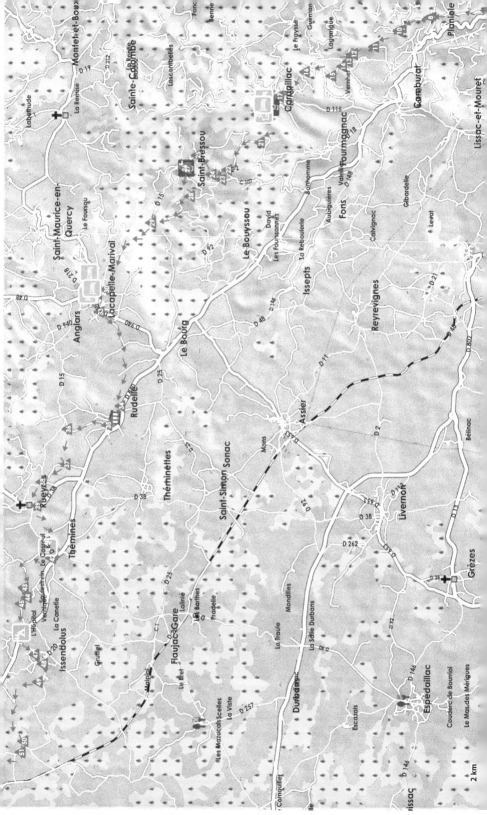

Waypoint	Total(km)	Directions	Verification	Compass	Altitude(m)
1	0.0	In **Figeac**, at intersection of boulevard Georges Juskiewenski and Le Célé River head north up boulevard away from Célé river on GR®6	Way markings continue to be the white and red bands of the GR®6	N	192
2	0.3	Turn left on rue des Maquisards		NW	199
3	0.5	Turn right onto avenue Marcenac	Keep church of Carmes to the left	N	200
4	0.6	Turn left onto chemin de la Curie and continue straight	Signpost	NE	200
5	0.9	Merge onto the road and continue straight through roundabout. Direction Cardaillac	Signpost	N	203
6	1.3	Leave Figeac and continue on the road	Follow stream (Ruisseau de Planioles)	NE	209
7	3.2	Keep left on road running alongside stream		NW	239
8	3.3	Pass picnic area on left and continue straight direction Escud	Signpost	NW	242
9	4.3	At fork keep left, direction Escudeyrie	Signpost	NW	259
10	4.4	Continue straight on track to the left of gate		NW	261
11	5.3	Continue straight on path		NW	263
12	6.1	Continue straight and then left on asphalt road and climb hill. Direction Cardaillac	Signpost	N	315
13	6.7	Turn right onto road D15 and take first left. Direction Le Pech	Signpost	N	381
14	7.0	Turn right, direction Le Pech	Signpost	N	385
15	7.4	Turn right and descend hill. Continue straight	Signpost. Ahead view of Cardaillac to left across valley	N	379
16	8.5	Merge left onto the D15 road to Cardaillac centre	Signpost	NW	365
17	9.7	Enter village of Cardaillac and continue straight on D15	Signpost	NW	361
18	10.2	Turn left onto rue du 11 mai 1944/D18 and immediately right towards medieval village	Signpost	W	364
19	10.2	Turn right at the entrance to **Cardaillac** and descend behind the information sign. Continue north on the track and cross the stream (Le Drauzou)	Information panel	NW	365
20	11.0	Turn left onto track and continue on path through forest	Signpost. Pass reservoir (Plan d'Eau des Sagnes) to the left	S	342
21	12.4	Keep right on road and take first left.	Signpost	NW	344
22	14.1	Turn right onto the C2 road and continue straight towards Pauly and then Espinadet		N	425

23	14.7	At Espinadet, turn right onto tree-lined path and continue straight towards Rabanel	Opposite concrete barn	N	423
24	15.0	Cross small street and continue straight until cross		NE	456
25	15.8	Turn left onto road and continue straight through Saint-Bressou	Signpost	N	530
26	16.4	At intersection turn left onto the D92 road (direction Le Bouyssou)	Cross	S	536
27	16.5	Turn right onto road (direction Girou) and then take the road to the right	Signpost	W	533
28	17.6	Merge left onto road and continue straight		N	505
29	19.5	At fork keep right on path that descends into forest	Signpost	W	554
30	22.4	Turn right onto street, then left onto the D15 road towards Lacapelle-Marival centre		N	375
31	22.7	Turn left onto the D653 road and enter the village of Lacapelle-Marival		W	371
32	22.9	In the centre of **Lacapelle-Marival** continue west on the D653 road and turn left onto the D940 road	Iron cross and pharmacy	W	375
33	23.5	Turn right off the D940 road onto small road D11. Cross road and continue in the same direction before turning right onto the N140 at Rudelle	Pass abandoned electricity building to the left	SW	376
34	26.7	Cross the village of **Rudelle** on a road to the right and parallel to the N140. At road's end turn left and then right to rejoin the N140. Continue straight	Fortified **church of Saint Martial** to the left	NW	362
35	27.5	Turn right on small street and climb straight passing through farmland	Stone cross.	N	354
36	28.8	At intersection turn left and continue straight	Keep farm to the right	W	412
37	29.9	Keep to the right	Signpost	NW	365
38	30.9	Turn left towards water tower and keep left until reaching the D38 road	Water tower and cross	NW	345
39	31.8	Turn right onto the D38 road (direction Rueyres), and then turn left on track. Cross the stream L'Ouysee before reaching the D40 road		NW	339
40	33.3	Turn left onto the D40 road and cross village of **Thémines**	Signpost	SW	314
41	33.7	After passing bakery on the left, veer right (uphill) on the road. Direction Le Cossoul	Signpost (Le Cossoul)	W	323
42	33.8	Keep right on road that passes to hamlet of Le Coussoul	Signpost.	NW	332
43	35.6	Continue on road through the hamlet of Gruffiel	Signpost	NW	339
44	36.0	Turn right on the road away from Lestrade (left). Direction Soulestrein	Signpost	N	337

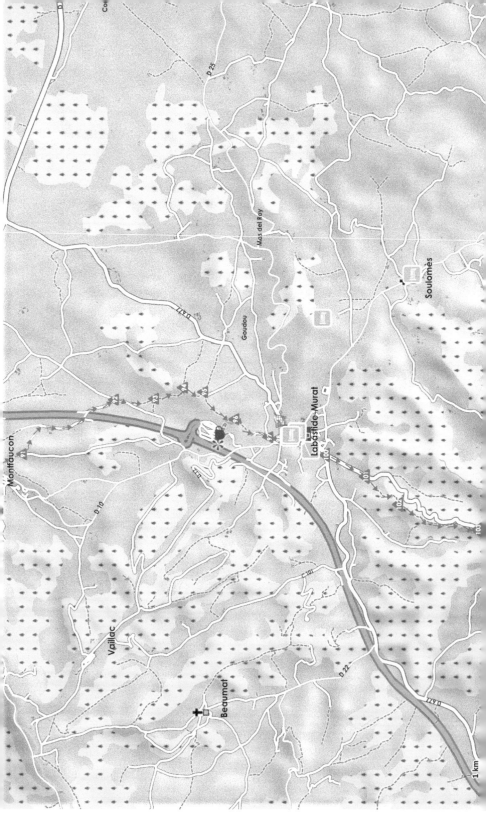

45	36.4	Turn left onto the road and continue straight through hamlet of Vernique. Keep right on track towards the D840 road and turn right	Signpost	W 326
46	37.8	Turn left and cross the D840 road. Continue straight direction Issendolus	Signpost	W 335
47	38.6	Continue straight. Then turn left to enter the village of Issendolus	Pass château to the left	SW 348
48	39.1	At fork keep right, passing a series of houses on the right		S 334
49	39.8	Continue straight on track, which then turns sharply left and passes through the village of Gary	Signpost	N 343
50	42.4	Keep right on track and cross hamlet of Saint-Chignes	Signpost	W 306
51	42.7	At fork turn left onto path. Continue straight until reaching road	Ahead pass farm on right.	W 310
52	46.7	Turn left onto N140 road and then right onto a small road that leads to Gramat	Signpost. The road follows the L'Alzou stream to the right	W 292
53	47.3	Pass under the D807 road and keep right on rue du Barry	Underpass	W 284
54	47.5	To leave **Gramat**, turn left on avenue des Cédres and continue straight	Follow cemetery wall on the left	NW 289
55	49.0	Turn right onto track and continue straight	Ahead pass under power lines	W 293
56	51.0	Turn left onto track and then turn right onto road. Continue straight to the entrance to the Vallée de l'Ouysse	Signpost	NW 312
57	52.4	Turn right onto a track that descends into the stunning Vallée de l'Ouysse natural reserve and which leads to Rocamadour	Signpost. Pass the Saut mill	NW 283
58	52.7	Keep left on rocky path that runs alongside the L'Alzou stream and leads to Rocamadour	Signpost. Pass several abandoned mills (Tournefeuille, Mouline, Sirogne, and Boulégou)	W 279
59	59.0	Turn left and rejoin road (D32) towards Rocamadour village		SW 147
60	59.4	Turn right up staircase to enter **Rocamadour** village		S 149
61	59.4	Leave Rocamadour by heading southwest on valley road (D32B). Follow the GR®46 to Vers	Signpost	S 148
62	59.8	Turn left off road (D32B) and continue straight	Pass mill and cross stream "Roquefraiche"	S 142
63	59.9	Turn right on track that climbs to the D32 road, and which offers beautiful views of Rocamadour	Pass house and Berthiol fountain on the left	SW 141
64	60.7	Cross road D32 and continue straight on footpath that climbs to plateau	Signpost	S 179
65	61.3	Take the path to the right of radio antenna and continue straight, before turning left onto the road	Signposts	S 262

66	61.7	Turn right and follow stone wall. Track eventually descends steeply before re-joining the D32 road	Stone wall. Signpost	SE	261
67	62.6	Turn left onto the D32 road	Signpost	SE	217
68	62.8	Turn right and then immediately left onto path that descends and climbs	Signpost	W	198
69	63.6	Turn left onto track direction Couzou	Signpost	SE	250
70	64.2	Turn right onto the road and continue straight towards village of Couzou	Farm	S	275
71	64.5	Merge onto the D32 road and continue straight towards hamlet of Couzou	Iron cross on the left	S	281
72	64.8	At fork keep right and cross hamlet of **Couzou**	Pass war monument, church and cemetery	SE	295
73	65.5	At road's end, turn right	Signpost	NW	292
74	67.0	Turn left and continue straight in ex-posed valley	Signpost	SE	197
75	68.0	Turn right through glade	Signpost	W	194
76	68.1	Stay right on track direction Montfau-con	Do not pass through gate. Signpost.	NW	200
77	70.2	Keep left	Stone cross	S	300
78	70.5	At fork stay right, direction Montfau-con	Signpost	S	302
79	71.6	Turn right onto track	Signpost	SE	305
80	72.0	At fork keep left. Pass through gate and continue left	Signpost	W	300
81	73.2	At road's end turn right, direction Montfaucon	Signpost	W	365
82	74.3	Turn left direction La Fontaine and continue straight. Take path/short cut off road, before rejoining road and turning right	Signpost	S	336
83	75.2	Turn left and climb up hill	Signpost	SE	269
84	76.5	Keep right leaving Rassiols and cross bridge over highway A20. Continue straight to hamlet of Places du Lac.	Signposts	SE	356
85	77.9	After traversing hamlet Places du Lac turn left	Cross on left	S	371
86	78.3	Cross road D801 with caution and con-tinue straight, direction Montfaucon	Signpost	SE	367
87	78.5	At fork turn right onto asphalt road through fields, which ends in a steep rocky descent to road D10	Signpost	SE	358
88	79.3	Turn left onto road D10 and pass through hamlet of Les Vitarelles	Signpost	S	318
89	79.7	At fork (with cross) keep right. Then turn left onto track, direction Montfau-con	Signpost	S	300
90	80.4	Turn left onto road and continue straight. The village of **Montfaucon** is to the right	Pass pond	SE	311
91	80.8	Turn left and cross bridge over A20 highway. Continue straight until road's end	A20 highway	E	319

92	82.5	At road's end turn right. Then take first left on rural road and continue straight	Turn away from highway A20. Further ahead pass farm	S	397
93	83.1	Continue south on road	Farm	S	408
94	83.6	Turn right direction Labastide-Murat	Signpost	S	384
95	83.9	At road's end turn right in the direction of Labastide-Murat and Lake Boutanes	Signpost	W	386
96	84.6	Keep right on track	Pass Lake Boutanes and picnic area to the right	S	400
97	85.2	Continue straight on gravel path towards village of Labastide-Murat	Garden	S	422
98	85.3	Cross road D10 and keep right at fork on rue Fortunière to enter centre of **Labastide-Murat**	Keep garden with stone cross to the left	S	426
99	85.7	Continue straight on rue du Causse/ D677	Pass church on the left	SW	447
100	86.1	At the fork stay left on the D32 road. Direction Saint Sauver La Valée.	Pass tennis courts on right. Signpost.	S	435
101	86.7	Veer right onto track, and continue straight through forest	Turn off is opposite a waste transfer station on the left	SW	424
102	87.4	At bottom of descent, keep left on path		S	364
103	88.7	Turn right onto the road D32. Continue straight		S	311
104	89.0	Turn right onto tree-lined path	Turn-off is before a sharp right curve in the road	S	300
105	89.3	Keep left on track	Pass field to the right	S	287
106	89.9	Turn left onto road and then an immediate right onto track. Continue straight		S	274
107	90.2	Cross street and continue straight on the road	Pass stone shed	SW	274
108	91.0	Pass through hamlet, and keep right on gravel road, which ascends	Pass farm buildings to the left.	W	333
109	92.1	Rejoin the road and continue straight. Climb hill ahead	Signpost	SW	378
110	93.3	At the road's end turn left and continue straight		SW	405
111	93.4	Take first left onto the D13 road (around pine trees). Continue straight through hamlet of Fages	Shrine to Virgen Mary	E	407
112	94.1	After passing goat farm on right, turn right onto track and continue straight		SE	417
113	94.4	Turn right onto the road through forest. Then take first left onto the track		S	405
114	95.5	Turn right onto road D7	Electrical lines on the right	SE	374
115	96.0	Turn left before house with tower. Then turn right onto footpath towards village of Cras	Village of Cras visible ahead. Signpost (Oppidum de Mucens - archaeological site)	E	372
116	96.5	Turn right onto the road, direction Cras. Then take first left direction Oppidum de Murcens (archaeological site)	Signposts	SW	364
117	96.8	At fork turn right, direction Le Barry	Signpost	SW	351

118	97.0	Turn left on grass road and continue straight	Cras village ahead	SW	356
119	97.5	Turn left onto the road and continue straight		S	358
120	98.2	Turn right onto track and continue descent direction Vers	Turn in opposite stone house. Signpost.	S	331
121	98.4	Turn left onto track and continue straight	Road passes between fields	SE	318
122	99.9	Keep straight on path, direction Vers	Thick woods and signpost	SW	219
123	100.0	Turn left onto track and continue straight on path, direction Vers	Signpost. Path follows the La Rauze stream to the right.	SE	207
124	101.2	Cross stone bridge over La Rauze stream and take immediate left. Continue on path to the hamlet of Guillot	La Rauze stream to the right	E	190
125	102.8	At road's end, turn right onto asphalt road. Then turn right again onto road D653 and cross hamlet of Guillot	Signpost	SE	191
126	103.4	After hamlet of Guillot, turn left off road D653 onto footpath. Climb		S	177
127	103.9	Turn left onto track. Direction Vers	Signpost	S	183
128	105.4	Continue straight on path towards the village of Vers	Pass house	S	159
129	106.1	Pass through thick woods/moss and keep right. Continue on path, which runs alongside Le Vers river	Le Vers to the right	W	159
130	107.9	Turn left off the road and continue straight on track to village of Vers	Stone building. Le Vers river to the right.	SE	147
131	109.9	Turn right onto the road and continue straight towards Vers village.	Signpost	SW	141
132	110.0	Turn right onto rue de la Plaquette. Continue straight to Vers village centre and cross Le Vers river	Signpost.	S	140
133	110.3	In **Vers** continue straight on the D653 road	Pass La Truite Dorée on the left	S	129
134	110.5	Keep left at fork and cross bridge over Lot River towards Béars	Signpost, bridge	SE	139
135	110.9	Keep right eventually rejoining the D49/route de Arcambal to pass through the hamlet of Béars	Signpost	SW	127
136	111.1	Keep to left	Abutting road	S	138
137	111.4	After passing through village of **Béars** and opposite the last house, turn left onto small road	Road is between a field and barn	E	153
138	111.5	Pass under power lines and turn right onto path that climbs steeply	Power lines	S	150
139	112.2	At summit continue straight on GR®36. Direction Les Mazuts. Here, the alternative route through the Célé Valley and the Rocamadour Route meet and both proceed on the GR®36 to Cahors	Signpost	S	205
140	113.4	Merge left onto road D49 and continue straight direction Les Mazuts	Signpost.	W	201
141	114.5	Turn right onto rocky footpath and climb	Signpost	S	236

142	114.8	Turn right, then again immediately right onto asphalt road. Direction Cahors	Signpost	W	265
143	115.3	Turn right onto the road and continue straight	Turn into forest	NW	294
144	116.1	Turn left onto rocky footpath, downhill	Signpost	SW	290
145	117.2	Continue straight on the road	Pass residential area to the right	W	205
146	118.0	Turn right onto route de Mondies	Signpost	NW	159
147	118.2	Continue straight on Impasse de la Tour, which descends steeply towards river	Signpost and stone wall	N	154
148	118.4	After steep descent, turn left following the Lot	Keep river Lot to the right	W	145
149	118.7	Turn right into parking lot and continue straight on path running alongside the Lot. Direction Arcambal	Signpost. River to the right	W	121
150	119.8	Pass under highway A20 and continue following the Lot	Underpass, Lot River to the right, pass locks "Ecluse de Arcambal" ahead on right.	SW	123
151	121.6	Keep to the right on GR®36, which runs alongside the Lot	Signpost and river to the right	NW	118
152	124.2	Pass locks Ecluse de Lacombe on right and continue straight on track running alongside the Lot	Locks, communal gardens to the left and river to the right.	W	116
153	125.6	Turn right onto chemin du Mas de Mansou	City of Cahors visible ahead	SW	120
154	126.7	Turn right onto rue de la Guinguette	Sports complex ahead	SW	121
155	127.0	At end of road turn left and continue straight towards city	Sport complex. River on the right as you approach the city.	S	119
156	127.8	Continue straight along the Lot to cross into Cahors from the south - Pont Louis Philippe bridge	Lot should be to the right	SE	115
157	128.3	Pass Moulin de Coty on the right and turn right on Promenade de Coty. Continue straight until Pont Louis Philippe bridge	Signpost and bridge	SE	119
158	128.9	Take staircase to the left to access bridge		SW	121
159	129.0	Turn right and cross Pont Louis Philippe bridge to enter **Cahors**			122

Cardaillac

Chambres d'Hôtes and Gîte d'Étape le Relais des Conques, (Jacky Fabre), Rue des Conques, 46100 Cardaillac, Lot, France; +33(0)5 65 40 17 22; +33(0)6 42 73 96 44; contact@relais-des-conques.fr; www.relais-des-conques.fr; €20/pers. (breakfast included); 4 rooms in B&B and one dormitory for 4.

Chambres d'Hôtes le Pressoir, (Mr. and Mrs. Labedie), Rue Sénéchal, 46100 Cardaillac, Lot, France; +33(0)5 65 34 68 75; +33(0)6 61 86 07 83; danl@orange.fr; www.lepressoir-cardaillac.cleasite.fr; €50/pers. €60/2 pers.; Located in the village centre 2 rooms in an 18th century home. Kitchen.

Lacapelle-Marival

Gîte d'Étape la Halte de Lacapelle-Marival, (Mr. and Mrs. Hequet), Place de la Halle, 46120 Lacapelle-Marival, Lot, France; +33(0)6 09 26 07 54; lahaltedelacapelle@yahoo.fr; www.lahaltedelacapelle.pagesperso-orange.fr; €23/pers. (includes sheet and breakfast); €12/dinner; Located in village. Tastefully decorated hostel with 10 places in 3 rooms.

Chambre d'Hôtes Boussac, (Marcel and Annie Boussac), La Garouste – route de Latronquière, 46120 Lacapelle-Marival, Lot, France; +33(0)5 65 40 84 15; +33(0)6 79 39 45 48; marcel.boussac@orange.fr; €40/pers. €54/2 pers.; Located outside the village centre. 1 room in lovely home with garden.

Chambre-Restaurant le Glacier, (Marc Gibrat), Rue Merlival, 46120 Lacapelle-Marival, Lot, France; +33(0)5 65 40 82 67; €34/pers. €36/2 pers., €40/3 pers., €6/breakfast ; Basic accommodation in 5 rooms.

Hôtel Restaurant Hostellerie la Terrasse, Route de Latronquière, 46120 Lacapelle-Marival, Lot, France; +33(0)5 65 40 80 07; hotel-restaurant-la-terrasse@wanadoo.fr; www.hotel-restaurant-la-terrasse.fr; €59-€73/single-double room, €83/half board, €8.50/breakfast; Across from the château, charming hotel with 13 rooms serving local specialities.

Office de Tourisme, Place de la Halle, 46120 Lacapelle-Marival, Lot, France; +33(0)5 65 40 81 11; lacapelle-marival@tourisme-figeac.com; www.lacapelle-marival-tourisme.fr

Thémines

Chambre d'Hôtes la Buissonière, (Elisabeth de Lapérouse Coleman), Le Bout du Lieu, 46120 Thémines, Lot, France; +33(0)5 65 40 88 58; +33(0)6 43 41 69 33; edelaperouse.coleman@wanadoo.fr; €55/2 pers. €65/3 pers., €18/dinner; 2 rooms. English spoken.

L'Hôpital

Au Coin des Granges, (Jean-Paul and Sylvie Brousse), Le Theil, 46500 Bio, Lot, France; +33(0)5 65 10 68 15; +33(0)6 80 88 76 40; contact@aucoindesgranges.com; www.aucoindesgranges.com; B&B: €68/2 pers. €78/2 pers. wagon, €100/2 pers. tree fort, €27/dinner; Located off the GR®65, accommodation in B&B, tree fort or antique wagon. Pool. English spoken. Horses welcome.

Gramat

Gîte les Petits Cailloux du Chemin, 1 avenue Louis Mazet, 46500 Gramat, Lot, France; +33(0)5 65 40 79 36; gite.gramat@gmail.com; www.gramatgitepelerin.com; Donation (for pilgrims with credentials), €30/half board for hikers; Welcoming and clean hostel run by volunteers. 11 places in 4 rooms. English spoken.

Béthanie d'Alzou, (Jean Baptiste), 5 rue Saint Félix, 46500 Gramat, Lot, France; +33(0)6 75 82 04 35; bethanie.dalzou@laposte.net or giteparoissialdegramat@laposte.net; www.giteparoissialdegramat.jimdo.com; Donation (breakfast and dinner included); Simple accommodation including 14 places (bunk beds) in 2 dormitories, communal dinner in the evening. Possibility to take part in religious ceremonies.

Les Sœurs de Notre Dame du Calvaire, (Sister Marie-Christine), 33 avenue Louis Mazet, 46500 Gramat, Lot, France; +33(0)5 65 38 73 29; +33(0)6 45 33 49 01; ndcalvaire@orange.fr; Rooms: €22/pers. €12/dinner, €5/breakfast; Several places in convent complex, including in dormitories of 5, 10 or 20 or in rooms as part of the hospitality service of the convent.

Chambre d'Hôtes la Ferme du Gravier, (Françoise and Michel), Lieu Dit le Gravier, 46500 Gramat, Lot, France; +33(0)5 65 33 41 88; +33(0)6 62 07 40 51; lafermedugravier@gmail.com; www.la-ferme-du-gravier.com; B&B: €60-70/pers. €70-€80/2 pers., €88-98/3 pers., Dormitory: €30/pers., €25/dinner; Highly rated B&B on restored farm, 500m from the GR before Gramat; with 5 rooms and 6 places in dormitory (dormitory not available in July and August). Pool. English spoken.

Aux Volets Blancs, (Marie-José Massé), 34 avenue Louis Mazet, 46500 Gramat, Lot, France; +33(0)5 65 33 70 96; +33(0)6 60 32 83 19; €50/double room, €85/room for 3/4 pers. €22/dinner; 9 places in various sized rooms.

Le Centre, Place de la Republique, 46500 Gramat, Lot, France; +33(0)5 65 38 73 37; le.centre@wanadoo.fr; www.lecentre.fr/; €65-€81/double room; Well run and clean hotel in village centre.

La Maison du Tourisme, Place de la République, 46500 Gramat, Lot, France; +33(0)5 65 33 22 00; contact@rocamadour.com; www.gramat.fr/fr/tourisme.html

Camping la Teulière, L'Hôpital Beaulieu Issendolus, 46500 Gramat, Lot, France; +33(0)5 65 40 86 71; +33(0)6 89 53 72 19; laparro.mcv@free.fr; www.laparro.mcv.free.fr; €28-€35/room, 40€/4 pers. mobile home/cabins (low season),€15/dinner; Well-run camping ground with cabins, rooms and mobile homes for let. Pool.

Rocamadour

Centre d'Accueil et d'Hébergement, Le Château, 46500 Rocamadour, Lot, France; +33(0)5 65 33 23 23; +33(0)6 27 95 28 51; centrendrocamadour@gmail.com; www.lerelaisdupelerin.fr; Starting at €33/room, €14/pers. in dormitory, €5/breakfast; Located in Rocamadour castle, above the village. 79 places in single or double rooms or dormitory.

Le Cantou, Rue de la Mercerie, 46500 Rocamadour, Lot, France; +33(0)5 65 33 73 69; +33(0)6 72 46 47 53; cantou.46@free.fr; €25/single room, €35/double room, €15/pers. in dormitory; Located in the old town near the sanctuary. 16 places in 6 single rooms, 2 double rooms and a dormitory for 6. Priority given to pilgrims on their way to Santiago. Possibility to take part in religious ceremonies. Kitchen.

Hôtel Amadour, L'Hospitalet, 46500 Rocamadour, Lot, France; +33(0)5 65 34 39 19; contact@amadour-hotel. com; www.amadour-hotel.com; €59-65/double room, €76/triple, €89/quadruple, €8.50/breakfast; Located in Hospitalet (a 10 min walk on the Sacred Way to Rocamadour) great value with beautiful views.

Hôtel-Restaurant du Lion d'Or, Cité Médiévale, 46500 Rocamadour, Lot, France; +33(0)5 65 33 62 04; contact@liondor-rocamadour.com; www.liondor-rocamadour.com; €50-€60/double room, €70/triple, €80/ quadruple, €8/breakfast; Low budget and friendly hotel located in old town centre. English spoken.

Hotel-Restaurant le Terminus des Pèlerins, Cité Médiévale, place Carretta, 46500 Rocamadour, Lot, France; +33(0)5 65 33 62 14; contact@terminus-des-pelerins.com; www.terminus-des-pelerins.com; €59/single, €64/ double, €8/breakfast; €68/half board; Located in the old town. 29 places.

Office de Tourisme, L'Hospitalet, 46500 Rocamadour, Lot, France; +33(0)5 65 33 22 00; www.vallee-dordogne.com/pratique/loffice-de-tourisme-vallee-dordogne

Carlucet

Camping and Restaurant –, (Sheila and Stuert Coe), Château de Lacomte, 46500 Carlucet, Lot, France; +33(0)5 65 38 75 46; +33(0)6 08 43 48 95; châteaulacomte@wanadoo.fr; www.campingchâteaulacomte. com; : €18-€38/for 2 pers. €18-€40/dinner, €5/poolr; Possibility to rent mobile homes or cabins in low season (call in advance). English spoken. Horses welcome. Pool.

Montfaucon

Chambre d'Hôtes le Clos des Roses, (Mr and Mrs Darolles), 1 rue du Lavoir, 46240 Montfaucon, Lot, France; +33(0)5 65 23 78 87; lcdr46@gmail.com; €50/pers. €55/2 pers.; Simple B&B in need of updating with 2 rooms.

Labastide-Murat

Gîte d'Étape le Savitri, (Mrs. Vanel), 64 Grand'rue du Causse, 46240 Labastide-Murat, Lot, France; +33(0)6 74 40 14 15; vero.vanel@laposte.net; www.giteetapesavitri.jimdo.com; €22/pers. (breakfast included); 11 places in bespoke house. Generous accommodation.

Auberge du Roy de Naples, 3 place Daniel Roques, 46240 Labastide-Murat, Lot, France; +33(0)5 65 21 11 39; €22/pers.; 9 places in double or single rooms in a former hotel/restaurant that was renovated in 2015 by the Commune. English spoken.

Chambre d'Hôtes-Domaine Equestre Centaure, (Erica de Graaf), La Devèze, 46240 Labastide-Murat, Lot, France; +33(0)5 65 20 19 24; +33(0)6 31 96 50 57; centaure@stage-attelage.fr; www.randonnee-cheval.net/ html/homepage.php; €55/pers. €60/2 pers., €80/3 pers., €20/dinner (upon reservation); 4 rooms. Located 2 km west of Labastide. Horses welcome.

Hôtel-Restaurant et Grignote la Garissade, (Hélène Recourt), 20 place de la Mairie, 46240 Labastide-Murat, Lot, France; +33(0)5 65 21 18 80; hotel@garissade.com; www.garissade.com; €78/double, €93/triple, €99/ quadruple, €9/breakfast, €19-€33/dinner; Centrally located with 19 rooms. English spoken. Accommodation for horses possible.

Office de Tourisme, 8 Grande rue du Causse, 46240 Labastide-Murat, Lot, France; +33(0)5 65 20 08 50; www. tourisme-labastide-murat.fr

Soulomès

Chambre d'Hôtes-Restaurant, (Adeline and Thomas Delqueux), Le Relais du Causse, 46240 Soulomès, Lot, France; +33(0)5 65 30 35 67; thomas.delqueux@gmail.com; www.relaisducausse.fr; €45/single; €55-115/2-4 pers. rooms; 5 rooms. English spoken. Pool. Located outside of the Labastide in village of Soulomès.

Cours

Auberge Rustica, (Eve and Lulu), Route de Figeac, 46090 Cours, Lot, France; +33(0)5 65 31 40 96; aubergerustica@orange.fr; €50/2 pers. €75/3 pers. (breakfast included), starting at €15/dinner (specializing and well regarded for its Madagascan cuisine); Charming B&B in a former mill, 3 rooms. English spoken.

stage 13

Vers

Hôtel-Restaurant la Truite Dorée, Rue de la Barre, 46090 Vers, Lot, France; +33(0)5 65 31 41 51; +33(0)5 65 31 46 13; latruitedoree@wanadoo.fr; www.latruitedoree.fr/; €42-€59/hostel, €59/half board, Hotel: €70-€93/room, €99-€113/half board; 7 rooms in hostel and 28 rooms in hotel, with one of the best restaurants in the area. English spoken.

Chambre d'Hôtes Thibaut, (Mr and Mrs. Thibaut), Rue de la Planquette, 46090 Vers, Lot, France; +33(0)5 65 31 29 11; +33(0)6 45 96 11 27; judithetdenis@sfr.fr; €35/pers. €43/2 pers., €80/4 pers., €17/dinner; 3 rooms in village centre. Welcoming.

Chambres d'Hôtes, (Colette Marsanne), Mas de Lucet, 46090 Vers, Lot, France; +33(0)5 65 31 38 60; +33(0)6 89 93 84 72; michel.marsanne@orange.fr; €68-€73/room; 3 rooms on a restored farm with garden and pool.

Mairie, Rue Montoi, 46090 Vers, Lot, France; +33(0)5 65 31 42 59

Arcambal

Chambres d'Hôtes les Rives d'Olt, (Evelyne Andlauer), 13 Impasse de l'Écluse, 46090 Arcambal, Lot, France; +33(0)5 65 30 18 62; +33(0)6 74 42 12 13; www.cybevasion.fr/go_annonce.php?id_annonce=35811; €60-€80/room, €21/dinner; Located in the village of Bears, about 2km after Vers on the other side of the Lot river. 5 lovely rooms of varying sizes. English spoken.

Walking to Saint-Cirq-Lapopie

LENGTH **71.8km**

STAGE ASCENT **2944m**

STAGE DESCENT **3030m**

Route - From Figeac, the alternative route through the Célé Valley, which also uses red and white way markings, takes five days (as opposed to four days on the GR®65), despite being about 10 kilometres shorter than the main route. It is generally considered more beautiful than the main route, as it crosses the limestone hills typical of the Causses region, beautiful villages built into the cliffs and follows the refreshing Célé river. The route, known as the GR®651, departs from the GR®65 in Mas-de-la-Croix, where it descends into the Célé Valley, and passes through the lovely medieval village of Espagnac. From there, it climbs and descends along the limestone cliffs, in dry and often difficult and rocky terrain, passing through several historic villages on the Célé River, before re-joining the Lot near the village of Bouziès. There, the route takes the GR®36, which runs alongside the Lot river to the city of Cahors, to reconnect with the main Way of Saint James (GR®65). In Bouziès it is also possible to make a day trip (recommended) to Saint-Cirq-Lapopie, considered one of the most beautiful villages in France, which is a lovely four kilometre walk along the Lot.

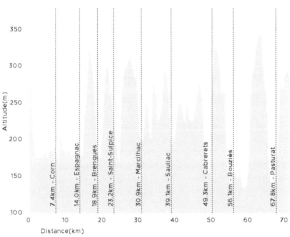

Pointers - The terrain is more challenging than the GR®65, and hikers should ensure that they have sufficient water and provisions. **Alternatives:** For a fun alternative to walking, especially if it gets hot, it is possible to travel by canoe or kayak down the Célé River from various points between Saint-Sulpice and Cabrerets. Several canoe rental companies organise trips: (1) Marcilhac-sur-Célé - Passion Aventure, Pont de Marcilhac Route de Saint-Chels, 46160 Marcilhac-sur-Célé, tel.: +33 6 10 73 73 12, www.location-canoe-cele.com, (2) Nature & Loisirs, Anglanat, 46330 Orniac , tel.: +33 5 65 30 25 69, www.nature-et-loisirs.net. Recommended intermediate resting places: Espagnac; Marcilhac-sur-Célé and Cabrerets.

CULTURAL DISCOVERIES

Espagnac

Espagnac (popl. 100, alt. 294m) developed in the 13th century around the convent of Val Paradis, which was founded by Aymeric Hébrard de Saint Sulpice, the son of a powerful Quercy family who became bishop of Coimbra, in Portugal. The convent suffered during the Hundred Years' War, during which time the church was set on fire and the cloisters destroyed. The church contains the tombs of local rulers, including Aymeric Hébrard.

Marcilhac-sur-Célé

The village of Marcilhac-sur-Célé (popl. 200, alt. 140m) developed around a 10th century Benedictine abbey, which was pillaged in 1368, during the Hundred Years' War. In the 15th century, the Hébrard de Saint-Sulpice family oversaw the abbey's reconstruction; however, in 1569, during the Wars of Religion, the abbey was attacked by French Protestants and burned. The structure was later converted into a parish church which contains lovely 17th century wood work.

There is an annual jazz festival in early August.

Sauliac-sur-Célé

Only ruins remain of the medieval "old Sauliac" which was built into the cliffs around a castle - *château des Anglais* - overlooking the Célé river in the valley. the castle of Géniez dates from the 13th century and was a protestant stronghold during the Wars of Religion.

Peche Merle Grotto (*La Grotte du Peche Merle*)

Located above Cabrerets, the museum and grotto of Peche Merle contain beautiful prehistoric cave paintings of bison, bears, horses and mammoths that are about 25 thousand years old.

Waypoint	Total(km)	Directions	Verification	Compass	Altitude(m)
1	0.0	At **Mas de la Croix**, continue straight on D21 road towards Béduer. Follow the GR®651 through the Célé valley	Signpost	NW	314
2	0.3	Descend into **Béduer** on the D21 road	Château of Béduer on the left	N	294
3	1.0	Turn right onto footpath steep descent into Célé River valley	Signpost	NE	274
4	1.8	At the end of the road, turn left onto the track through corn fields and cross the D21 road	Célé River to the right	NW	180
5	4.9	Turn right and cross the bridge over the Célé River. At road's end turn right onto the D41 road	Bridge	N	180
6	5.3	In Boussac, before church, turn left, direction Manden, and continue straight	Signpost	NW	180
7	6.1	Continue straight on track	Pass château on left	NW	189
8	6.7	Merge right onto D41 road and continue straight on road (caution) to arrive in village of Corn	Pass large property on the left	N	183
9	7.4	Turn right into **Corn** on narrow passage that passes church.	Signpost and church	SW	192
10	7.5	Cross the D113 road and take the footpath along the stream. Cross the D41 road to leave Corn.	Church and D41	W	183
11	7.6	Cross road and continue straight on track	Pass cross on the right	S	185
12	7.9	Cross bridge over Célé River and then turn right and continue straight	Célé River to the right	S	176
13	8.0	Turn right and continue straight on main road		SW	174
14	8.5	At fork in hamlet of Goudou keep left	Château	SW	193
15	8.8	Turn right onto track and continue straight through forest	Signpost	S	215
16	10.2	Merge left onto track that runs alongside the Célé River and pass through the hamlet of Sainte-Eulalie	River	W	179
17	10.7	At fork, keep left on high road to leave hamlet of Sainte Eulalie and continue straight		S	175
18	11.3	Take left onto footpath before bridge to enter forest. Turn left, crossing over iron pipe, and continue straight on path.	Célé River to the right	NW	189
19	12.3	Continue straight on path until Espagnac	Pass stone houses to the right	W	184
20	14.0	Merge right onto road leading to the village and **Espagnac**. Then turn right at cross to enter village of Espagnac	Signpost	NW	181
21	14.3	From church, continue straight on D211 road to leave Espagnac. Cross bridge over Célé River.	Church on the left	N	183
22	14.5	Turn right onto the D41 road, direction Corn	Signpost	NW	172
23	14.8	Turn left into hamlet of Pailhès. Keep left onto a path that switchbacks through forest until it joins a road, and turn left.	Cross	NW	170

ALTERNATE ROUTE VIA THE CÉLÉ VALLEY

24	16.1	Turn left onto a path through the forest and then cross the D38 road. Continue straight		SW	280
25	17.1	Turn right onto the D38 and then left onto a path that leads to cliffs and the ruins of the Tour des Anglais	Signpost	S	322
26	18.0	Continue to follow path in its rocky descent to the D38 road, and turn left to Mas de Bessac.	Signpost	SE	282
27	18.6	Keep right on the D38 road as it descends towards the valley into the village of Brengues.	Signpost	SW	214
28	18.9	In **Brengues** turn right towards Vignes-Grandes.	Road runs parallel to the D41	SW	189
29	19.3	Keep right on path that climbs through forest, then turn right on a road that climbs to a fork.		SW	181
30	20.6	Keep left, and at the fork turn left on a path that climbs towards the crests and then descends parallel to the valley floor.	Signpost	SW	278
31	22.7	Turn left onto the D13 road and descend towards the valley	Pass iron cross	S	259
32	23.2	Turn right onto a track and pass the Château of Saint-Sulpice, continue straight to leave **Saint-Sulpice**	Pass château on right	SE	243
33	24.1	Turn left onto path that descends into valley, then turn right onto path that climbs the hills and passes Pech Merlu.	Iron cross	S	217
34	27.0	Turn right onto the D17 road and at the fork keep left on the D17	Cross	NW	299
35	27.3	Turn left onto path that climbs to Pech Peyroux, and then descends south to the D14 road		SW	300
36	30.8	Keep right on the D14 road	Continue straight to visit village of Marcilhac (off GR®)	SW	181
37	30.9	Turn right in Jean-Fabret square, and continue straight away from D14 to leave **Marcilhac**	Signpost	W	177
38	31.0	Turn left on a road that climbs between houses, and then switchbacks.		W	169
39	31.6	Turn left and continue straight, on path until reaching the route de Combes-Basses, turn left.	Pass access road to B&B Le Picarel on left	SW	238
40	33.1	Turn right on switchback path. Keep left	Cross	W	197
41	34.6	Turn left on road direction Montagnac and then turn right (opposite farm)		SE	277
42	35.5	At fork, turn left on path that follows ledge of plateau before descending to a small road	Ahead pass farm	NW	230
43	37.1	Turn left onto road, and at the first bend continue straight on path that descends to Sauliac-sur-Célé	Signpost	S	296
44	39.1	Continue straight and pass along cliffs through old **Sauliac**. Road curves to right	Turn left to visit village (off GR®)	NW	214
45	40.0	At fork keep left, and continue on path that switchbacks uphill. Keep left and then turn left on wall lined path, to road leading to Château de Cuzals		NW	199

46	42.0	Turn left at castle gate, and continue straight.	Pass musée de plein-air du Quercy on right	S	258
47	42.1	Continue straight		S	248
48	42.8	Turn right onto track through fields and pass through gate. Continue straight until the D40 road	Signpost	W	233
49	44.5	Cross the D40 road and continue straight through village of Espinières	Signpost	SW	219
50	44.9	Continue straight on the shrub-lined road, which becomes a rocky path. Keep right until arriving at a small road before the D42 road		SW	227
51	46.2	Turn left onto the road and continue straight. Then turn right on footpath between an oak tree and field. Cross hilltop fields with amazing views of the Causse region		S	266
52	47.6	After crossing field follow path along stone walls, and descend towards Cabrerets. At road's end, turn right		S	272
53	48.1	Continue straight on steep rocky descent into Cabrerets.		S	219
54	48.7	Merge right onto road running alongside the Célé River. Take first right and cross through Cabrerets centre.	Pass bridge and Célé river to the left	SW	159
55	49.1	Keep left, cross main road and head towards church.	Church and signposts	SW	160
56	49.3	At top of hill, beside the church in **Cabrerets**, turn left onto road next to cemetery and take the rocky path to Grotte du Pech Merle	On path pass picnic area on left	NW	152
57	50.1	Pass through gate and continue to **Grotte du Pech Merle** and museum, and then climb stairs to the right.		W	254
58	50.2	Cross through the Pech Merle car park and then turn left onto road		N	281
59	50.6	Turn left on rock path, direction Bouziès.	Signpost	S	300
60	50.7	Turn left at fork and continue straight on path along hill crest	Beautiful valley views to the left	SE	312
61	52.5	Turn left, direction Bouziès and continue straight on path along the crest of the hill	Signpost	E	279
62	53.8	Continue straight on long descent that switchbacks towards the Lot River valley		S	271
63	54.8	Rejoin the road to the right, which descends to the D41 road	Pass château on right	W	211
64	55.0	Turn right onto the D41 road with care, and continue straight direction Bouziès. Turn left and cross bridge and enter Bouziès.	Célé river to the left	NW	208
65	56.1	In **Bouziès**, after crossing bridge, turn right to follow the GR®36 to Cahors. The alternative route to Saint-Cirq-Lapopie - GR®36 - departs from the church/ bridge in Bouziès and follows the Lot River south.	Signpost	W	132
66	56.4	Cross bridge over abandoned railway tracks, and at cross turn right onto road and continue straight	Signpost	SW	141

67	57.9	At fork, keep right heading towards shed in the distance. At the shed, take immediate right towards river	Cross	SW	153
68	58.4	Cross railway tracks and continue on the road as it turns left and runs alongside river. Before reaching the bridge, turn right onto footpath running alongside a field		W	152
69	59.5	Keep right on path running alongside Lot River	River to the right	S	138
70	59.9	Turn left and pass under bridge, followed by long climb towards the D8 road.	Head away from river	SE	139
71	62.7	Turn right on path towards Pasturat and then merge onto the D8. Continue straight	Cross and picnic area	W	346
72	63.1	Turn right off D8 road onto track running parallel. Continue straight	Signpost	W	341
73	63.7	Turn right onto track, heading away from the D8 and continue straight. Cross hamlet of Saint-Gery	Signpost	NW	354
74	65.1	Pass electrical tower and cross street, before steep descent towards D10 road		NW	282
75	66.0	Turn right towards forest. Direction Pasturat. Pass under bridge and descend towards Lot River	Signpost	N	170
76	66.1	Merge left onto road and take immediate left before bridge onto path. Continue straight	Bridge	N	168
77	66.3	Pass under bridge and descend towards river, keep left and continue straight on path bordering the Lot River	Lot River to the right	NW	153
78	67.0	Continue along path that, which veers left before bridge	Bridge	W	126
79	67.0	Cross street and continue straight on long climb to Pasturat.		NW	127
80	67.8	At road's end, turn left and enter Pasturat.	Head towards church	SE	155
81	67.8	Before the church in **Pasturat** turn right on Route du Travers Rouge	Signpost	SW	157
82	67.9	Turn left on small footpath	Before lovely stone house	SE	160
83	68.0	Turn right onto the road, and continue straight on long climb out of valley		SE	166
84	68.5	Turn right and continue straight, steep climb	Path passes between houses	SW	217
85	68.8	Turn right onto track, direction Les Mazuts, and continue straight	Pass farm house on left	SW	277
86	69.6	Turn right onto road and continue climb, direction Les Mazuts		W	268
87	70.0	Turn right onto track, direction Vers (on GR®36)		N	289
88	71.6	Beautiful view of valley, continue straight	Pass radio tower on left	SW	249
89	71.8	At end of path, turn left onto GR®36 towards Cahors. Direction Les Mazuts. At this point, the alternative routes from Rocamadour and Célé valley meet and proceed to Cahors on the Rocamadour route	Signpost		249

stage 13

LENGTH **7.6km**

STAGE ASCENT **439m**

STAGE DESCENT **440m**

Route - The alternative route to Saint-Cirq-Lapopie is approximately 3.8 kilometres one-way; it is possible to make a day trip to the village. The route, which is well-marked with the white-red way markings of the GR®36, is mostly flat, as it follows the Lot river at the foot of impressive limestone cliffs, but for a short steep climb to the medieval village of Saint-Cirq-Lapopie, which is perched on a cliff overlooking the Lot river. The village boasts 13 historic monuments and has been classified as one of the most beautiful villages in France.

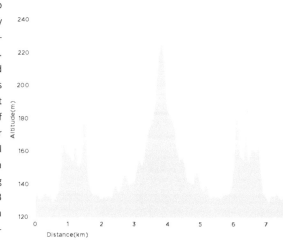

CULTURAL DISCOVERIES

Saint-Cirq-Lapopie

The medieval village of Saint-Cirq-Lapopie (popl. 200, alt. 120m) is perched on a cliff overlooking the Lot river and boasts 13 historic monuments. It is classified as one of the most beautiful villages in France. In the 20th century, the site was appreciated by artists and writers, including French writer and founder of surrealism, André Breton, who lived in the village and famously said "I have ceased to wish myself elsewhere." In July and August, the village holds a market on Wednesday afternoons (4p.m. to 8p.m.).

Waypoint	Total(km)	Directions	Verification	Compass	Altitude(m)
1	0.0	From **Bouzies** church, descend to the left of the bridge towards river and turn right	Signpost	NE	140
2	0.3	Take GR®36 to Saint-Cirq-Lapopie		SE	131
3	0.5	Cross camping grounds and join path. Continue straight with river to the left on footpaths and roads.		S	136
4	2.2	Turn right, away from river, and then take first left and continue straight on the road towards Saint-Cirq		S	140
5	3.4	Turn right onto footpath to climb out of river valley. Steep	Signpost	S	141
6	3.8	Turn left out of staircase, and arrive in **Saint-Cirq.** To return to the Célé valley route, retrace your steps to Bouziès	Place du Sombral, village centre	W	216
7	7.6	Rejoin the Célé Valley route beside the church in Bouziès			133

ACCOMODATION & TOURIST INFORMATION

Boussac

Chambre d'Hôtes Mas de Lum, (Mrs. Skura), Domaine Villedieu, 46100 Boussac, Lot, France; +33(0)5 65 40 06 63; +33(0)6 89 19 90 02; contact@mas-del-lum.fr; www.mas-del-lum.fr; €90-€115/2 pers. €140/3 pers., €165/4 pers.; Top-rated B&B on 18th century estate. 4 rooms and a 4-pers. cottage. Closed in July and August. English spoken. Eco-pool.

Corn

La Maison de Cécile, (Madame Chiminello), Lapparot, 46100 Corn, Lot, France; +33(0)5 65 40 01 24; +33(0)6 79 42 77 36; raymonde.roques123@orange.fr; €22/pers. €5/breakfast; 400m from the GR, beautiful stone house with sweeping valley views. 4 places. English spoken.

Espagnac-Sainte-Eulalie

Maison du Passant Pèlerin, (Gaby Sénac), Le Bourg, 46320 Espagnac-Sainte-Eulalie, Lot, France; +33(0)5 65 40 05 24; gabysenac@wanadoo.fr; Donation (meals not provided); 4 places in dormitory.

Gîte d'Étape Communal d'Espagnac, Chemin des Dames, 46320 Espagnac-Sainte-Eulalie, Lot, France; +33(0)5 65 11 42 66; +33(0)5 65 40 09 17; mairie.espagnac@wanadoo.fr; www.espagnac-ste-eulalie.fr/fr/tourisme/le-gite-detape-et-les-gites-de-sejour-communaux.html; €12/pers. €25/single room, €30/double room, €42/triple room, half board possible.; 21 places in a historic tower in the heart of the medieval village. Kitchen.

Mairie and Office de Tourisme, Chemin des Dames, 46320 Espagnac-Sainte-Eulalie, Lot, France; +33(0)5 65 40 09 17; mairie.espagnac@wanadoo.fr; www.espagnac-ste-eulalie.fr/fr/tourisme/office-du-tourisme.html

Brengues

Gîte la Brenguoise, Le Bourg, 46320 Brengues, Lot, France; +33(0)9 63 26 31 46; contact@labrenguoise.fr; www.labrenguoise.fr; €20/pers. €7/breakfast, €18/dinner (upon reservation); Located in the village of Brengues. 8 places in 2 rooms. English spoken. Horses welcome.

Camping le Moulin Vieux, Lieu-Dit le Moulin Vieux, 46320 Brengues, Lot, France; +33(0)5 65 40 00 41; +33(0)6 81 09 65 01; lemoulinvieux@gmail.com; www.camping-lemoulinvieux.com; €17.50/pers. (mobile home), €14/pers. (tent), €6.50/breakfast, €17/dinner; Located on the Célé river, possibility to rent mobile home (2 rooms) or tent. Pool. English spoken. Accommodation for horses. Possibility to canoe a stage(s) down river (instead of walking).

Saint-Sulpice

Camping du Célé, Camping le Célé, 46160 Saint-Sulpice, Lot, France; +33(0)5 81 48 06 13; +33(0)6 29 46 48 22; contact@camping-du-cele.fr; www.camping-du-cele.fr/; Caravan: €15/pers. Tipi: €15/pers., €50/5 pers., €6/breakfast; Located next to the Célé river. Possibility to rent 5-pers. tipi or caravan.

Marcilhac-sur-Célé

Chambre d'Hôtes Ferme de Cazals, (Fabienne and Jean-Michel Bos), Route de Pailhès, 46160 Marcilhac-sur-Célé, Lot, France; +33(0)5 65 50 07 89; fab.bos@orange.fr.; www.fermedecazals.hautetfort.com; €42/pers. €64/2 pers., €20/dinner (upon reservation); 2 km before Marcilhac, organic farm with 4 rooms run by couple who moved from the city. English spoken. Horses welcome.

Gîte de Galance, (Véronique and Jean), Chemin de Pailhès, 46160 Marcilhac-sur-Célé, Lot, France; +33(0)5 65 34 23 97; +33(0)6 15 94 91 97; contact@gitedegalance.fr; www.gitedegalance.fr/; €24/pers. with private bath, €18/pers. €6/breakfast, €15/dinner, €4/horse; Recently built and fully equipped hostel, with 15 places in 6 rooms. English spoken. Horses welcome.

Gîte d'Étape Accueil Saint-Pierre, (Ombeline and Cédric), Ombeline and Cédric, 46160 Marcilhac-sur-Célé, Lot, France; +33(0)5 81 24 06 30; +33(0)6 34 36 54 60; gitemarcilhac@gmail.com; www.accueilsaintpierre.sitew.com; €16/pers. €6/breakfast, €12/dinner; Located in the village. 11 places. Horses welcome. Kitchen.

Chambres d'Hôtes le Picarel, (Lyn and Ian Thomas), Mas de Picarel, 46160 Marcilhac-sur-Célé, Lot, France; +33(0)5 65 34 47 13; lepicarelbandb@gmail.com; www.lepicarelbandb.eu; €40/pers. €58/2 pers., €25/dinner; Located after village on the GR, lovely B&B owned by British couple. 4 double rooms. English spoken.

Sauliac-sur-Célé

B&B - Château de Génièz, (Pascal and Béatrice Byé), Geniès, 46330 Sauliac-sur-Célé, Lot, France; +33(0)5 65 30 27 39; ch.genies@orange.fr; www.facite.com/site/index.php?R=genies; €20/pers. (breakfast included), €15/dinner, €4/horse; 2 room B&B located off the GR, across the river from the village of Sauliac, in the spectacular château de Génièz. English spoken. Horses welcome.

L'Autre Chemin, (Alain Marsal), Les Fargues, 46330 Sauliac-sur-Célé, Lot, France; +33(0)5 65 31 91 64; +33(0)6 87 14 96 28; lautrechemin@sfr.fr; www.lautrechemin.fr; €52/pers. €62/2 pers., €92/3 pers.; 3 rooms in lovely Quercy-style house in village centre. English spoken.

Orniac

Gîte la Flèche Bleue, Les Granges, 46330 Orniac, Lot, France; +33(0)5 65 23 36 72; +33(0)6 32 31 97 09; laflechebleue46@gmail.com; www.laflechebleue.com; €14/pers. €6/breakfast, €14/dinner; Before Cabrerets and 1km from the GR®651 (but worth the detour), 32 places in 11 various sized rooms. Kitchen. English spoken. Horses welcome. Nature and bird watching walks organized.

Cabrerets

Gîte du Barry, (Christelle Peyron), Le Bourg, 46330 Cabrerets, Lot, France; +33(0)5 65 22 91 79; +33(0)9 66 88 20 15; Christelle.Peyron46@gmail.com; €17/pers. (sheets included), €9/breakfast, €42/half board; Located in the village centre. 15 places in 5 rooms for 4 to 6 pers. Pool. Accommodation for horses.

Refuge du Célé, Le Bourg, 46330 Cabrerets, Lot, France; +33(0)9 66 88 20 15; refugeducele@gmail.com; www.refugeducele.wix.com/refugeducele; €15/pers. in triple room, €40/double room, €16/dinner, €9/breakfast; Located near village centre and the Célé river, 5 triple and double rooms. English spoken. Pool.

Chambre d'Hôtes Un Jardin Dans la Falaise, (Cathy Beloeil), Le Bout du Lieu, 46330 Cabrerets, Lot, France; +33(0)7 83 57 01 23; unjardindanslafalaise@gmail.com; www.unjardindanslafalaise.com; €60-€80/2 pers. €95/3 pers., €22/dinner; 3 rooms in B&B with private bath and kitchenette on the GR with beautiful views. English spoken. Cathy, an avid hiker, lived in the U.S. for 30 years, and returned France to run the B&B with her husband.

Equestrian Centre and Commercial Hostel, (Pascal Gaudebert), Ferme Équestre du Pech Merle, 46330 Cabrerets, Lot, France; +33(0)6 11 93 25 23; +33(0)6 24 25 76 52; randocheval@gmail.comvvvv; www.pechmerle.fr; €40/double room, €15/pers. in dormitory, €6/breakfast, €17/dinner, €6/horse; 800m from the GR. 2 double dooms and dormitory sleeping 4. English spoken. Horses welcome. Possibility to organize horse rides.

Office de Tourisme, Lieu-Dit Bourg, 46330 Cabrerets, Lot, France; +33(0)5 65 21 41 19

Bouziès

Gîte les Deux Vallées, Gare de Conduché, 46330 Bouziès, Lot, France; +33(0)5 65 24 58 92; info@les2vallees.com; www.les2vallees.com; €17/pers. €6/breakfast; Located at the confluence of the Lot and Célé rivers in a former train station. 8 places in 3 rooms. Restaurant and boutique selling regional products on-site. English spoken. Horses welcome.

Chambres d'Hôtes, (Mrs Yvette Marmiesse), L'Oustalou, 46330 Bouziès, Lot, France; +33(0)5 65 31 25 70; €45/single, €55-€65/double, €95/triple; Charming B&B located in centre of Bouziès.

Hotel-Restaurant les Falaises, Lieu-Dit Bourg, 46330 Bouziès, Lot, France; +33(0)5 65 31 26 83; hotelfalaises@gmail.com; www.hotel-falaises-bouzies46.fr; €54-€89/double room, €69-€119/triple room, €74-€139/quadruple; Charming hotel on the Lot with views on cliffs. Pool. English spoken. 45 simple rooms. Good restaurant.

Saint-Cirq-Lapopie

Maison d'Hôtes a la Source, (Claquin Bérengère), Lieu-Dit Castan, 46330 Saint-Cirq-Lapopie, Lot, France; +33(0)5 65 23 56 98; +33(0)6 21 72 43 56; bclaquin@hotmail.fr; www.alasource46.fr; €50-€55/pers. €55-€70/2 pers., €20/dinner; Located between Bouziés and Saint Cirq Lapopie, a charming B&B with 3 spacious rooms. Ideal for those wanting to make a detour to visit the beautiful village of Saint Cirq. English spoken. Horses welcome.

Office de Tourisme, Place Sombral, 46330 Saint-Cirq-Lapopie, Lot, France; +33(0)5 65 31 31 31; info@saint-cirqlapopie.com; www.saint-cirqlapopie.com

Arcambal

Gîte d'Étape-Chambre d'Hôtes le Relais de Pasturat, (Jacques and Anne-Marie Charazac), 54 route du Travers Rouge, 46090 Arcambal, Lot, France; +33(0)5 65 31 44 94; +33(0)6 13 46 46 85; gitescharazac@hotmail.com; Hostel: €22/pers. (breakfast included), €35/half board, €16/dinner; 15 places in hostel and 4 B&B rooms. Horses welcome.

Chambre d'Hôtes les 3 Cochons d'Olt, (Ulrike Currie), 135 route de Saint-Cirq-Lapopie, 46090 Arcambal, Lot, France; +33(0)5 65 21 20 51; +33(0)6 42 82 30 54; ulrikecurrie46@orange.fr; €55/pers.; €65/2 pers. €80/3 pers., €18/dinner; 1 room in family house 300m from the GR®36. English spoken.

Chambre d'Hôtes les Mazuts, (Carmen and Pierre Nouyrit), 219 route des Mazuts, 46090 Arcambal, Lot, France; +33(0)5 65 23 95 29; +33(0)6 74 85 96 68; carmenpierre@orange.fr; www.lesmazuts.free.fr/Accueil.html; €50-€60/2 pers.; In the village of Mazuts, before Arcambal. 5 rooms in a restored Quercy farmhouse.

View of Cajarc

DISTANCE **28.3km**

ASCENT **806m**

DESCENT **882m**

FROM LE PUY **275km**

TO RONCEVAUX **499km**

Route - The route continues to be well-marked as it crosses the arid Causses Region. It consists mostly of asphalt roads and paths through oak forests and dry sheep pastures. The rocky descent to the Lot River valley and the city of Cajarc is steep, as is the climb out of the valley to Saint-Jean-de-Laur.

Pointers - **Advance planning:** Ensure sufficient water, as the Causses region is particularly demanding due to the heat, rocky terrain and dryness.

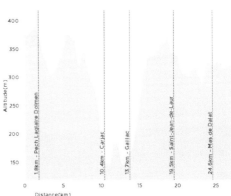

CULTURAL DISCOVERIES

Pech Lagaire2 Dolmen

Dolmens were built some 3,500 years ago as monumental stone funerary tombs or sepulchres. Some 600 dolmens have been found in the department of Lot in Quercy. The Pech Laglaire2 Dolmen is one of three dolmens built on the Pech Lagaire hilltop site, and it is classified as a historical monument. It consists of a square sepulchral chamber with a large stone cover, all of which would have originally been buried under a mound of earth and stone (called a tumulus).

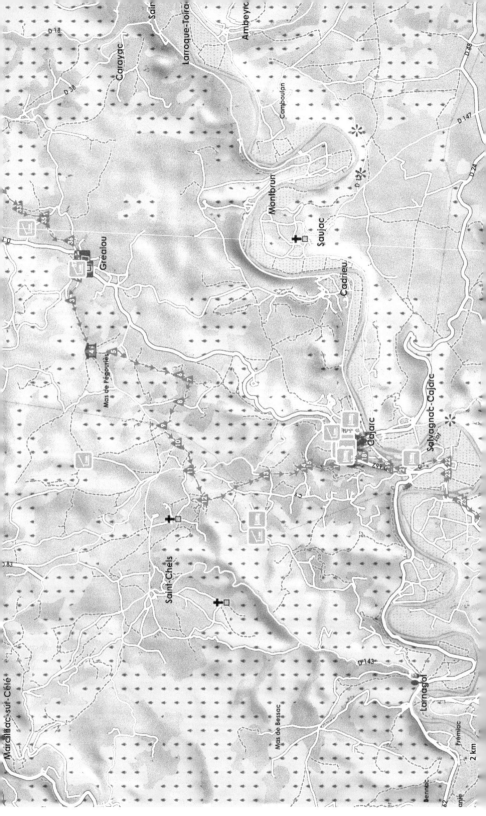

Cajarc

In Cajarc (popl. 1,140, alt. 160m), following a revolt against the Bishop of Cahors in 1256, the town's citizens were granted a charter recognizing their "customs and privileges." Specifically, the charter set forth a new relationship between the baron and his subjects and provided for certain fundamental rights, such as due process, which the baron was to respect. With this, Cajarc was one of the first communes in Quercy to gain rights and a degree of independence from the barony. During the Hundred Years' War, thanks to its strategic position encircled by cliffs as well as strong walls, the city was never captured by the English. In the Middle Ages, Quercy was also an important producer of saffron, a precious spice made from the saffron crocus flower. Since 1997, saffron production has been revived and an association of producers is based in Cajarc. An annual saffron fair is held on the last weekend of October.

ROUTE INSTRUCTIONS

Waypoint	Total(km)	Directions	Verification	Compass	Altitude(m)
1	0.0	From **Gréalou** church turn right and continue straight towards cemetery.	Church	NW	388
2	0.2	Continue straight	Pass cemetery on the right	W	385
3	0.7	Turn left and continue straight on track	Cross on the right	W	380
4	1.8	After the **Pech Laglaire Dolmen**, turn left on track that descends to the D82 road.		S	382
5	2.3	Cross the D82 road and continue straight on path and pass farm Martigne on the left.		S	363
6	3.8	Turn right onto asphalt road and continue straight towards Le Verdier.		S	311
7	4.0	At fork in the hamlet of Le Verdier turn right and continue straight.	Signpost	W	309
8	4.5	At intersection, climb straight until the D82 road	Cross to the right	NW	334
9	5.2	Turn left onto the D82, and before curve in road keep left on track.		W	352
10	5.7	Continue straight at intersection		SW	376
11	6.3	Cross D17 road and continue straight on path		SW	372
12	7.0	At road's end, turn left and continue straight and cross road.	Pass cut tree trunk on left	S	328
13	8.4	Merge left onto asphalt road and then turn left onto track		SE	311
14	9.3	Turn left and descend on road. Direction Cajarc.	Signpost	SE	283
15	9.4	Turn right onto path that descends sharply into village of Cajarc.	Turn before tree and area with beautiful views of Cajarc	S	269
16	10.0	Turn right on narrow path		S	194
17	10.4	In **Carjac** turn left onto avenue de la Capelette, then immediately right on rue du Cuzoul.	Continue straight on avenue de la Capelette to visit Cajarc centre.	E	163
18	10.7	Pass camping ground on the right and continue straight		S	150
19	11.2	Turn right before underpass and follow path around house. Steep climb out of valley to the D662 road.		W	149
20	11.4	Turn left onto the D662 road (use caution), and continue ascent.		SW	158

21	11.6	Keep left at fork and continue straight on chemin de la Route Vieille	Pass Chapel Madeleine to the left and wooden cross to the right.	S	187
22	12.6	Turn right	Pass car garage to the right	SW	153
23	12.9	Merge onto the D19 road (caution) and continue straight to cross the Lot River and climb to the village of Gaillac	Signpost	W	149
24	13.7	After rounding corner in **Gaillac**, turn left onto path	Signpost and access to path via stone wall to the left.	SW	165
25	13.8	Keep left on asphalt road, then turn right onto path running along wall to climb into forest		SW	164
26	14.3	Keep left on path through woods. Climb		S	191
27	14.8	At fork keep to right	Signpost	S	236
28	15.8	Keep right at fork		S	317
29	16.6	Turn right onto asphalt road and continue straight		SW	340
30	18.6	Turn right onto path	Stone cross	SW	371
31	19.5	On the outskirts of **Saint-Jean-de-Laur** turn right onto asphalt road.	Picnic area and refuge on left	W	344
32	19.8	Cross the D79 road and continue straight on path to leave Saint-Jean-de-Laur		NW	343
33	21.0	At fork keep left		NW	311
34	21.1	Turn left	Signpost	SW	311
35	21.8	Continue straight	Farm to the right	S	307
36	22.0	Merge right onto asphalt road and continue straight through village of Mas de Bories		SW	318
37	22.2	Continue straight on road, leave village	Cross on left	SW	323
38	23.2	Turn left onto path. Direction Limogne-en-Quercy	Signpost	S	296
39	23.9	Keep right on path	Following fence to the left	W	325
40	24.2	Turn right at end of path and descend	House and yard	S	327
41	24.5	Turn right and climb into village of Mas de Dalat		SW	321
42	24.6	Turn left at fork and traverse village of **Mas de Dalat**	Pass cross on the left	S	318
43	24.6	Keep right on road to leave village		SW	321
44	24.8	Turn right off asphalt road and continue straight on track		W	322
45	24.9	Turn left onto footpath	Follow stone wall	SW	324
46	25.2	Turn left	Pass farm	S	328
47	25.4	Turn left onto asphalt road D143 and continue straight through Mas de Palat		SE	330
48	25.6	Turn right and again right (U-turn) and follow the wall of the farm	Farm with concrete buildings	SE	329
49	25.8	Turn right onto track.	Keep left of cross	W	329
50	26.3	Turn right		SW	325
51	27.6	Merge left onto road and continue straight in the direction of Limogne-en-Quercy		W	312
52	28.0	Merge left onto road D911 to enter village of Limogne-en-Quercy	Signpost	W	302
53	28.3	Arrive at **Limogne-en-Quercy** centre - Place d'Occitanie	Office of Tourism		299

Saint-Chels

La Source d'Ussac (Dominique Pourcel), Ussac, 46160 Saint-Chels, Lot, France; +33(0)5 65 40 79 89; dominique. pourcel@orange.fr; www.source-ussac.fr; €60/double room ; €15/pers. in shared rooms (no sheets) €5/breakfast €13/dinner; About 600 metres off the GR after Gréalou, but worth the detour, 12 places in 4 rooms in peaceful and beautifully renovated farm located near the natural spring of Ussac. Warm welcome and use of farm and garden products. Accommodation for horses.

Cajarc

Chez Annie et Claude, (Annie and Claude Doucet), 8 Impasse des Lilas, 46160 Cajarc, Lot, France; +33(0)3 56 54 06 10 0; +33(0)6 30 65 43 26; €25/pers. €5/breakfast; 2 rooms in hosts home. Very welcoming.

Le Pèlerin, (Mr and Mrs. Cajarc de Lagarrigue), 11 rue Lacaunhe, 46160 Cajarc, Lot, France; +33(0)5 65 40 65 31; +33(0)6 74 32 44 40; €15.50/pers. (rooms); €12/pers. (dormitory); €5/breakfast.; In a modern building close to the village centre, designed for pilgrims. 15 places in rooms of 2-3 or in 10-pers. dormitory. Kitchen. Accommodation for horses.

Gîte d'Étape Communal, Rue de la Cascade, 46160 Cajarc, Lot, France; +33(0)6 14 66 54 89; accueil@cajarc.fr; €12.60/pers.; Located behind the office of tourism. 20 places in very basic conditions.

Chambres d'Hôtes-Gîte la Galinette, (Anne Conseil), Semberot, 46160 Cajarc, Lot, France; +33(0)5 65 11 03 44; lagalinette46@orange.fr; www.galinette.dormiton.free.fr; B&B: €56/1 pers.; €64/2 pers.; €84/3 pers.; Hostel: €21/pers. (breakfast included) €35/half board.; Located 4 km before and on the decent into Cajarc, an eco-friendly recently renovated house. 2-4 person rooms or separate hostel located in a cabin with 2 4-pers. rooms. English spoken.

Chambre d'Hôtes, (Evelyne and Roland Lemoine), La Peyrade, 46160 Cajarc, Lot, France; +33(0)5 65 50 15 28; +33(0)6 09 64 32 18; roland.lemoine46@orange.fr; €42/pers.; €52/2 pers.; 2 rooms. English spoken.

Chambre d'Hôtes Delvit, (Michel Delvit), Pech d'Andressac, 46160 Cajarc, Lot, France; +33(0)5 65 40 70 00; +33(0)6 24 11 11 69; €30/1 pers.; €45/2 pers.; 1.5km after Cajarc on the GR®65. 2 rooms in welcoming and calm home with lovely view of Cajarc.

La Ségalière, 380 avenue François Mitterrand, 46160 Cajarc, Lot, France; +33(0)5 65 40 65 35; hotel@lasegaliere.com; www.lasegaliere.com; €75-€125/1 to 4 pers. rooms; €10.50/breakfast; €23.50/dinner; Located on the banks of the Lot river, this basic but well maintained hotel with 23 rooms is located a few minutes from Cajarc centre. Lovely pool and garden.

Office de Tourisme, Boulevard du Tour de Ville, 46160 Cajarc, Lot, France; +33(0)5 65 40 72 89; www.cajarc.fr/fr/tourisme

Saint-Jean-de-Laur

Gîte d'Étape, (Colette and Roger Sohn), Mas de Jantille, 46260 Saint-Jean-de-Laur, Lot, France; +33(0)6 88 85 07 18; masdejantille@gmail.com; www.masdejantille.com; €16/pers. €5/breakfast; Just off the GR®65, this hostel is housed in a lovely 18th century restored farm house. The owners are former pilgrims that fell in love with the Causse region and decided to create a gîte. 10 places in dormitory. Kitchen. Food available for purchase. English spoken.

Les Deux Pigeonniers-, (Marie-Claude and Maxime Boisset), Mas Delpech, 46260 Saint-Jean-de-Laur, Lot, France; +33(0)5 65 40 70 13; +33(0)6 09 93 05 48; maxime.boisset854@orange.fr; €21/per. €5/breakfast, €13/dinner; 7 places in a typical Quercy-style home with lovely garden.

Puyjourdes

Gîte le Poulailler, (Françoise Pillon), Le Bourg, 46260 Puyjourdes, Lot, France; +33(0)5 65 14 06 95; +33(0)6 88 10 57 34; cepierefanoche@gmail.fr; €30/half board; About 2 km from the GR®65, 5 places in dormitory including in the lovely restored 20m2 poulailler (hen house) with private Moroccan styled terrace. English spoken

Limogne-en-Quercy

Gîte la Maison en Chemin, (Marie and Yves Paillas), 99 rue de Lugagnac, 46260 Limogne-en-Quercy, Lot, France; +33(0)5 65 23 24 41; +33(0)6 77 57 83 64; la.maison.en.chemin.GR®65@orange.fr; €22/pers. (sheets included); €6/breakfast; €42/half board; One of the nicest hostels on the Chemin both for its hospitality and fine accommodation. The owners are former pilgrims that realized their dream of having a gîte. 14 places in 6 rooms with 1-3 beds and courtyard/garden. English spoken.

Dalat'Etape, (Dominique and Françoise David), Mas de Dalat, 46260 Limogne-en-Quercy, Lot, France; +33(0)6 07 31 69 61; contact@dalatetape.fr; www.dalatetape.fr; €20/pers. €25/single room, €5/breakfast, €14/dinner; Hostel located 3km before Limogne housed in an 18th century Quercy style house. 15 persons in 5 rooms and dormitories. Hot tub and garden.

Gîte d'Étape Communal, Avenue de Cahors, 46260 Limogne-en-Quercy, Lot, France; +33(0)5 65 24 34 28; +33(0)6 12 84 86 47; gite.limogne@orange.fr; www.lalbenque.net/dormir/g%C3%AEtes-d-%C3%A9tape-et-de-groupe/communal-limogne/; €13/pers.; 10 places in 3 rooms. Basic accommodation.

La Hulotte, (Claudine and Lionel Baudin), Mas de Games, 46260 Limogne-en-Quercy, Lot, France; +33(0)5 65 31 58 51; +33(0)6 17 38 84 47; www.chambreslahulotte.fr; €48-€58/1 pers.; €58-€68/2 pers.; €75-€90/3 pers.; €19/dinner (upon reservation); On the GR®65 2.5km before Limogne, in a 4-room B&B housed in a lovely Quercy-style restored farmhouse with garden. Kitchen. Accommodation for horses. English spoken.

Office de Tourisme, 55 place d'Occitanie, 46260 Limogne-en-Quercy, Lot, France; +33(0)5 65 24 34 28; tourisme. limogne@wanadoo.fr; www.lalbenque.net

stage 15

DISTANCE **22.1km**

ASCENT **376m**

DESCENT **410m**

FROM LE PUY **304km**

TO RONCEVAUX **471km**

Route - The route continues to be well-marked, as it crosses the Causses Region, becoming largely flat and straight from Bach, where it follows a former Roman road, le Cami Ferrat, for 15km to Mas de Vers.

Pointers - **Culture:** The 26 km section of the GR®65 from Bach to Cahors is on the UNESCO world heritage list. **Reservations:** Advance reservations are recommended in Mas de Vers, as accommodation possibilities in this sparsely populated stretch of the route are few and sometimes several kilometres from the main route. There are also no grocers/restaurants, though meals may be reserved with accommodation.

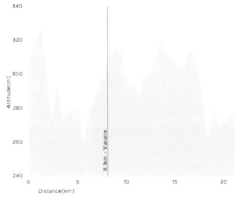

CULTURAL DISCOVERIES

Varaire - Cami Gasco

Varaire (popl. 300, alt. 240m) boasts a defensive tower from a 13th century fortress that belonged to the Cardaillac family as well as an impressive large *lavoir* (communal laundry) with butterfly-designed washing stones.

From Varaire, the GR®65 follows an ancient Roman road, known as the *Cami Gasco*, which connected the cities of Caylus and Cahors.

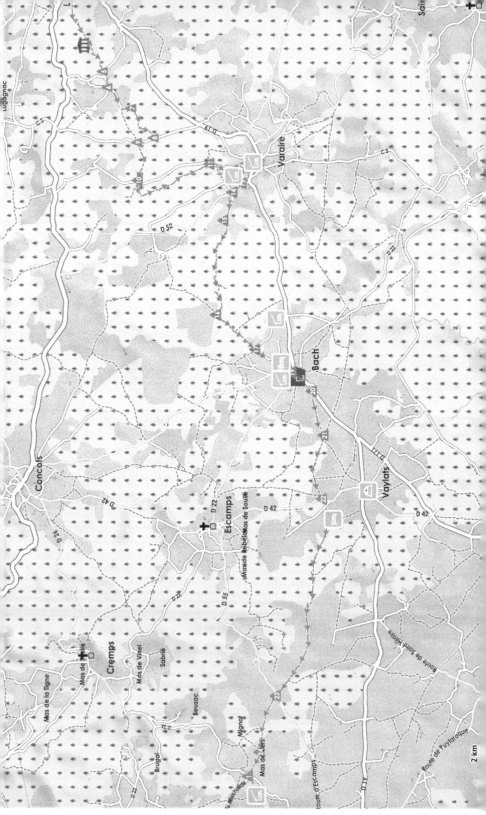

Waypoint	Total(km)	Directions	Verification	Compass	Altitude(m)
1	0.0	In **Limogne-en-Quercy,** from Place d'Occitanie ascend avenue de Cahors		SW	299
2	0.2	At fork keep left on the D19 road	Total gas station	SW	307
3	0.5	Turn right on chemin du Joncas and continue straight		W	315
4	0.6	Turn left onto track at fork	Oak tree	SW	324
5	2.4	Turn right onto asphalt road. Direction Ferrieres Bas and continue straight	Signpost	W	276
6	2.8	At fork keep left direction Ferrieres le Dolmen and continue straight	Stone cross, signpost	SW	286
7	3.5	Turn right off track onto path and continue straight	Ahead pass farm on the right	SW	277
8	4.3	At road's end, turn right onto asphalt road		N	279
9	4.7	Turn left onto track and continue straight		W	275
10	5.5	Keep straight on asphalt road and then turn left on track.	Signpost	NW	268
11	7.4	Merge right onto asphalt road and continue straight towards village of Varaire		S	297
12	8.1	On the outskirts of **Varaire** turn right	Signpost. Keep left to visit Varaire village and facilties.	W	305
13	8.4	Turn right onto D52 and continue straight to leave village of Varaire		NW	312
14	8.7	Turn left onto track towards the hamlet of La Plane.	Signpost for Bach. Pass Farm on the left.	W	311
15	9.3	Turn left, continuing south on track.		W	315
16	11.3	Turn left	Signpost	SW	291
17	12.4	Arrive in Bories-Basses and continue straight through intersection	Building to the right	SW	302
18	13.0	Turn left and enter village of **Bach**	Signpost	SW	304
19	13.3	At road's end turn right onto road and continue straight through village	Church	SW	315
20	13.9	Turn right onto track	Opposite beige house	W	314
21	14.8	Turn right at road's end. Direction Vaylats and Mas de Vers	Signpost	NW	308
22	16.2	Cross the D42 road and then a smaller road. Continue straight on path	Pass cross on right	SW	308
23	20.4	Cross asphalt road and continue straight		NW	275
24	21.6	Continue straight ahead, direction of Cahors		W	267
25	22.1	Arrive at **Mas-de-Vers**			273

Varaire

Clos des Escoutilles, (Mariëtte and Robert), Lieu-Dit Escoutilles, 46260 Varaire, Lot, France; +33(0)5 65 24 50 84; +33(0)3 67 34 70 23 6; info@clos-des-escoutilles.fr; www.clos-des-escoutilles.eu; €17-€21/1 pers.; €6/breakfast; €15/dinner; €33-€37/half board; 50 metres from the GR, the hostel is in a recently renovated separate building from the 19th century. Offers 12 places in 2 double rooms and 2 4-person rooms. Kitchen. English spoken. Very welcoming.

Gîte-Café-Restaurant des Marronniers, (Marie-Claire Bousquet), Le Bourg, 46260 Varaire, Lot, France; +33(0)5 65 31 53 85; lesmarronniers46@sfr.fr; €15/dinner ; €15/person (dormitory) ; €40/double room; €35/half board (dormitory) ; €80/half board 2 pers. (double room); 25 places in rooms or dormitory. Reputed for its gourmet restaurant's fixed-menu serving regional specialities, rather than for its basic accommodation.

Bach

Le Relais Arc-en-Ciel, (Michelle Prade), Les Moulins, 46230 Bach, Lot, France; +33(0)5 65 22 72 64; +33(0)6 45 25 92 97; michele.prade@laposte.net; www.relais-arcenciel.com; €15/pers. €5/breakfast, €5/dinner (soup/salad); Famous for its warm welcome, the gîte is in a tastefully restored farm, consisting of 12 places in 4 3-person rooms, with garden and living room with large fire place. English spoken. Accommodation for horses. Located about 1km before Bach.

La Grange Saint Jacques, (Michelle and Mike Spain), Les Nougayrols, route-de-Concots, 46230 Bach, Lot, France; +33(0)5 65 31 08 75; +33(0)6 45 38 37 61; lagrangesaintjacques@gmail.com; www.gitecompostellebach.weebly.com; €14.50/pers.; €5.50/breakfast; €60/2 pers. double room; €13.50/dinner; Lovely gîte located at the entrance to Bach. Owner Mike (English) is a former pilgrim who with his wife Michelle (French) renovated the 19thCentury granary to accommodate pilgrims, includes 10 places in 3 rooms (hostel) and 1 double room (B&B).

Vaylats

Monastère des Filles de Jésus-Association sur les Chemins de Compostelle, Le Couvent, 46230 Vaylats, Lot, France; +33(0)5 65 31 63 51; filles.de.jesus@wanadoo.fr; www.couventdevaylats.fr; €28/half board; An easy detour from the GR®65 (maps are available on the convent's website), the convent has a history of welcoming pilgrims. 15 1-4 pers. rooms and a dormitory with 26 places. Ability to take part in religious services.

Les Yourtes de Bascot, (Pascal Pons), Chemin de Bascot, 46230 Vaylats, Lot, France; +33(0)6 71 50 54 17; ponspascal@yahoo.fr; www.lesyourtesdebascot.com; €50/pers.; €60/2 pers. (breakfast included); €15/dinner (upon reservation); A unique experience. 8 places in 2 comfortable yurts situated on the GR in the forest of the Parc Régional des Causses du Quercy. Accommodation of horses. Host, Pascal, very welcoming.

Lalbenque/Mas de Vers

Gîte d'Étape de Poudally, (Elsa and Manu), 440 Chemin de Poudally, 46230 Lalbenque, Lot, France; +33(0)5 65 22 08 69; manu.elsa@poudally.com; www.poudally.com; €13-€20/pers.; €5/breakfast; €15/dinner, €5/foot soak; A restored farm run by a young couple 300 metres from Mas de Vers on the GR®65. 27 places in 9 1-6 pers. rooms. Accommodation for horses. English spoken. Very welcoming; dinner is recommended.

DISTANCE **17.7km**

ASCENT **388m**

DESCENT **537m**

FROM LE PUY **326km**

TO RONCEVAUX **448km**

Valentré Bridge Cahors © Alexandra Huddleston

Route -The route continues to be well-marked, as it descends into Cahors and the Lot River Valley. From Mas de Vers, it follows the Roman road, the Cami Ferrat, to Pech. From Pech there is a long descent on mostly small asphalt roads, into Cahors. This stage is short in order to arrive earlier and have time to explore the historic city of Cahors.

Pointers - Pilgrim welcome: The GR®65 enters Cahors by the Louis-Philippe bridge. A pilgrim welcome and information centre is set up on the left hand (western) side of the bridge. **Market:** Cahors' old town (Place Chapou) hosts a large and colourful market each Wednesday morning and the first and third Saturday of the month.

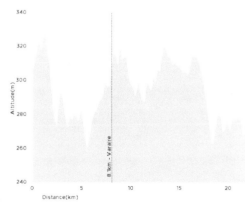

Cahors

Cahors (popl. 20,000, alt. 120m) is the largest city in the Quercy Region. It was founded by the Romans in the 1st century, in a bend in the Lot River. In addition to benefiting from navigation and protection (being surrounded on three sides) afforded by the Lot river, Cahors was also the meeting place of Roman roads leading to Toulouse, Bordeaux and Rodez. Roman ruins include a forum, Diane's arch (a remnant of the former baths), the remains of a large amphitheatre and the fountain of Chartreux.

Cahors was a rich merchant city in the 12th-14th centuries and an important intellectual and administrative centre in the 16th-18th centuries, due in part to its famous university (which no longer exists). Commerce, wine and administration formed the heart of the city.

Cahors remains famous for its wine (once called "black wine" by the English), which is made from Malbec grapes and was historically an important export, as it survived transport and could be kept over long periods. Black truffles (or "black diamonds") are another delicatessen. These grow on the roots of oak trees on the limestone plateau and are harvested in winter with the help of pigs or dogs. Other specialities include *croustilot* bread (made from local wheat), melons and *Pastis du Quercy* (a cake made with filo pastry and apple purée made with alcohol). Cahors hosts a lively market each Wednesday (Place Chapou).

Cathedral of Saint Stephen (*Cathédrale Saint-Étienne*)

According to legend, the Cathedral of Saint Stephen and its ecclesiastical complex was built in the 7th century by Saint Didier. However, most of the structure dates from the 12th century, when Pope Calixtus II consecrated the cathedral's two main altars. The cathedral has undergone several additions and renovations over the centuries. It remains, however, one of the best examples in France of a Romanesque Dome-church, with its 17 metre cupola stretching across the central nave. The tympanum over the northern entrance is from the middle of the 12th century and depicts Christ's Ascension and the preaching and martyrdom of Saint Stephen, one of the first Christian martyrs and the cathedral's patron saint. The cathedral also contains important Romanesque frescoes depicting Old Testament scenes, including the story of Genesis.

Valentré Bridge

Built in the second half of the 14th century, the Valentré Bridge is the oldest surviving bridge across the Lot River. The bridge was extensively restored in the 19th century - its military defences were reinforced and a small devil-figure was added to the central tower as a symbol of the legend that Satan had a role in the bridge's completion. With its three imposing towers, the Valentré Bridge is one of the best examples in France of a medieval fortified bridge.

Cathedral of Saint Stephen

Waypoint	Total(km)	Directions	Verification	Compass	Altitude(m)
1	0.0	In **Mas-de-Vers**, continue straight on road.	Pass cross on the right	NW	273
2	1.5	Cross the D10 road and continue straight on track		NW	278
3	2.6	Cross asphalt road and continue straight on track		W	273
4	3.6	Turn left onto asphalt road	Pass *lavoire* on right	W	248
5	4.9	Turn right towards Le Pech and then immediate left on asphalt road direction Cahors	Signposts	N	200
6	5.8	Turn left and follow path running along road. Cross road and turn left onto footpath		W	193
7	6.1	Go through underpass below the A20 highway and take path to the right, which runs alongside road.		W	187
8	7.2	Turn right onto footpath and continue climb. Direction Cahors.	Signpost. Farm building to the left	NW	235
9	7.4	Turn right onto asphalt road and continue straight		NE	248
10	7.9	Turn left onto track and continue straight	Ahead pass sports pitch to the right	N	259
11	9.0	Enter village of **Flaujac-Poujols** and keep left. Continue straight on chemin de Saint Jacques	Signpost	NW	278
12	10.4	Turn left on path	Before D22 road	N	194
13	12.0	Keep to the right of stone shed and continue straight on path		NW	227
14	12.6	Turn right onto the D6 road and then take first right onto route de la Marchande	Signpost	N	263
15	12.7	Turn left after house number 71 onto chemin de la Marchande		NW	270
16	13.2	Cross D6 and continue straight on chemin de Cabridelle	Cross residential area followed by barren hilltop.	NW	281
17	15.7	Merge onto chemin du Pech de Fourques and begin descent into Cahors		NW	251
18	17.2	At road's end turn left, pass under train tracks and continue straight towards Lot River.	Signpost	NW	134
19	17.4	Turn right onto rue St Georges and take staircase on left to cross bridge Pont Louis Philippe. Here, on bridge Louis Philippe, the alternative routes from the Célé Valley and Rocamadour rejoin the Way of Saint James - GR®65.	Pilgrim Welcome Centre on the left-hand side of the bridge	NE	120
20	17.7	Arrive at **Cahors**			112

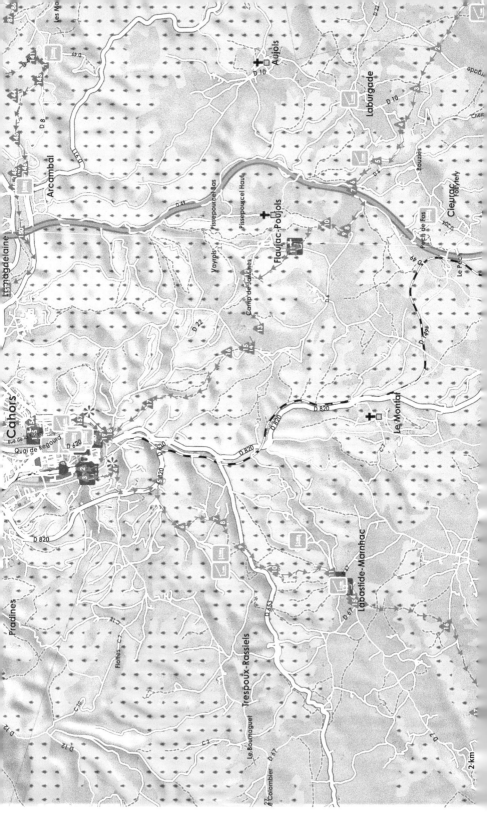

Laburgade

Gîte Privé Elisa, (Eliane Sarrut), La Bouyssière, 46230 Laburgade, Lot, France; +33(0)5 65 31 60 46; +33(0)6 69 58 01 32; sarrutp@wanadoo.fr; Starting at €14/pers. €5/breakfast, €12.50/dinner; 1km off the GR. 5 places in 2 rooms. Kitchen, garden and pool. English spoken.

Gîte Communal, (Annelise and Alex Latour), Le Pech, 46230 Laburgade, Lot, France; +33(0)5 56 24 72 84; haneliese@hotmail.com; www.gitelepechlatour.fr; €15/pers. €50/double room, €12/dinner (reservations required), €4/breakfast; 10 places in comfortable hostel. Kitchen. Horses welcome. English spoken.

Cieurac

Chambres d'Hôtes, (Gabrielle Bataille), Mas de Graniou, 46230 Cieurac, Lot, France; +33(0)6 82 18 10 55; gabriellebataille@orange.fr; www.lemasdegraniou.fr; €60-€70/double room, €20/dinner; 500m from the GR®65, lovely and calm B&B offering 5 double rooms and gourmand dinner. English spoken. Possibility to accommodate horses. Pool and garden.

Cahors

Habitat de Jeunes en Quercy, 129 rue Fondue Haute, 46000 Cahors, Lot, France; +33(0)5 65 35 29 32; afjq46@yahoo.fr; www.logement-cahors.fr; €17/pers. €3.50/breakfast, €8.50/dinner; Basic budget accommodation, including 18 places in 10 rooms (based on availability). English spoken. Garden.

Gîte d'Étape le Relais des Jacobins, (Serge Bouquet), 12 rue des Jacobins, 46000 Cahors, Lot, France; +33(0)5 65 21 00 84; +33(0)6 87 86 89 01; lerelaisdesjacobins@hotmail.fr; www.lerelaisdesjacobins.fr; €14.50/ pers.; €5.50/breakfast; €14/dinner; Down to earth budget hostel with 15 places in 5 rooms. A short walk to the Cathedral and famous for its welcoming and knowledgeable owner, Serge. Large garden. English spoken.

Gîte le Papillon Vert, (Eden Chalumeaau), 51 rue du Tapis Vert, 46000 Cahors, Lot, France; +33(0)5 81 70 14 09; +33(0)6 75 80 58 42; papillonvert.cahors@gmail.com; €15-€25/pers.; €5/breakfast; Located in a quiet street next to the Cathedral, tastefully decorated town-house with 9 places in 3 rooms, but every additional amenity is priced. Kitchen. English spoken.

Chambre d'Hôtes Chez Pierre, (Pierre Capredon), 62 rue Etienne Brives, 46000 Cahors, Lot, France; +33(0)6 09 96 28 32; noderpac@orange.fr; €30/pers. €50/2 pers., €70/3 pers.; 11 places in rooms of 1 to 3 persons. English spoken. Located in the historic centre. Pierre comes from Cahors and knows the region well.

Hôtel Jean XXII, (Sandrine and Guy), 2 rue Edmond Albe, 46000 Cahors, Lot, France; +33(0)5 65 35 07 66; jeanxxii@gmail.com; www.hotel-jeanxxii.com; €57/single, €68-€77/double, €85/triple, €89/4 pers. €7.80/ breakfast; Charming two-star hotel in the old town and housed in the former 13th century palace of Duèze with 9 rooms for 1 to 4-persons.

Le Coin des Halles, 30 place Saint-Maurice, 46000 Cahors, Lot, France; +33(0)5 65 30 24 27; www. lecoindeshalles-hotel.com; €67/simple, €77/double, €97/triple; Centrally located, simple but welcoming hotel.

Office de Tourisme, Place François-Mitterrand, 46000 Cahors, Lot, France; +33(0)5 65 53 20 65; www. tourisme-cahors.fr

DISTANCE **23.5km**

ASCENT **652m**

DESCENT **590m**

FROM LE PUY **344km**

TO RONCEVAUX **431km**

Route - The route continues to be well-marked, and uses mostly footpaths and tracks. After crossing Cahors' beautiful Valentré bridge, there is a short but steep climb up cliffs, offering beautiful views of the city. The route becomes more moderate as it passes through villages, pine forests and sunflower and wheat fields, typical of the high plateau of Quercy Blanc, before arriving in Lascabanes.

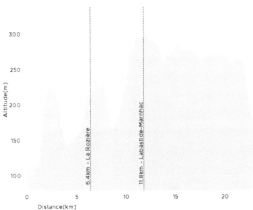

CULTURAL DISCOVERIES

Labastide-Marnhac

Labastide-Marnhac (popl. 1,200, alt. 140m) is a medieval fortified village founded by baron Guillaume de Lard of Cahors. In the 13th century, a castle and hospital were built of which only the current Romanesque chapel remains.

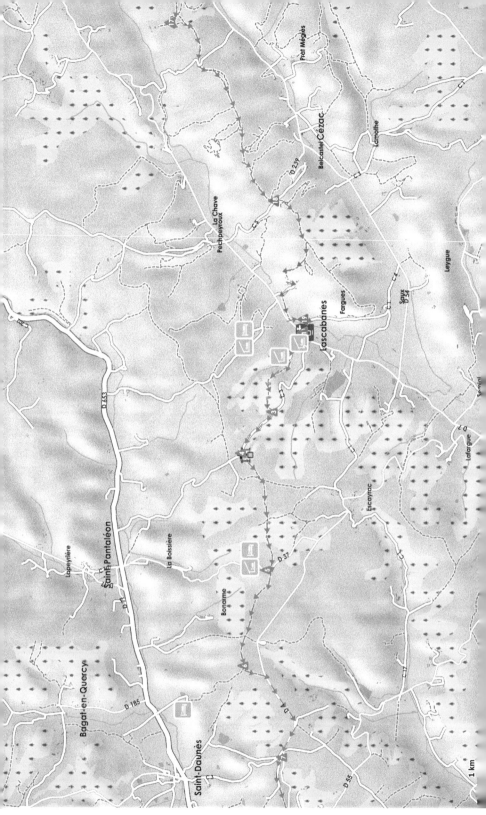

Waypoint	Total(km)	Directions	Verification	Compass	Altitude(m)
1	0.0	In **Cahors**, turn left from Pont Louis Philippe bridge and walk along the Quai of the Lot River until Pont Valentré bridge	River should be to the left	SW	112
2	1.1	Cross Valentré bridge	Bridge	W	114
3	1.4	Cross C21 road and climb steep footpath that leads to plateau. Keep left on a path that runs alongside the cliffs	Signpost	S	111
4	2.3	Turn right onto asphalt road, and then left to descend to the D820 road. Use underpass	Signposts	W	219
5	4.1	Turn left onto road running next to the D820 road, and then continue straight	D820 road on the right	NW	142
6	5.5	Continue straight on chemin de la Combe Nègre towards La Rozière	Signpost	SE	163
7	6.4	In **La Rozière** turn right towards church, and afterwards turn right again	Pass salle des fêtes on right and basketball court	S	219
8	6.6	Turn right and continue straight on track to leave village. At road's end turn left towards **Domaine des Mathieux**	Cross	W	212
9	8.4	Go through underpass and cross road D653. Continue straight then turn right	D653 road	SE	189
10	9.9	At fork keep left and continue straight through forest		W	223
11	11.5	Cross street and continue straight on path to the left of the road to enter Labastide-Marnhac		SW	298
12	11.8	In **Labastide-Marnhac** continue straight on main road, direction commerce	Pass church on left	SW	295
13	12.0	Continue straight on asphalt road	Pass town hall (*Mairie*) on left	SW	301
14	12.4	Turn right at stop sign and immediate left onto D7 road.	Signpost	W	297
15	12.5	Turn left on chemin du Roy and continue straight	Sign post	S	293
16	14.9	Turn left and then right onto road towards Fabre		SE	276
17	17.5	Turn left and continue straight towards Lascabanes		SW	266
18	20.8	Turn left onto asphalt road and then keep right. Descend into the valley towards the village of Baffalie		S	259
19	23.3	Enter Lascabanes. Turn right and cross stream (Le Verdanson) towards village centre	Signpost and stream	S	180
20	23.5	Arrive at **Lascabanes**			178

Labastide-Marnhac

Gîte de l'Eglise, (Patrice Michenaud), Centre Bourg, 46090 Labastide-Marnhac, Lot, France; +33(0)5 65 23 91 50; +33(0)6 27 70 59 89; michenaud.patrice@orange.fr; €20/pers. (breakfast included); Basic accommodation. 3 places in dormitory. Kitchen.

Gîte des Mathieux, Domaine des Mathieux, 46090 Labastide-Marnhac, Lot, France; +33(0)5 65 31 75 13; domainedesmathieux@gmail.com; www.domainedesmathieux.com; Dormitory: €20/pers. breakfast included; €35/pers. half board; B&B: €49/pers. half board; Owned by a former pilgrim; 28 places in dormitory, rooms or B&B. English spoken. Pool.

Chambre d'Hôtes Kerzazou, (Evelyne and Alain Deschamps), Impasse Monredon, 46090 Labastide-Marnhac, Lot, France; +33(0)5 65 23 21 69; +33(0)6 45 80 77 33; www.kerzazou.thierry-dollon.net; €55/pers.; €60/2 pers.; Lovely B&B that can accommodate 1 to 5 persons in 3 rooms. English spoken.

Lascabanes

Gîte le Nid des Anges, (Mrs. Cécile Maupoux), Le Bourg, 46800 Lascabanes, Lot, France; +33(0)5 65 31 86 38; chiha-maupoux@wanadoo.fr; €13.50/pers. €32/half board, €6/breakfast, €13.50/dinner; 17 places in rooms of 2 to 5 pers. Housed in the former presbytery, with a large vaulted dining room and piano. The dinner, using local products, is recommended.

Yourte le Sabatier, (Laetitia Lethé and Jean-Sébastien André), Lieu-Dit Sabatier, 46800 Lascabanes, Lot, France; +33(0)5 65 23 98 54; jslascabanes@gmail.com; €25-€29/pers.; €38-€42/2 pers.; €55-€59/3 pers.; €65-69/4 pers.; €13/dinner; €5/breakfast; Choose between a Mongol or Inuit yurt, each accommodating between 1- 4 pers. Pool. English spoken. Accommodation for horses possible.

L'Étape Bleue, (Marie-Claude et Jean-Michel Cayon-Glayère), Lieu-Dit Durand, 46800 Lascabanes, Lot, France; +33(0)5 65 35 34 77; mc.cayon-glayere@orange.fr; www.gite-etape-bleue.com; B&B: €52/2 pers.; Hostel: €13/pers.; €14/dinner; €5/breakfast; About 800m off the GR®65 and 1km before Lascabanes. The B&B is a restored farmhouse owned by welcoming former pilgrims, offering 1 B&B room and 4 dormitories with 2 to 4 places.

DISTANCE **23.8km**

ASCENT **698m**

DESCENT **654m**

FROM LE PUY **367km**

TO RONCEVAUX **407km**

Lauzerte

Route - The route, which uses mostly asphalt roads and tracks, continues to be well-marked, as it passes through a rich agricultural zone including sunflower and wheat fields, vineyards and medieval villages perched atop hills.

Pointers - Be careful on the brief but steep descent after Montlauzan (Pech-de-la-Rode), which can be slippery when wet. **Market:** Lauzerte hosts a market each Wednesday and Saturday morning (8a.m. to 1p.m.). **Festival:** Lauzerte also hosts an annual nocturnal contemporary arts festival the first weekend in August (5-7 August 2016). www.nuitsdelauzerte.fr

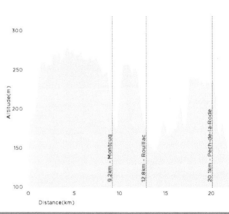

CULTURAL DISCOVERIES

Montcuq

The medieval walls that once surrounded Montcuq (popl. 1300, alt. 150m) were raised by order of the king in 1229. Only some vestiges remain, including a 12th century square 24 metre tower that dominates the village, and which today houses a medieval history exposition. The 14th century **Church of Saint Hilary** (*Eglise Saint-Hilaire*), with an octagonal clock tower, has impressive frescoes. More recently, the village became famous for a 1970s comic skit that poked fun at the name Montcuq. In French, Montcuq is pronounced (mon kü), or *mon cul*, meaning my backside, while in the native Occitan language the pronunciation is mon kük. A local market is held on Thursday and Sunday mornings.

Lauzerte

The village of Lauzerte (popl. 1488, alt. 200m) was designed as a *castelnau*, or settlement founded around a castle for defensive purposes. It was perched on a summit, and included a fortress, surrounding walls, towers and six gates. Despite these defences, Lauzerte fell to the English during the Hundred Years' War and passed between Protestant and Catholic control in the Wars of Religion. The main street, Grand Rue, is lined by impressive medieval houses from the 14th-16th centuries that attest to a former prosperity from the wheat trade. The village is considered one of the most beautiful in France and has a lively artistic community. A local market takes place on Saturday mornings.

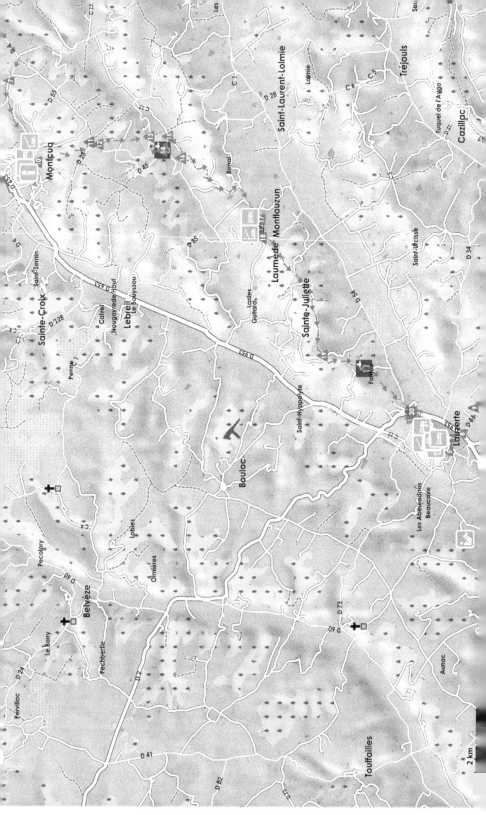

stage 18

Waypoint	Total(km)	Directions	Verification	Compass	Altitude(m)
1	0.0	Leave **Lascabanes** on main street (D7) and take immediate right on road C3	Alternatively, make your way to the church, from whence the path departs	W	177
2	0.2	Take first right and head towards church. Stay left on road to the left of church (route de Saint-Géry) and continue straight	Signpost and bridge	NE	187
3	1.6	Turn right onto C3/Route de Saint-Pantaléon and continue straight		NW	261
4	2.3	Turn left at Chapel Saint-Jean-le-Froid and continue straight past the turn off on the left to Escayrac	Water spring (la fontaine de Saint-Jean) near chapel was once revered as "miraculous."	SW	258
5	4.1	Turn left on the D37 road and then right onto track, direction Montcuq	Signpost	S	271
6	5.7	Turn left and then right onto the D4 road. Continue straight		SW	272
7	7.4	Turn right and continue straight on track descending to village of Montcuq		NW	264
8	9.2	Turn right to visit **Montcuq** village centre (off the GR®). The main route continues to the left	Signpost	W	212
9	9.3	Keep left south on the D28 road to leave the village	Opposite church	SW	207
10	9.5	Continue straight on the D28 road. After bridge turn left onto footpath next to fields and continue straight		SE	189
11	10.8	Turn right, direction Lauzerte and then left onto the D28 road	Signpost and Château of Charry visible	SW	257
12	11.0	Turn left on footpath, direction Charry	Signpost	S	259
13	12.2	Turn right onto the D28 road and then left onto track, which descends towards Rouillac		S	232
14	12.8	Leave **Rouillac** by turning left at the church, direction Berty	Church and signpost	SE	183
15	13.2	In Berty, turn right onto C17 road and continue straight	Pass farm on left	S	170
16	13.7	Turn left off road and cross stream (Ruisseau du Tartuguié). Continue straight towards Montlauzun	Stream. Further south, pass farm on the right	SW	149
17	16.5	Turn right to visit hilltop village of Montlauzun (off the main route)		SW	189
18	16.9	Turn left onto the D45 road and then right on track through forest towards Le Pech-de-la-Rode		S	196
19	20.1	In **Pech-de-la-Rode** cross street and continue straight (steep descent). Continue on path until reaching the D54 road, and turn right towards Lauzerte		SW	233

20	22.7	At roundabout, continue straight on road (crossing the D953). Climb towards Lauzerte.	Supermarket on right	W	128
21	23.1	Take path to the right and continue steep climb towards Lauzerte centre	Pass Gîte Les Figuiers on right	SW	134
22	23.6	Turn right and continue climb towards village of Lauzerte. Then turn left to enter village centre.		SW	183
23	23.7	Continue straight through village	Signpost	SE	201
24	23.8	Arrive at **Lauzerte**	Place des Corniers		213

100 m
1 : 5 241

Lascabanes

La Grange de Grizou, (Alain and Claire Brulé), Grizou, 46800 Lascabanes, Lot, France; +33(0)5 65 23 36 30; +33(0)6 75 39 73 35; alaincbrule@live.fr; www.lagrangedegrizou.fr; €15/pers. (hostel), €6/breakfast; €15/dinner, €54/2 pers. (B&B); In a restored farmhouse after Lascabanes and approximately 250m off the GR®65. Offering 13 places, including 6 places in 2 rooms (hostel) and 3 rooms (B&B). English spoken. Possibility to have vegetarian and gluten free dinner (but call in advance).

Saint-Daunès

Chambres d'Hôtes, (Gisèle and Jean-Pierre Couture), Ferme de Labouysse, 46800 Saint-Daunès, Lot, France; +33(0)5 65 31 84 39; +33(0)6 32 90 83 41; leauthier.joselyne@cegetel.net; €30/pers. half board; Located midway between Lascabanes and Montcuq, and about 1.5 km off the GR®65, this very welcoming 3-room B&B is housed in an old castle from the 17th century. Accommodation for horses.

Montcuq

Gîte d'Étape le Souleillou, (Detlev Bahler), 22 rue du Souleillou, 46800 Montcuq, Lot, France; +33(0)5 65 22 48 95; +33(0)7 61 51 69 41; contact@le-souleillou.fr; www.le-souleillou.fr; €13-€17/pers. (dormitory); €22/ pers. (double room), €27/single room, €6/breakfast; €14.50/dinner.; Located a few minutes before Montcuq, and about 200m off the GR®65, 29 places in rooms of 2-6 pers. Accommodation for horses. English spoken.

Gîte À L'ombre de la Tour, (Nancy Vandecasteele), 22 rue du Faubourg-Saint-Privat, 46800 Montcuq, Lot, France; +33(0)6 59 34 45 66; legite46@hotmail.fr; €29/pers. (breakfast and sheets included); Located in the medieval village centre. 3 double rooms. Kitchen. English spoken.

Chez Joelle Simon, 12 rue du Faubourg-Saint-Privat, 46800 Montcuq, Lot, France; +33(0)5 65 36 97 46; +33(0)6 70 37 65 59; joelle.simon0428@orange.fr; www.cadoline.com/simon/index.htm; €25/pers. (breakfast included); Located near medieval village centre 5 rooms. Kitchen.

Office de Tourisme, 8 rue de la Promenade, 46800 Montcuq, Lot, France; +33(0)5 65 22 94 04; info@ tourisme-montcuq.com; www.tourisme-montcuq.com

Montlauzun

L'Ancien Presbytère, (Chris and Eileen Gillon), Le Bourg, 46800 Montlauzun, Lot, France; +33(0)5 65 36 04 02; +33(0)6 73 44 26 39; lap46montlauzun@orange.fr; B&B: €38/pers. €61/2 pers.; €52/half board; €89/half board 2 pers.; Hostel: €15-€17/pers.; €34-€36/half board; A charming B&B located in the hilltop village of Montlauzan, in a renovated presbytery, with a capacity of 12, including 3 rooms (B&B) and 2 dormitories capable of sleeping 6. Owners are English and both former pilgrims.

Lauzerte

Gîte Communal, 15 rue du Millial, 82110 Lauzerte, Tarn et Garonne, France; +33(0)5 63 94 61 94; +33(0)6 19 70 89 49; corinne.segard6@orange.fr; €12/pers. in dormitory, €13/pers. in 3-4-pers. room, €15/double, €5/breakfast, €12/dinner.; Basic accommodation offering 15 places in the medieval village centre, run by former pilgrim. Kitchen. Possibility to have vegetarian or gluten free meal (but call in advance).

Les Figuiers, (Michel and Bernadette Reversat), Chemin du Coudounier, 82110 Lauzerte, Tarn et Garonne, France; +33(0)5 63 29 11 85; +33(0)6 85 31 71 31; michel.reversat@wanadoo.fr; www.lesfiguiers-lauzerte.com; B&B: €29/single room; €44/double room; Hostel: €11-€17/pers.; €5/breakfast; €14/dinner.; Located on the ascent to the village of Lauzerte, 30 places in modern facility. The hosts are famous for their hospitality.

Le Jardin Secret, (Mrs. Sara Costelloe), 37 rue de la Garrigue, 82110 Lauzerte, Tarn et Garonne, France; +33(0)5 63 94 80 01; costelloesara82@gmail.com; €70-€85/room; 5 rooms for 2 to 3 pers.. In village centre with interior garden, pool and views. English spoken.

Hôtel-Restaurant du Quercy, Faubourg d'Auriac, 11 route de Cahors, 82110 Lauzerte, Tarn et Garonne, France; +33(0)5 63 94 66 36; hotel.du.quercy@wanadoo.fr; www.hotel-du-quercy.fr; €48-€60/double room; €66/half board 1 pers. €969-€104/half board 2 pers.; €7:breakfast; In need of refreshing, but reasonably priced 11 rooms. The restaurant is better than the hotel, with nice terrace. English spoken.

Office de Tourisme, 3 place des Cornières, 82110 Lauzerte, Tarn et Garonne, France; +33(0)5 63 94 61 94; www.lauzerte-tourisme.fr

Moissac Cloister

DISTANCE **27.1km**

ASCENT **681m**

DESCENT **829m**

FROM LE PUY **391km**

TO RONCEVAUX **383km**

Route - The route continues to be well-marked, and uses mostly asphalt roads as it passes through farms and orchards to makes its way to Moissac, a major stop along the Way of Saint James.

Pointers - **Treats:** Possibility to buy local produce at a farm stand before Durfort-Lacapelette (bring coins). **Advance planning:** Ensure that you have enough water and provisions between Durfort-Lacapelettte and Moissac, as there are no watering points or grocers in this stretch.

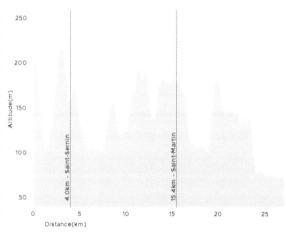

CULTURAL DISCOVERIES

Moissac

Moissac (popl. 12,570, alt. 70m) occupied a strategic position on the main land and water routes that connected Toulouse, Bordeaux, Quercy and Gascony. It is most famous, however, for the **Abbey of Saint Peter** (*Abbaye Saint-Pierre*). According to legend, the abbey was founded in the mid-7th century by Clovis, the first Christian French King. In the mid-11th century, the abbey became affiliated with the powerful Cluny order, after which important building projects began, including a new church, consecrated in 1063, and the cloister finished in 1100. With its 76 intricately sculpted capitals (topmost part of a column), depicting saints and biblical and creation scenes (such as flora and fauna), the cloister of Saint Peter is a treasure of Romanesque art. Later in the 12th century, the church's magnificent tympanum over the southern entrance was sculpted, depicting Christ in Majesty (as recounted in the Book of Revelation). A market is held each Saturday morning (Place des Récollets).

Detail of Prophet Jerome

stage 19

Waypoint	Total(km)	Directions	Verification	Compass	Altitude(m)
1	0.0	Depart **Lauzerte** from Place des Cordieleieres	Signpost	SE	218
2	0.0	Turn right onto Grand Rue, then turn left onto stairs at end of road	Staircase before Retirement home (*Maison de retraite*)	SW	220
3	0.3	Turn left and descend staircase		SW	219
4	0.4	Turn right on Passage du Pèlerin	Signpost	SW	207
5	0.5	At path's end, turn left	Cemetery	E	197
6	0.7	Turn right onto chemin de Ruppe and descend		S	177
7	0.9	Turn right onto steep path and descend to the D953 road	Pass modern building	S	159
8	1.1	Cross D953 road and continue straight on the D81 road crossing stream (Le Lendou)	Signpost	SE	129
9	1.8	Turn right and continue straight, climbing. Keep to right on track and pass pond to the right		E	111
10	2.8	Turn left onto asphalt road and continue straight to Charton. After passing *pigeonnier* (dovecote), turn right onto path to Chapel of Saint-Sernin		E	209
11	4.0	Pass Chapel of **Saint-Sernin** on left and continue to the right on path	Chapel	S	166
12	4.4	Turn right at fork and continue straight to the D57 road		SW	170
13	6.1	At road's end, turn right and continue straight on the D57 road		SW	105
14	7.5	Turn left off the D57 road and climb footpath. Keep left on road towards Mirabel	Signpost	S	102
15	9.3	Turn left before asphalt road and continue on track through fields		SE	123
16	10.1	Turn right and climb hill, which can be covered with sunflowers in summer		SW	122
17	11.1	Turn left onto small street before D2 road. Then turn right on path next to residential area and rejoin the D2 and enter Durfort-Lacapelette		SE	183
18	11.8	At roundabout continue straight towards **Durfort-Lacapelette** centre	Sign post	SW	178
19	12.0	Pass through Durfort. At intersection with the D2 road, continue straight on the D16 road	Sign post	S	183
20	12.3	Turn left (before houses) onto path. Then keep right and walk around a small pond (to the left)	Houses and pond	SE	186
21	12.9	Turn right onto footpath and climb through orchards until reaching a small road. Turn right.	Pass through orchards and a farm to the left	S	139
22	14.0	Cross the D16 road and continue straight to the hamlet of Saint-Martin		W	186

23	15.4	Turn left and pass the chapel of **Saint-Martin** on the right. Continue straight until reaching the D16 road	Signpost	S	180
24	16.9	Cross the D16 road, and then the stream (Ruisseau de Laujol). Continue straight		S	136
25	17.2	Cross road and continue straight on footpath between hedges, following stream	Hedge and stream to the right	S	113
26	17.9	Turn right and then left onto the D16 road		W	106
27	18.4	Turn left onto path and continue straight		SE	107
28	19.4	At top of steep climb turn right and then keep right towards Carbonnières (farm). Continue straight		SE	137
29	24.3	Turn left on the D957 road and continue straight towards Moissac	Signpost	S	77
30	24.9	Turn right onto the chemin des Vignes, and then right onto the D927 road		SW	83
31	25.9	Before bridge, turn right onto chemin de Richard, keeping train tracks to the left		W	75
32	26.2	Turn left and then right on rue du Faubourg Sainte-Blanche/D927 and continue straight towards city centre		S	80
33	26.7	At roundabout, continue straight on rue Malaveille	Signpost	W	74
34	27.0	Turn right onto rue de la République	Direction Abbey	NW	76
35	27.1	Arrive at **Moissac** centre	Abbey of Saint-Pierre		76

ACCOMODATION & TOURIST INFORMATION

Lauzerte

Centre Equestre, (Isabelle Favrot), Domaine du Pigeonnier, 82110 Lauzerte, Tarn et Garonne, France; +33(0)5 63 94 63 46; equi-sejour-lauzerte@wanadoo.fr; www.equi-sejour-lauzerte.com; €38/half board, €12/horse (feed included); Located on the hill facing Lauzerte 3km off the GR®65, this equestrian centre offers a hostel, mobile homes and pool. Accommodation for horses. English spoken.

Durfort-Lacapelette

Gîte À la Ferme la Bayssade, (Camille Favarel and Claudette Moriquet), Saint-Hubert, 82390 Durfort-Lacapelette, Tarn et Garonne, France; +33(0) 63 04 51 47; earldebayssade@wanadoo.fr; €20/pers. (breakfast included), €15/dinner; 9 places in 3 rooms on a working farm (fruits and dairy), located 1.5 km after Durfort, and 1.5 km off the GR, possibility to take a short cut the next day to rejoin the GR. Accommodation for horses.

Gîte du Mourelet, (Hans and Anja Maliepaard), Lieu-Dit Mourelet-Saint-Hilaire, 82390 Durfort-Lacapelette, Tarn et Garonne, France; +33(0)5 63 04 75 57; +33(0)6 85 97 87 69; hans.maliepaard@gmail.com; www.freewebs.com/mourelet; €40/half board; Located on a lovely renovated farm with large property and lake, 2.5km from the GR®65 (north of the village of Saint Martin). 8 places in 2 dormitories. English spoken. Pool. Accommodation for horses.

Le Soleil Levant, (Christophe Delmas), Le Bourg, 82390 Durfort-Lacapelette, Tarn et Garonne, France; +33(0)6 14 96 00 30; gitedusoleillevant@hotmail.fr; €15-€20/pers.; Located on the GR®65. 6 places in 2 rooms. Basic. English spoken. Accommodation for donkeys possible.

Moissac

Accueil de la Communauté Religieuse Marie Mère de l'Eglise, 20 Boulevard Camille Delthil, 82200 Moissac, Tarn et Garonne, France; +33(0)5 63 32 28 87; prieure@mariemeredeleglise.fr; www.mariemeredeleglise.com; Donation (breakfast and dinner included); 7 places in 2 rooms in a working convent located in the centre of town. Possibility to take part in religious ceremonies. Run by volunteers. Kitchen.

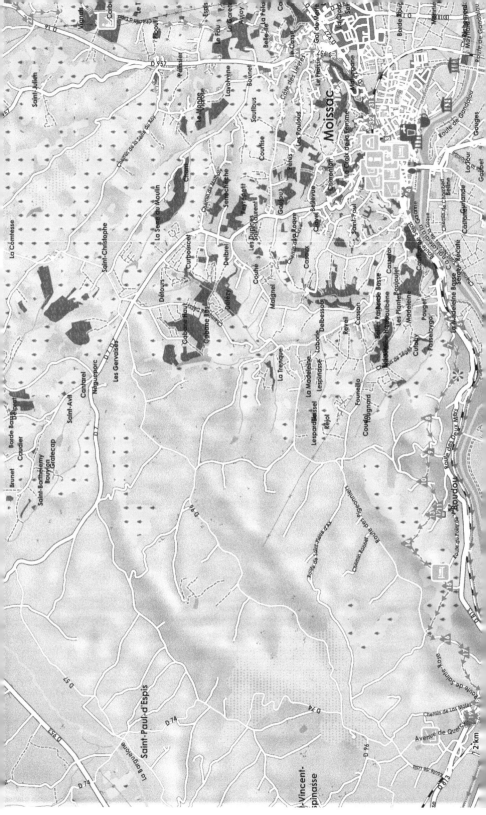

Gîte l'Ancien Carmel, 5 Sente du Calvaire, 82200 Moissac, Tarn et Garonne, France; +33(0)5 63 04 62 21; +33(0)9 64 48 71 99; contact@giteanciencarmelmoissac.com; www.giteanciencarmelmoissac.com; €14/pers. €5.40/breakfast, €33/half board; Located in a former convent, with extensive capacity, basic accommodation. Run by volunteers. English spoken. Dinner is served under the arcades in the courtyard.

Gîte la Petite Lumière, Panorama du Calvaire, 82200 Moissac, Tarn et Garonne, France; +33(0)5 74 68 12 94; +33(0)6 62 62 73 72; lapetitelumiere@free.fr; www.lapetitelumiere.org; Hostel: €15/pers. €33/ half board; B&B: €37/double room, €14/dinner; €5.50/breakfast; A lovely and welcoming little house with 8 places located on the heights of Moissac next to the statute of the virgin (a worthwhile climb). Beautiful views, terrace, piano. English spoken. Accommodation for horses.

Ultreia, (Rom and Aideen Bates), 45 avenue Pierre Chabrié, 82200 Moissac, Tarn et Garonne, France; +33(0)5 63 05 15 06; +33(0)6 71 74 03 14; info@ultreiamoissac.com; www.ultreiamoissac.com; Hostel: €15/pers.; €5/breakfast, €14/dinner, B&B: €43/single room, €57/double room; €78/triple room.; Owned by an Irish couple, this charming gîte with garden offers 14 places in small dormitories and 4 B&B rooms and is located on the GR®65 across from the train station.

La Maison du Pont Saint Jacques, (Christine et Michel Fournier), 20 Quai Magenta, 82200 Moissac, Tarn et Garonne, France; +33(0)5 81 78 12 09; +33(0)6 11 09 73 53; info@chambresdhotesmoissac.fr; www.chambresdhotesmoissac.fr; €53/pers. €65/2 pers.; A lovely and welcoming B&B with garden on the Canal des deux Mers, close to the city centre, offers 5 rooms.

Office de Tourisme, 6 place Durand de Bredon, 82200 Moissac, Tarn et Garonne, France; +33(0)5 63 04 01 85; tourisme@moissac.fr; www.tourisme-moissac.fr

Gîte l'Escapade et Centre Equestre, (Henri and Svetlana), 2105 Chemin d'Espis, 82200 Moissac, Tarn et Garonne, France; +33(0)5 63 04 48 96; +33(0)6 72 24 68 45; escapade@moissac82.fr; www.moissac82.fr; €20/pers.; On the GR®65, 6 km before Moissac. A familial equestrian centre and hostel with 13 places in 3 rooms. English spoken. Horses welcome.

Moissac Tympanum

100 m

GASCONY

Gascony Fruit Stand © Alexandra Huddleston

Gascony's historic natural borders were the Atlantic ocean to the west, the Pyrenees mountains to the south, and the Garonne River, which originates in the Pyrenees and flows northwest through Toulouse to Bordeaux. Gascony also includes the vineyards of Armagnac that grow on the hills between the Garonne and Adour rivers.

Over the centuries, Gascony has been occupied by several different cultures — in pre-historic times it was the land of the Vascones, or Basques, who were later conquered by the Romans (1st century), Visigoths (5th century), Franks (6th century), Basques (7th century), Norsemen (9th century) and finally by the English in 1154. By the 13th century, England's last small possession in France was the duchy of Gascony. When King Philip VI of France (1328-1350) seized Gascony in 1337, King Edward II of England declared war, thus starting the devastating Hundred Years' War. The region was taken from the English in 1453 and was united with France in 1607 under the rule of Henry IV of France.

The land in Gascony is fertile. Close to the Garonne river are fruit orchards (including plums for which the region is famous), and further south, crops such as corn for animal feed and wheat. It is renowned for its natural and hearty foods, such as duck *confit* (duck legs cooked in fat), blood sausage, prunes, *foie gras* (a French delicacy made from duck liver) and *garbure* (a stew made from cabbage, vegetables and preserved meats). Gascony also produces Armagnac (a type of brandy distilled from grapes) and *floc*, a lighter aperitif made from local grapes and fortified with Armagnac. The Gascon dialect is a variant of Occitan and is different from the Basque language.

stage 20

DISTANCE **21.5km**

ASCENT **586m**

DESCENT **549m**

FROM LE PUY **418km**

TO RONCEVAUX **356km**

Canal Leaving Moissac © Alexandra Huddleston

Route - Except for Moissac centre, the route continues to be well-marked as it follows the Tarn river and the Canal of Garonne, before climbing into the river-side hills, which offer beautiful views of orchards, vineyards and the confluence of the Tarn and Garonne rivers. From Malause, the route is mostly flat and on asphalt roads, as it makes its way to the historic city of Auvillar.

Pointers - Choice of routes: After Moissac, at the Ecluse (lock) de l'Espagnette, it is possible to take the flat alternative route that continues along the canal and re-joins the GR®65 at Malause. This avoids the main route, which has several steep climbs and descents, but equally beautiful views of the Tarn and Garonne rivers. **Market:** Auvillar hosts a local produce market every Sunday morning (8a.m. to 1p.m).

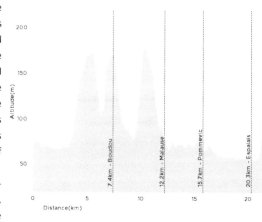

CULTURAL DISCOVERIES

Auvillar

The fortified village of Auvillar (popl. 942, alt. 65m) was built in the 10th century on a point over-looking the Garonne River. By the 11th century it housed a viscount, whose castle stood at Place du Château, which offers panoramic views of the river valley. The village fell to successive rulers, including the Counts of Armagnac and the Kings of Navarre, before being joined to the French crown under King Henry IV. By the 19th century, Auvillar had become a busy port and an important producer of earthenware and goose-feather quills. It was during this period, in 1830, that the *Halle*, the circular market hall, which is supported by 20 columns and designed in a Tuscan style, was built. Also of note is the elegant late 17th century clock tower, which replaced a fortified gate and drawbridge. Auvillar is classified as one of the most beautiful villages in France.

Waypoint	Total(km)	Directions	Verification	Compass	Altitude(m)
1	0.0	Facing the **Moissac** church (tympanum) turn left onto passage rue Marcassu, and then left onto Allée Marengo and continue straight joining the D7 road	Church	SW	76
2	0.3	Cross boulevard Lakanal and continue straight on avenue Pierre Chabrié towards the train station		SW	78
3	0.7	Descend staircase opposite train station and continue straight on Quai Antoine Hebrard	Cross the Canal Latéral à la Garonne	SW	73
4	0.8	Turn right on Promenade Saint-Martin	Canal to the right and Tarn River to the left	W	72
5	3.2	Turn right and cross bridge over train tracks and turn right onto the D813 road	An alternative route, which avoids the steep climbs, continues straight along the canal and rejoins the main route after about 7.5km in Maulause	SW	69
6	3.5	Turn left into parking lot, and then left onto route de la Roquette, which climbs and switchbacks		NE	74
7	4.2	Turn left onto track and continue climb.	Pass orchards and vineyards on the left	SE	117
8	5.8	Turn left onto track to descend into valley and then merge left on asphalt road	Pass farmhouse on the left	W	171
9	6.4	Turn right onto path, and then take first left to climb out of valley (steep)		NW	112
10	6.9	Turn left onto main road and continue straight towards Boudou	Signpost	SW	156
11	7.4	In **Boudou**, turn right at central square - Place Bertrand de Montaigut	Signpost	W	171
12	7.5	Turn right at church, and continue straight on chemin Roubiac		N	173
13	7.6	Continue straight on Impasse des Roseaux, running alongside orchard		NW	174
14	8.3	Turn left at end of path, and continue straight on track along valley bottom		SW	109
15	9.3	Turn right onto track. After climb, turn left on D4 road and continue straight		SW	79
16	10.6	Keep left on Route du Phare		SW	180
17	11.0	Turn right onto track after passing church of Sainte-Rose to descend into Malause	Stone cross	W	162
18	12.0	Turn left and descend Route Royale towards village centre	Signpost	NW	92
19	12.2	In **Malause** cross the roundabout (left) and continue down rue de la Marie towards the canal		S	84
20	12.4	Turn right onto rue Paul Riquet and then immediately left to cross the train tracks and the Canal Latéral à la Garonne		W	80

21	12.8	Turn right and continue straight alongside canals	Canals on both sides	NW	65
22	15.7	Turn right and cross bridge. Continue straight until reaching the D813 road and turn left to pass through village of **Pommevic**		N	72
23	16.5	Turn left onto the D116E1 road and cross the Canal de Golfech. Continue straight		SW	69
24	17.1	Keep right on road, direction Espalais. Continue on road through Espalais.	Signpost	SW	63
25	20.3	After crossing **Espalais** turn left onto the D11 road and cross the Garonne River. Turn left onto Rue-Saint-Catherine which climbs to the centre of Auvillar	Bridge and Pass Chapel Saint-Catherine	W	63
26	21.5	Arrive at **Auvillar**	Place de la Halle		111

Auvillar Market Hall © Alexandra Huddleston

Boudou

Chambre d'Hôtes, (Jenny Smither), Pugnal, 82200 Boudou, Tarn et Garonne, France; +33(0)9 63 01 40 21; +33(0)6 66 59 38 72; jennysmither@wanadoo.fr; www.pugnal.com; €25/pers. in 4-pers. room, €30/pers. in triple room, €70/double room (breakfast included); €18/dinner; Located on an 18 hectare property on the GR®65, 1km after the village of Boudou and 8km after Moissac. Spacious and reasonably priced B&B with 5 rooms and pool. English spoken. Horses welcome.

Malause

Gîte Boudet, (Mrs. Yolande Boudet), Avenue de Quercy, 82200 Malause, Tarn et Garonne, France; +33(0)5 63 39 64 23; +33(0)6 79 44 09 77; yolande.boudet@wanadoo.fr; €20/pers.; 12 places in 4 rooms in a small house with garden and terrace. Kitchen. Possibility to accommodate horses.

Espalais

Le Par Chemin, (Vincent and Sylvie Bernard), 34 avenue Montplaisir, 82400 Espalais, Tarn et Garonne, France; +33(0)5 63 94 73 78; +33(0)6 33 74 48 63; parchemin82@orange.fr; Donation (organic breakfast and dinner included); Mythic stop on the Chemin, famous for hospitality, familial atmosphere, communal dinners and music room. The owners are both former pilgrims who were drawn to this special place. Worth stopping in for refreshments even if you don't spend the night.

Auvillar

Gîte d'Étape Desprez, (Marie-Thérèse Desprez), Chemin Neuf, 82340 Auvillar, Tarn et Garonne, France; +33(0)5 63 39 01 08; +33(0)6 10 93 56 25; desprezmarie@orange.fr; €20/pers. (breakfast included); Located 1km from the town, 4 places in bunk beds in small pavilion. Pool and Garden. English spoken. Very welcoming.

Gîte d'Étape Privé Chez le Saint-Jacques, (Gerhard and Marie-José Schneider-Ballouhey), 14 place de la Halle, 82340 Auvillar, Tarn et Garonne, France; +33(0)5 63 29 14 23; +33(0)9 62 30 85 78; gemijo@orange.fr; €20/pers. (breakfast included); Welcoming hostel with 6-8 places in 4 rooms in an old house in the village. English spoken. Reserved for pilgrims.

Un Autre Auilleurs, (Kriss and Steff), Rue Sainte-Catherine, 82340 Auvillar, Tarn et Garonne, France; +33(0)6 88 36 78 69; unautreailleurs@yahoo.fr; €12/pers. €5/breakfast; 4 places in dormitory. Garden. Very welcoming hosts. English spoken.

Gîte d'Étape Communal d'Auvillar, Ancien Presbytère, 82340 Auvillar, Tarn et Garonne, France; +33(0)5 63 39 89 82; office.auvillar@wanadoo.fr; www.auvillar.fr/fr/tourisme/le-gite-detape.html; €14.50/pers.; Located in the old town centre, renovated in 2015 a former presbytery with garden. A comfortable hostel with 18 places in 6 rooms of 2 to 4. Kitchen. English spoken.

Le Petit Baladin, (Caroline and Jean-Pierre Wojtusiak), 5 place de la Halle, 82340 Auvillar, Tarn et Garonne, France; +33(0)5 63 39 73 61; les-crapettes-dauvillar@wanadoo.fr; Hostel: €38/half board in 4-pers. room, €42/half board for double room; Located in the main square, the hostel includes 15 places in rooms of 3-4 persons, and the B&B has 4 rooms. Very original decoration. Garden with café. English spoken. Accommodation for donkeys possible.

Chambre d'Hôtes Brune, (Anne-Marie and Francis Brune), 9 rue Marchet, 82340 Auvillar, Tarn et Garonne, France; +33(0)6 64 62 07 52; brune.anne-marie@wanadoo.fr; www.monvillageetvous.com/accueil.php; €52/pers. €66/2 pers.; Located 500m from the village centre, follow signs for 'Gîtes de Marchet, 3 rooms'. Gardens and pool. English spoken.

L'Entre Garonne et l'Olivier, (Stephanie), 11 rue Marchet, 82340 Auvillar, Tarn et Garonne, France; +33(0)6 83 09 51 37; stephanie_cx@hotmail.fr; www.lentregaronneetlolivier.fr; €38/single room, €60/double room, €104/4 pers. room; Located 300m from the town centre, considered one of the best B&Bs in Auvillar. 4 places. With pool and garden. English spoken.

Office de Tourisme, Place de la Halle, 82340 Auvillar, Tarn et Garonne, France; +33(0)5 63 39 89 82; office.auvillar@wanadoo.fr; www.auvillar.fr/fr/tourisme/office-de-tourisme.html

DISTANCE **21.8km**

ASCENT **698m**

DESCENT **654m**

FROM LE PUY **554km**

TO RONCEVAUX **561km**

Route - The route continues to be well-marked, as it crosses the rolling and rich agricultural region of Gascony, with endless wheat and sunflower fields. The route follows principally asphalt roads and paths through fields or along-side roads.

Pointers - Advance planning: The route is highly exposed, be sure to have sun protection (hat, sunscreen, etc.) as well as sufficient water

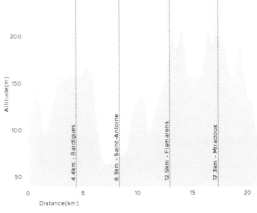

Wheat-scape © Alexandra Huddleston

Castle of Flamarens

The 13th century Castle of Flamarens (popl. 130, alt. 100m) was given as a dowry to the niece of Pope Clement V in 1289. During the 100 Years' War it was used as a fortress and in 1469 the main body of the building and an enormous keep were added. In the 17th century and at the beginning of the 18th century the castle was luxuriously furnished. However by the 20th century the place was abandoned, and its roof destroyed in a fire. Since 1983, it has been privately owned and restored.

Miradoux

The fortified village of Miradoux (popl. 530, alt. 280m) appears to have been founded in 1253, making it one of the oldest *bastides* in the region. The village became an important trading centre in the 17th century. During *La Fronde* (a series of French civil wars from 1648 to 1653 that sought to limit King Louis XIV's power), the loyalist village was captured by the Prince of Condé's troops, forcing the villagers to take refuge in the church. De Condé's troops were eventually and heroically pushed back by loyalist forces. The village continues to celebrate the battle through re-enactments. The large 16th century church, is dedicated to and houses a reliquary of Saint Orens (the 5th century Bishop of Auch (a town in south-western France)). The region is dependent on agriculture and produces wheat, garlic, melon and oil seeds. A market is held on Saturday mornings.

Castet-Arrouy

Casetet-Arrouy (popl. 200, alt. 107m) has a 16th century church dedicated to Saint Blandine (a 2nd century Christian martyr from Lyon), which is classified as a historic monument. It has lovely 19th century wall paintings by the celebrated local artist Paul Lasseran (1868-1935, a French painter and poet from Lectoure).

ROUTE INSTRUCTIONS

Waypoint	Total(km)	Directions	Verification	Compass	Altitude(m)
1	0.0	From Place de la Halle in **Auvillar** continue south on rue de l'Horloge/ D11, direction Bardigues	Pass through clock tower	S	113
2	0.7	Turn left onto small road between houses. Continue south-west on path, which passes through Lafume and then rejoins the D11 road	Signpost	S	146
3	1.6	Turn left onto the D11 road. Cross under A62 highway and continue on D11 road until Bardigues.	Highway A62	SE	96
4	4.4	After passing **Bardigues**, turn right onto asphalt road and continue straight, direction Pessanton		W	157

5	5.9	Turn right and then immediate left onto footpath, and descend to the D88 road	Path runs parallel to large power-lines to the right	W	163
6	6.8	Cross the D88 and continue straight. Then turn left and cross the Arrats river. Continue straight to Saint-Antoine.	Signpost	W	80
7	8.3	On entering **Saint-Antoine** turn left and pass through village on rue de la Commanderie. Continue straight through village.		SW	82
8	8.5	Leave Saint Antoine, and continue straight on the D953 road.		SW	75
9	9.0	At fork, keep right on the Voie Communal 13 and continue straight	Signpost	SW	77
10	10.1	Continue straight through intersection and then on path through woods which descends to the stream (Ruisseau de la Teulère)		W	127
11	11.1	Cross stream and continue straight climbing to Flamarens		W	100
12	12.9	Turn left and then right to enter **Flamarens** centre.		S	161
13	13.0	Turn left at war monument and pass in front of church	Monument	SW	193
14	13.1	Turn left and continue straight on the D953 road to leave Flamarens	Pass château on left	W	201
15	14.0	Turn left on small street, direction Miradoux	Signpost	S	201
16	14.1	Turn right on the path and descend towards the D953. Then turn left onto path running alongside the D953 road and continue straight	Signpost	S	208
17	16.1	Turn left and climb steep path along pine grove (to the right), then turn right onto asphalt road		SW	161
18	16.7	Turn left onto the D953 road and continue straight on D953 through village of Miradoux	Signpost	SW	202
19	17.3	Continue straight on D953 road and leave **Miradoux**, direction Lectoure		S	208
20	18.6	Turn left (opposite reservoir) onto small road and climb on path through fields	Reservoir and signpost.	S	156
21	19.7	Keep right and continue straight to rejoin the D23 road and enter Castet-Arrouy	Pass Château du Gachepouy on right.	W	180
22	21.5	Turn left and immediately right to pass through centre of Castet-Arrouy	Signpost	S	99
23	21.8	Arrive at **Castet-Arrouy** centre	Beside the church		105

Saint-Antoine-de-Pont-d'Arratz

L'Oustal, (Famille Dupont), Au Coin et Clos Sous l'Eglise, 32340 Saint-Antoine-de-Pont-d'Arratz, Gers, France; +33(0)5 62 28 64 27; +33(0)6 42 10 46 23; loustal.dupont@orange.fr; www.loustaldupont.e-monsite.com; €12-€16/pers. €5/breakfast, B&B: €50-€60/double room.; Located in a relaxing farm house at the exit of the village, very welcoming host. 30 places in dormitory or rooms of 2-9 persons. B&B: 3 rooms. Dinner is served at local restaurant, La Coquille, upon reservation.

Chambres d'Hôtes, (Rose-Anne and Renaud des Courtis), La Ferme de Villeneuve, 32340 Saint-Antoine-de-Pont-d'Arratz, Gers, France; +33(0)5 62 28 21 75; +33(0)6 10 33 67 99; contact@la-ferme-de-villeneuve.fr; www.la-ferme-de-villeneuve.fr; B&B: €60/single room and half board; €95/double room and half board for 2 pers. Hostel:€23/pers. (breakfast included), €39/half board for 1 pers.; Located on the GR®65, 1.5km after Saint Antoine, 15 places in 5 rooms with private baths and 1 dormitory in a beautiful 18th century farmhouse owned by former pilgrims. Pool, views and garden. English spoken. Horses welcome.

Flamarens

Accueil Pèlerin, (Xavier and Isabelle Ballenghien), La Patte d'Oie, 32340 Flamarens, Gers, France; +33(0)5 62 28 61 13; Donation (breakfast and dinner included); On left 1 km after Flamarens, 4-5 places in Christian home that has been welcoming pilgrims for more than 20 years. Reservations possible 48 hours in advance.

Miradoux

La Pause Verte, (Thérèse Fardo), 17 route de Valence, 32340 Miradoux, Gers, France; +33(0)5 62 28 66 57; +33(0)6 74 65 89 58; therese.pause.verte@hotmail.fr; Donation (breakfast and dinner included); A legendary stop on the Chemin, due to the generosity and uniqueness of its host. Worth stopping for a visit and sharing refreshments and fruit with Thérèse.

Bonté Divine, (Stephane and Nathalie Chevillion), 5 rue Porte d'Uzan Nord, 32340 Miradoux, Gers, France; +33(0)5 62 68 30 80; +33(0)6 20 50 09 70; contact@bontedivine.net; www.bontedivine.net; €15/pers. €5/breakfast, €13/dinner, €33/half board; Located in the village centre, 12 places in dormitory with bunk beds. Garden. English spoken.

Camping À la Ferme-Gîte d'Étape, (Jan Laville), Biran, 32340 Miradoux, Gers, France; +33(0)5 62 28 64 65; +33(0)6 20 29 90 70; plaville52@gmail.com; €30/double room, €15/pers. in cabin; Camp ground with 2 double rooms and 3 cabins sleeping 2-3 pers. located 2 km before Miradoux off the GR®65. Kitchen. Horses welcome.

Chambres d'Hôtes les Tournesols, (Josiane Wachill), 4 place de la Halle, 32340 Miradoux, Gers, France; +33(0)5 62 28 68 53; +33(0)6 46 24 82 49; josiane.wachill@wanadoo.fr; €45/double room, €12/dinner (upon reservation); 11 places in 2 rooms in an 18th century building opposite the market square. Garden and views. English spoken. Accommodation for horses.

Chambres d'Hôtes la Cordalie, (Family Abbal), 3 place de la Mairie, 32340 Miradoux, Gers, France; +33(0)5 62 28 84 35; +33(0)6 75 57 49 29; lacordalie@free.fr; www.lacordalie.free.fr; €45-€60/1-2 pers.; 8 places in 3 rooms in a beautiful 18th century home located in the old town centre, across from the town hall. English spoken. Possibility to accommodate horses.

Le Bonheur, (Wilma and Karel Thissen), 6 Grande rue, 32340 Miradoux, Gers, France; +33(0)5 62 28 69 19; karelwilma@sfr.fr or info@lebonheurmiradoux.com; www.lebonheurmiradoux.com; €55-€72/double room, €21/dinner; One of the best B&Bs in Miradoux, 4 rooms in a regal 19th century building with garden and terrace in village centre. English spoken.

Castet-Arrouy

La Lièvre et la Tortue, (Clément), La Tardanne, 32340 Castet-Arrouy, Gers, France; +33(0)9 54 43 97 35; +33(0)6 02 30 11 87; accueil.lievre.tortue@gmail.com; Donation (breakfast and dinner included); Very welcoming accommodation in shared rooms and large tent.

Gîte d'Étape Communal de Castet Arrouy, Mairie de Castet-Arrouy, 32340 Castet-Arrouy, Gers, France; +33(0)5 62 29 28 43; +33(0)6 84 92 73 96; gitecomcastetarrouy@orange.fr; www.gite-castet-arrouy.fr; €18/pers. (breakfast included); Located next to the town hall, 18 places in shared rooms of 4 to 6 persons. Kitchen. Horses welcome.

Chambre d'Hôtes Chez Nat, (Nathalie Arnulf), Rue Principale, 32340 Castet-Arrouy, Gers, France; +33(0)5 62 29 19 40; +33(0)6 22 39 54 07; nat.arnulf@orange.fr; https://www.facebook.com/Chez-Nat-676422275742611/; €42/half board; 8 places in 3 rooms. Very welcoming host. Possibility to accommodate horses.

Chambres d'Hôtes Albert Sala, (Mr Albert Sala), Place de l'Eglise, 32340 Castet-Arrouy, Gers, France; +33(0)6 22 18 42 76; albert.sala@aliceadsl.fr; €30/pers. €50/2 pers.; 12 places in 4 rooms in a restored stone house next to the church of Saint Blandine. English spoken. Horses welcome.

Lectoure Cathedral

DISTANCE 11km
ASCENT 305m
DESCENT 229m
FROM LE PUY 461km
TO RONCEVAUX 313km

Route - The route, which mainly follows asphalt roads, continues to be well-marked, as it crosses the rolling and rich agricultural region of Gascony to arrive at the hilltop city of Lectoure, which is popular with British tourists. This stage is short in order to arrive early and have time to explore the historic city.

Pointers - **Relaxation:** Lectoure is famous for its natural thermal springs (known as *thermes*). The spa, which is located in the town centre, offers half-day pilgrim passes, including access to the spa and foot and water massages (€35). Thermes de Lectoure, 125 rue Nationale, 32700 Lectoure, tel. : +33 5 62 68 56 00, www. valvital.fr/stations-thermales/lectoure

Recreation: (1) Lectoure has a beautiful public pool with views of the Pyrenees, entrance fee (around €4). Located next to the town hall, Place du général de Gaulle 32700 Lectoure, (2) Flea market (known

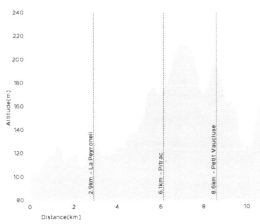

as a *brocante*): more than 20 antique dealers show off their wares in the Château des Comtes d'Armagnac, located in the town centre. **Market:** Lecoutre hosts a large and colourful produce market every Friday morning (8a.m. to 1p.m.)

Lectoure

The fortified city of Lectoure (popl. 3,700, alt. 200m) knew two periods of great prosperity: during the Middle Ages, when it was the main residence of the powerful counts of Armagnac, and in the 17th and 18th Centuries, when economic growth was driven by tanneries and agriculture. It was also during this latter period that several citizens of Lectoure gained powerful positions under Napoleon and that a number of private mansions (*hôtel-particuliers*) were built. Also of note is the former **Cathedral of Saint Gervasis and Saint Protasius** (*Cathédrale Saint-Gervais-et-Saint-Protais*), which was built on the site of a pagan sanctuary to Cybele (mother/earth goddess) and later a church dedicated to Saint Thomas (one of Jesus' 12 apostles). The church was built in 1325, and incorporated certain parts of a former 12th century monastery. A large part of the original church was destroyed in the 15th century, and was subsequently rebuilt in a Gothic style.

ROUTE INSTRUCTIONS

Waypoint	Total(km)	Directions	Verification	Compass	Altitude(m)
1	0.0	From the church in **Castet-Arrouy**, continue west through village centre. Then turn left onto the D23 road, and continue straight alongside the D23 road		SW	109
2	2.5	Turn right and cross the D23 road. Continue straight through agricultural fields		W	112
3	2.9	Beside **La Peyronell**, continue straight	Woods on the right	W	120
4	3.4	Turn left, and then keep right on path running alongside stream	Stream to the left	S	125
5	4.2	Turn right onto footpath and continue to follow path alongside stream	Stream	W	125
6	5.1	Merge left onto road and then turn right onto path towards Pitrac	Pass farm on left	SW	142
7	6.1	Keep left on road (passing **Pitrac** on the right) and continue south-west until reaching the N21 road.		SW	171
8	6.9	Turn left and then right, crossing the N21 and continue straight towards Lectoure		SE	206
9	8.0	Turn right onto road (C30) and climb to Petit Vaucluse	Signpost	NW	183
10	8.6	In **Petit Vaucluse** turn left. At end of road turn left towards Lectoure	Signposts	SW	196
11	10.7	Enter Lectoure. Turn left after roundabout on rue Barbacane		SW	160
12	10.8	Turn right on rue de Corhuat and then left on rue Saint-Gervais. Continue straight until reaching Cathedral.		W	164
13	11.0	Arrive at **Lectoure** in front of the Cathedral	Place de Gaulle		176

Lectoure

Accueil Presbytère de Lectoure, 30 rue Nationale, 32700 Lectoure, Gers, France; +33(0)5 62 68 83 83; paroisselectoure@wanadoo.fr; Donation (breakfast and dinner included); Located next to the Cathedral, 10 places in simple shared rooms in an imposing presbytery. Run by volunteers, most of whom are former pilgrims.

La Halte Pèlerine, (Véronique Pautrel), 28 rue Sainte Claire, 32700 Lectoure, Gers, France; +33(0)5 62 28 50 35; +33(0)6 88 90 55 74; vp.merlette@gmail.com; www.halte-pelerine.com; €21.50/pers. (breakfast included); €56.65/double room (breakfast included); Located in the town centre, simple accommodation in dormitory. Kitchen. English spoken. Large garden on the ramparts. Try the home made hot chocolate at breakfast.

L'Etoile Occitane, (Isabelle Fournier), 140 rue Nationale, 32700 Lectoure, Gers, France; +33(0)5 62 68 82 93; +33(0)6 74 45 11 17; isabelfournier@hotmail.fr; www.giteletoileoccitane.com; €20/pers. (breakfast included). €56.65/double room (breakfast included). €20/pers. (breakfast included). 14 places (bunk beds) in two rooms. English spoken. Possibility to accommodate horses.

Ferme de Barrachin, (Christine and Guy Esparbès), Barrachin, 32700 Lectoure, Gers, France; +33(0)5 62 68 84 57; barrachin2@wanadoo.fr; €30/pers. €45/2 pers., €13/dinner, Hostel: €8/pers., €5/breakfast.; Located 3.5 km after Castet Arrouy and 200m off the GR, on a traditional working farm with garden and beautiful views. Hostel includes 5 places in a simple dormitory, and 1 B&B double room. English spoken. Horses welcome.

Chambres d'Hôtes le Clos, (Joëlle Pons), 87 rue Nationale, 32700 Lectoure, Gers, France; +33(0)5 62 68 49 58; +33(0)6 32 02 81 64; leclos.lectoure@gmail.com; www.chambresdhotesleclos.jimdo.com; €47/single, €59/double, €82/3pers. €105/4 pers.; 15 places in 5 rooms in a recently restored building in the historic centre and near thermal baths.

Chambres d'Hôtes l'Horloge, (Béatrice Sager), 101 rue Nationale, 32700 Lectoure, Gers, France; +33(0)5 62 28 99 62; +33(0)6 76 86 30 42; beajl.sager@free.fr; www.chambres-horloge-lectoure.com; €68/double room, €110/2 pers. suite; 3 rooms in tastefully decorated historic home in village centre with garden terrace. Basic English spoken.

Chez Ginette et Michel Sellin, (Ginette et Michel Sellin), Tarissan, 32700 Lectoure, Gers, France; +33(0)5 62 68 92 73; +33(0)6 78 38 60 60; €36/pers. €48/half board; Lovely and welcoming farmhouse with 5 rooms, located 4 kilometres before Lectoure.

La Mouline de Belin, (Aline Salinié), Chemin de la Fontaine Saint Michel, 32700 Lectoure, Gers, France; +33(0)5 62 28 57 31; +33(0)6 26 18 52 00; mouline-de-belin@orange.fr; www.lamoulinedebelin.com; €75/1 pers. €82/2 pers., €96/3 pers., €110/4 pers.,€15/dinner; 1km before Lectoure on the GR®65, one of the best rated B&Bs. A restored 12th century mill and farmhouse, that includes 2 rooms and a gîte for 4 persons, as well as pool, stream, piano and fountain on more than 15 hectares of land. English spoken.

Le Marquisat, Chemin du Marquisat, 32700 Lectoure, Gers, France; +33(0)5 62 68 71 27; contact@lemarquisat.com; www.lemarquisat.com; €60/double room, €45/single room (breakfast included); 3 rooms in a comfortable B&B in lovely stone house with garden. Very welcoming. Wife speaks English.

Hôtel-Restaurant de Bastard, (Mr and Mrs. Arnaud), Rue Lagrange, 32700 Lectoure, Gers, France; +33(0)5 62 68 82 44; hoteldebastard@wanadoo.fr; www.hotel-de-bastard.com; €85-€120/room, €12/breakfast; 28 rooms in this sumptuous hotel, with gourmet restaurant, terrace and pool. English spoken. Accommodation for horses possible through the office of tourism.

Office de Tourisme, Place Gén de Gaulle, 32700 Lectoure, Gers, France; +33(0)5 62 68 76 98; contact@mairie-lectoure.fr; www.tourisme-lectoure.fr

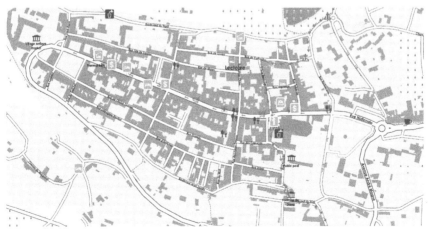

DISTANCE **18.8km**

ASCENT **444m**

DESCENT **443m**

FROM LE PUY **472km**

TO RONCEVAUX **302km**

Collegiate St-Pierre

Route - The route, which mainly follows tracks and asphalt roads, continues to be well-marked, as it crosses sunflower and wheat fields and some forests, to arrive in the UNESCO-listed world heritage site of La Romieu.

Pointers - **Culture:** The 35 km section of the GR®65 from Lectoure to Condom (including La Romieu) is on the UNESCO world heritage list. **Advance planning:** The route is highly exposed, be sure to have sun protection (hat, sunscreen, etc.) as well as sufficient water. **Choice of Routes:** It is possible to reach Condom and avoid La Romieu by taking a shortcut (mostly on asphalt road) at La Maurage.

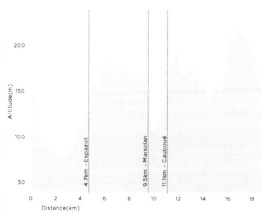

CULTURAL DISCOVERIES

La Romieu

According to legend, La Romieu (popl. 535, alt. 187m) was founded in the 11th century by the Benedictine monk Albert when he returned from pilgrimage to Santiago de Compostella; the word *romieu* meaning pilgrim in Gascon. The village has an impressive collegiate church that was patronized by the Avignon Papacy (the period from 1309 to 1377 when seven successive popes resided in Avignon (as opposed to Rome)). The church complex was built rapidly between 1314 and 1321, and includes a church, a sacristy with beautiful 14th century frescoes, a cloister and two towers, including a square tower with an impressive defensive staircase. Throughout the village are lovely statutes of cats by French sculptor, Maurice Serreau. These refer to the legend of Angéline's cats, which supposedly saved the village and its harvest from rats in the 14th century.

Waypoint	Total(km)	Directions	Verification	Compass	Altitude(m)
1	0.0	From **Lectoure** Cathedral head south descending rue Fontelie		S	178
2	0.2	Keep left (pass Diane's Fountain on left) and then turn right on rue Claude Ydron to leave Lectoure		SE	185
3	0.5	Cross and turn left onto the N21/ avenue ville de Saint-Louis and at intersection turn right on footpath chemin de la Tride		SW	135
4	1.0	Turn right onto the D36 road and take first left, crossing over railway tracks		NW	95
5	1.3	Turn right on avenue de la Gare and continue straight	Railway tracks to the right	NW	91
6	2.0	Turn left onto the D7 road, cross the Gers river and then right onto a track, before bridge over stream. Continue straight	Signpost	NW	83
7	3.1	Cross the D36 road and continue straight on small road that passes alongside corn fields	Pass farm on the left and Laslèbes on the right	NW	81
8	4.1	Keep left and descend path that runs alongside stream		SW	101
9	4.7	Turn left towards **Espazot** and then right at road's end. Continue straight through fields		S	128
10	7.5	Turn right onto footpath and continue straight	Stone shed and signpost	NW	179
11	8.8	Turn left to enter Marsolan	Pass cemetery on the left as approaching village	SW	174
12	9.4	Turn right at road's end and descend, passing next to Marsolan village	Pass church on the left	W	174
13	9.5	Leave **Marsolan** by descending on road and crossing the D166 road. Cross the Auchie stream and continue straight		W	169
14	11.1	Keep left towards the hamlet of **Cauboué** and then continue straight on track to Montravail	Pass hamlet on the left	SW	142
15	14.0	Turn right, direction La Romieu, on path that leads to forest	Signpost and pass reservoir on the right. Possibility to take unmarked alternative route (short cut) on asphalt road that continues straight towards Castelnau	N	175
16	16.1	In forest, turn left. At asphalt road, turn right		NW	188
17	16.8	Turn left on road. Then turn right before farm and continue straight to La Romieu	Road runs alongside forest	NW	209
18	18.8	Arrive at **La Romieu**	Village centre straight ahead		187

Larroque-Engalin

Lagarde-Fimarcon

D 283

D 166

Marsolan

La Romieu

D 166

Castelnau-sur-
l'Auvignon

Blaziert

D 7

D 41

1 km

Espazot/Marides

Gîte d'Étape, (Catherine Coustols), La Ferme d'Espazot, 32700 Lectoure, Gers, France; +33(0)6 37 64 89 80; peregrine32@orange.fr; €20/pers. (sheets included), €5/breakfast; 5 kilometres after Lectoure, on the GR®65 on farm in quiet agricultural area. 4 double rooms. Horses welcome. English spoken.

Chambre d'Hôtes, (Laetitia Brécy), Marides, 32700 Marsolan, Gers, France; +33(0)5 81 68 15 08; +33(0)6 34 27 41 94; laetitia.brecy@hotmail.fr; www.marides-lectoure.fr; €35/1 pers. €40/2 pers., €55/3 pers., €17/dinner; Located approximately 6km after Lectoure, a simple B&B with 3 rooms on a working farm, with garden and terrace. English spoken. Horses welcome.

Marsolan

Gîte d'Étape le Bourdon, (Philippe and Monique de Laval), Le Village, 32700 Marsolan, Gers, France; +33(0)9 54 10 78 68; lebourdondemarsolan@gmail.com; www.lebourdondemarsolan.fr; €15/pers. €5/breakfast; A simple but welcoming hostel only for pilgrims with 14 places in 3 rooms, owned by former pilgrims, located on the village ramparts with lovely views. English spoken.

Gîte-Chambres d'Hôtes, (Sylvie and Richard Musset), L'Enclos du Tabus, 32700 Marsolan, Gers, France; +33(0)5 62 68 79 40; lenclosdutabus@hotmail.fr or isabelfournier@hotmail.fr; Hostel: €35/half board, B&B: €43-€60/half board.; On a property located 300m from Marsolan centre, with 18 places in small shared rooms and 3 B&B rooms for 1 to 4 pers. Pool. English spoken. Horses welcome.

Chambres d'Hôtes, (Edith and Guy Tardin), Mieucas, 32700 Marsolan, Gers, France; +33(0)5 62 68 90 53; edith.tardin@wanadoo.fr; www.mieucas.fr; €58-€72/1 pers. €63-€77/2 pers., €23/dinner; Located 1.5 km after Marsolan and half a kilometre from the GR, a comfortable B&B on a 17th century working farm with 4 rooms, pool table and pool. Horses welcome.

La-Romieu

Gîte de Beausoleil, (Isabelle and Oscar Coupey), Moncade, 32480 La-Romieu, Gers, France; +33(0)5 62 28 84 61; +33(0)6 71 58 50 21; iocoupey@club-internet.fr; https://gitelaromieu.wordpress.com; €18/pers. €4.50/breakfast; 35 places in double rooms on lovely property 1 km before La Romieu. English spoken. Horses welcome.

Gîte Privé, (Francis and Marie), Domaine de Pellecahus, 32480 La-Romieu, Gers, France; +33(0)5 62 28 03 89; contact@pellecahus.com; www.pellecahus.com; €45/pers. €63-€66/2 pers., €84/3 pers.; 5 rooms in separate buildings on a restored farm. 1.5km from La Romieu. Pool.

Le Couvent de la Romieu, (Frédérique Larribeau), Rue Réglat, 32480 La-Romieu, Gers, France; +33(0)5 62 28 73 59; +33(0)6 88 47 36 17; leveupas@orange.fr; www.lecouventdelaromieu.fr; Dormitory: €20/pers. €32/single room, €48/double room (breakfast included); Dormitory (very spacious) and rooms in an 18th century former convent.

Chambre d'Hôtes-Café-Restaurant Angeline, (Mr. Martin), 6 place Bouet, 32480 La-Romieu, Gers, France; +33(0)5 62 28 10 29; +33(0)6 69 63 88 99; etapeangeline@orange.fr; www.chambre-hotes-restaurant-la-romieu.fr; €43/pers. €58/2 pers., €75/3 pers., €93/4 pers., €16/dinner; 5 rooms in main square in charming B&B with fine restaurant. English spoken.

Chambres d'Hôtes Va Bene, (Denis and Caterine Beaugé), 1 place Bouet, 32480 La-Romieu, Gers, France; +33(0)5 62 68 25 91; +33(0)6 82 13 25 17; caterine.beauge0081@orange.fr; www.chambresdhotesvabene.com; €70/double room, €85/double room separate beds; Lovely B&B with 2 rooms in the village centre, across of the cloister, in a bourgeois house. English spoken.

Office de Tourisme, Rue Doct Lucante, 32480 La-Romieu, Gers, France; +33(0)5 62 28 86 33; la-romieu.i@wanadoo.fr; www.la-romieu.com

Camp de Florence, Le Camp de Florence, 32480 La-Romieu, Gers, France; +33(0)5 62 28 15 58; info@lecampdeflorence.com; www.lecampdeflorence.com; €45/1 pers. half board, mobile homes: €50-€60/4-6 pers. (may require a 2 night stay), 6.50/breakfast, €19/dinner; 1 night lodging not available in July or August. 500m from La Romieu, camp-ground on 15 hectares with pool, offering mobile homes and cabins for 2 to 6 persons. English spoken. Horses welcome.

Larressingle

DISTANCE **19.6km**

ASCENT **483m**

DESCENT **519m**

FROM LE PUY **491km**

TO RONCEVAUX **283km**

Route - The route is well-marked and mainly follows asphalt roads, as it makes its way to the city of Condom. The stage ends in Larressingle, one kilometre off the GR®65 in a fortified medieval village, considered to be one of the most beautiful in France. Backtrack from Larressingle to re-join the GR®65.

Pointers - **Market:** Condom hosts a large and colourful produce market each Wednesday and Sunday morning (8a.m. to 1p.m.)

CULTURAL DISCOVERIES

Castelnau sur-l'Auvignon

Castelnau sur-l'Auvignon (popl. 180, alt. 166m) was built around a 12th century fortress that was perched on a rocky outcrop overlooking the Auvignon valley. Only a watchtower remains. In 1943, the village was an important centre of French and English resistance against Nazi Germany. On 21 June 1944, Nazi forces attacked and burned the village. Before retreating, the resistance fighters destroyed a tower of the former castle which served as an arsenal, preventing the arms from falling into enemy hands. There is a monument to the Resistance in the village centre.

Castelnau sur-l'Auvignon Tower

Condom

The Three Musketeers

Condom (popl. 7,000, alt. 73m) developed around the confluence of the Baïse river and Gèle stream, from which its name is derived; *condatòmagus* is Galois for marketplace at the confluence. A Benedictine abbey dedicated to Saint Peter was built in 1011. Later, in 1317, while under English occupation during the Hundred Years' War, Condom became an important bishopric (the area for which a bishop is in charge), with 130 parish churches falling under its domain (including Larressingle). In the 16th century, the flamboyant gothic-styled former **Cathedral of Saint Peter** (*Cathédrale Saint-Pierre*) was built on the spot of the original abbey church. The city experienced a period of prosperity in the 18th century when flat-bottomed barges began to export Armagnac down the Baïse river to Bordeaux. Both the Armagnac Museum and boat rides permit visitors to discover the history of the Armagnac trade. D'Artagan, from Alexandre Dumas,' *The Three Musketeers*, was said to born in the Armagnac region; there is a statue of the trio outside the church. A market is held every Wednesday, Saturday and Sunday morning.

Larressingle

Larressingle is an amazingly well-preserved tiny fortified medieval village. In the 13th century, during the Hundred Years' War, the village was entirely walled. At that time, there were about 40 homes, housing 250-300 people. The homes lined the defensive walls, thus buttressing them and creating a communal space in the village centre. The village also housed a castle (13th century), built for the abbots and bishops of Condom, and the Church of Saint Sigismond (12th century). Larressingle is classified as one of the most beautiful villages in France and as a historic monument.

ROUTE INSTRUCTIONS

Waypoint	Total(km)	Directions	Verification	Compass	Altitude(m)
1	0.0	Leave **La Romieu**, heading south-west on D41/ avenue Roger Lacroix direction Condom	Signpost	W	190
2	0.9	At bend, turn right on path running alongside corn field. Continue straight until road, and turn right.		NW	194
3	1.8	Turn left at intersection, and continue straight, direction **Château de Maridac**	Pass Château on the left	W	177
4	2.6	Turn left onto asphalt road and continue straight to the D41 road		SW	180

5	3.2	Cross the D41. Turn left, followed by first right and climb towards Castelnau sur l'Avignon	Signpost	S	151
6	4.4	Arrive in **Castelnau-sur-l'Auvignon**. To leave village, continue straight on road that descends to valley	Signpost	W	160
7	4.8	Continue straight on trail and cross stream Le Grand Auvignon. Keep left and climb through fields		W	121
8	5.8	Keep right and pass Chapel of Sainte-Germaine on the left. Continue straight towards village of Le Baradieu		W	140
9	6.2	In **Le Baradieu** turn left and then take first right	Pass farm on the left	S	165
10	7.3	Keep left and then right, on path circumscribing the Lake of Bousquètara		S	146
11	8.3	Keep left and continue straight until reaching the D204 road		NW	133
12	10.0	Cross the D204 and continue straight towards Condom		W	176
13	12.1	Turn left on path and descend towards the D7 road	Signpost	SW	112
14	12.5	Turn right onto the D7 road and continue straight towards city centre		W	85
15	12.8	In **Condom** turn left onto avenue des Anciens Combattants and take rue Jean-Jaurés	Keep right of war monument	SW	82
16	13.3	Turn left to rejoin the D930/ avenue Général de Gaulle and descend towards roundabout. Turn right.		W	95
17	13.6	Cross bridge over the Blaise River and turn left on path that runs along the river	Bridge	W	81
18	14.2	Cross the D15 road and continue straight on road through bamboo grove. Then turn left onto chemin des Capots de Testé		W	75
19	15.0	At roundabout turn right onto "voie verte" passing through trees	Signpost and Tènaréze information panel on the right	W	90
20	15.1	Turn left onto small road		SW	90
21	17.6	Keep left on footpath that passes between fields.		W	154
22	18.5	Turn right on chemin de Valence and continue straight to reach Larressingle	Signpost	NW	178
23	19.4	Turn left to enter Larressingle, historic centre.	Signpost	SW	150
24	19.6	Arrive at **Larressingle**	Beside the gates of the medieval village		146

Castelnau-sur-l'Auvignon

Accueil Bénévole l'Ancre sur l'Auvignon, (Jean-Pierre Knobel), Le Mourelot, 32100 Castelnau-sur-l'Auvignon, Gers, France; +33(0)5 62 28 93 15; +33(0)6 40 05 10 48; Donation (breakfast and dinner included); 1km before Castelnau, house providing 8 places in 2 rooms. Kitchen. Horses welcome.

Gîte le Relais du Maçon, (Philippe et Nicole Pillon), Le Maçon, 32100 Castelnau-sur-l'Auvignon, Gers, France; +33(0)6 16 93 84 70; n.pillon80@laposte.net; www.lerelaisdumacon.fr; €15/pers. €5/breakfast, €32/half board; Opened in 2014, lovely gîte located on a renovated farm 500m from the GR®65, includes garden, pool and billiard room. 15 places in 7 rooms.

Gîte-Chambre d'Hôtes, (Jeanine and André Rodriguez), Les Arroucasses, 32100 Castelnau-sur-l'Auvignon, Gers, France; +33(0)5 62 68 12 24; jeaninne32@hotmail.fr; www.lesarroucasses.com; Hostel: €34/half board, B&B: €60/half board 1 pers. €84/2 pers. half board; Former pilgrims share their lovely home with garden and pool, including a communal dinner on the terrace. 13 places in 5 rooms.

Chambre d'Hôtes la Maison du Lézard, (Sylvia Schneider), Avenue 24 Juin 1944, 32100 Castelnau-sur-l'Auvignon, Gers, France; +33(0)5 62 68 26 75; +33(0)6 56 79 37 92; sylvia@maison-du-lezard.fr; www.maison-du-lezard.fr; €55/double room, €14/dinner; 4 places in 2 double rooms in historic home in village centre. English spoken. Kitchen.

Condom

Gîte de Gabarre, (Eric and Isabelle Lanxade), 42Bis avenue des Mousquetaires, 32100 Condom, Gers, France; +33(0)6 86 41 58 39; lanxade.eric@orange.fr; www.gitedegabarre-condom.com; €15/pers. €5.50/breakfast, €35/half board; Located on a lovely property on the Blaise river, once a 14th century Armagnac wine storehouse, after Condom, 10 minutes from the city and 200m from the GR®65. 40 places. English spoken.

La Halte du Kiosque, (Fabienne Rouilhès), 2 Square Salvandy, 32100 Condom, Gers, France; +33(0)5 62 68 37 76; +33(0)6 84 32 30 01; contact@lahaltedukiosque.fr; www.lahaltedukiosque.fr; €19/pers. €5/ breakfast, €34/half board; Close to the city centre, 10 places in 3 rooms. Cottage with garden and terrace. English spoken.

Relais de Saint Jacques, (Alain Laurent and Arnaud), 2 avenue du Maréchal Joffre, 32100 Condom, Gers, France; +33(0)6 13 28 52 66; +33(0)6 21 78 47 86; laurent_crassous@orange.fr; www.relais-saintjacques. fr; €20/pers. (breakfast included), €15/dinner; Located in an 18th century former post office at the entrance of Condom, 15 places in rooms of 2 to 4. English spoken.

Gîte l'Ancien Carmel, 35 avenue Victor Hugo, 32100 Condom, Gers, France; +33(0)5 62 29 41 56; +33(0)3 64 10 91 24 3; contact@lanciencarmel.com; www.lanciencarmel.com; €25/pers. (breakfast included), €35/ half board, Dormitory: €15/pers. (breakfast included) €25/half board.; Located at the entrance to Condom, 600m from the GR®65, a former convent dating back to the 13th century, 37 places in rooms of 1 or 2, and dormitory for 12. Kitchen. English spoken. Horses welcome.

Le Champ D'etoiles, (Anne Charlotte), 18 rue du Maréchal Joffre, 32100 Condom, Gers, France; +33(0)6 08 05 26 84; lechampdetoiles@gmail.com; €15/pers. €5/breakfast, €13/dinner; Located at the entrance of the city, on the GR65, 100m from the centre. Three rooms in a house with a large garden and kitchen. English spoken. Horses welcome.

Office de Tourisme, 5 place Saint-Pierre, 32100 Condom, Gers, France; +33(0)5 62 28 00 80; contact@ tourisme-tenareze.com; www.tourisme-condom.com

Larressingle

Ferme de Tollet, (Mr and Mrs Carrère Tollet), D507,, 32100 Larressingle, Gers, France; +33(0)5 62 28 02 45; +33(0)6 87 36 04 34; €15.50/pers. €32.50/half board; Basic accommodation on a working farm, which produces local specialities in Armagnac. 10 places, welcoming hosts.

La Halte de Larressingle, (Martine Valeri), Cahuzac, 32100 Larressingle, Gers, France; +33(0)6 62 77 29 72; haltedelarressingle@yahoo.com; www.lahaltedelarressingle.com; Hostel €16/pers. €29-€34/half board (in shared rooms), B&B: €45/pers. half board, €68/half board 2 pers.; Run by a former pilgrim who is very welcoming, located 500m from the GR®65 and 250m from Larressingle, with lovely views. 9 places, including 5 places in dormitory and 3 B&B rooms.

Maison d'Hôtes - Lacassagne, (Maïder Papelorey), Lacassagne, 32100 Larressingle, Gers, France; +33(0)5 62 28 26 89; contact@lacassagnechambresdhotes.fr; www.lacassagnechambresdhotes.fr; €65-€95/ double room, €8/breakfast.; Located 500m from the medieval village, luxurious B&B in a spacious 18th century farmhouse. 4 double rooms. English spoken.

Auberge de Larressingle, Coulomet, 32100 Larressingle, Gers, France; +33(0)5 62 28 29 67; contact@ auberge-de-larressingle.fr; www.auberge-de-larressingle.fr; €65-€95/double room, €8/breakfast.; Located next to the historic village, 12 rooms, which can accommodate 2 to 4 pers. Sauna and spa. Hoses welcome. English spoken.

Office de Tourisme, Au Village, 32100 Larressingle, Gers, France; +33(0)5 62 68 22 49; contact@tourisme-tenareze.com

stage 25   LARRESSINGLE TO ÉAUZE

DISTANCE **29.2km**

ASCENT **643m**

DESCENT **626m**

FROM LE PUY **511km**

TO RONCEVAUX **263km**

Hiker before Éauze © Alexia Adamski

Route - The route is very well marked, as it makes its way to the former Roman city of Éauze, crossing fields and vineyards. From Lamothe, the route is straight and monotonous (following former railway tracks) for 6km as it leads to Éauze.

Pointers - **Market:** Éauze hosts a local produce market every Thursday morning as well as Sunday mornings in July and August.

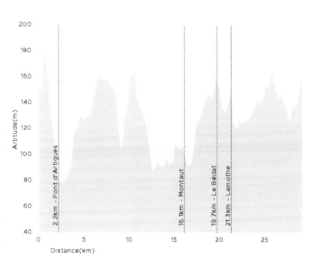

198

LARRESSINGLE TO ÉAUZE

Pont d'Artigues

Pont d'Artigues is a 12th century Romanesque bridge over the Osse river on the former Roman road connecting Agen to Éauze, and is considered a world heritage site. The Knights of Malta built a hospital and chapel nearby (now destroyed).

Montréal du Gers

Considered one of the most beautiful villages in France, Montréal du Gers (popl. 1,185, alt. 100m) is one of the oldest *bastides* in the region. Founded in 1255 by Alphonse de Poitiers on a summit overlooking the Auzoue river, it follows the typical design of *bastides*, with its narrow streets leading to a central square.

Éauze

Main Square Éauze

In the 1st century, Éauze (pronounced ōze, popl. 4,000, alt. 140m), which was held by the Aquitanians, fell to the Roman armies of Julius Caesar. By the 4th century, it had become the Roman capital of Novempopulana (meaning nine people - the southern part of the Roman imperial province of Aquitaine). By the 5th century, Éauze was one of the most important Catholic dioceses in France. King Henry IV (1553-1610), who played an important role during the Wars of Religion, had significant ties with Éauze and repeatedly visited the city, including with his wife, Marguerite de Valois (also known as *Reine Margot*). Most of the town's principal monuments date from this period.

In 1985, an important Roman treasure, the **Treasure of Éauze** (*Le Trésor d'Éauze*) was discovered outside the city, including 30,000 gold pieces and

jewellery from the 3rd century. The treasure is on display at the archaeological museum, which also describes Roman occupation of the region.

Of note is the former **Cathedral of Saint Luperc** (*Cathédrale Saint-Luperc*), constructed from the remains of the Roman city, as well as the old timber buildings and the home of Jeanne d'Albert (Queen Regent of Navarre from 1555 to 1572, mother of King Henry IV and leader of the French Protestants).

Today, Éauze is also famous for its Armagnac, as it is surrounded by some of the most prestigious Armagnac vineyards.

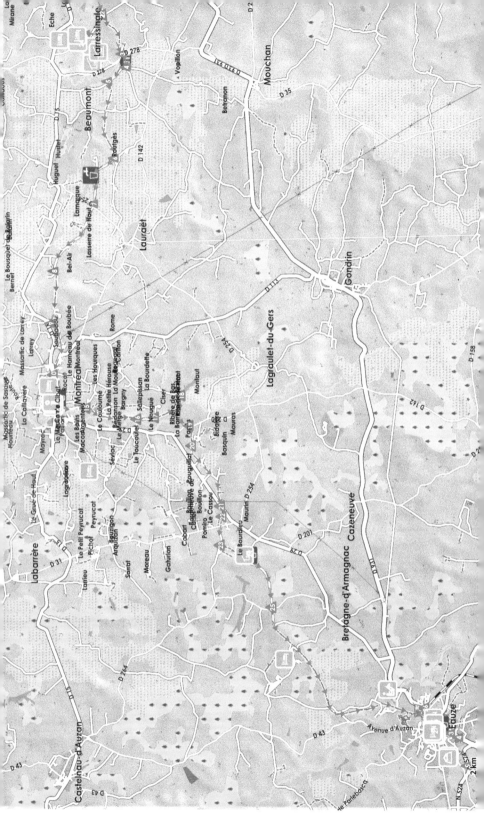

Waypoint	Total(km)	Directions	Verification	Compass	Altitude(m)
1	0.0	Retrace the route to rejoin the GR®65: from **Larressingle** turn right onto the chemin de Valence and then right onto the GR®65		NE	145
2	1.0	Descend charming path through forest to the D278 road.		SW	176
3	2.2	Cross the D278 road and cross the bridge (**Pont d'Artigues**) over the L'Osse river. Continue straight	Romanesque bridge dating from the 12-13th century	W	98
4	2.6	Turn right on asphalt road and continue straight		N	81
5	3.2	Turn left onto track that passes through fields. Continue straight	Signpost	W	81
6	5.2	Turn right onto asphalt road, descend left until junction with D254 road.	Pass church of Routgès on the right	NW	127
7	6.6	Cross the D254 road and continue straight		NW	160
8	8.6	Turn left onto path. Continue straight crossing the stream		W	145
9	9.9	Keep left on path that converges with the D113 road. Turn right onto D113 and cross to Montréal-du-Gers		S	136
10	11.3	At fork, keep right, and continue straight on rue Auresan towards village centre	Pass gas station to the left	W	137
11	12.0	Turn left into central square of **Montréal-du-Gers**		S	124
12	12.1	From central square take road next to church, passing through historic gates		SW	123
13	12.1	Turn right onto boulevard des Pyrenees and descend village ramparts to route de Condom/D15		W	125
14	12.5	Turn right on D15 road and immediately left on small road that runs alongside stream Ruisseau de Lazoue. Continue straight	Stream on right	W	98
15	13.3	Continue straight on path	Lac de la Tènaréze on the left	S	92
16	14.7	Continue straight on asphalt road	Pass Ribère de Bas on the left	S	94
17	15.2	Turn right onto path towards Montaut		S	109
18	16.1	In **Montaut** pass under metal bridge, use ramp and turn left onto tree-lined path that goes to D230 road. Turn left.		E	107
19	17.1	Turn right onto track through vineyards. Attention, poorly way-marked		W	107
20	17.6	Turn right onto road and then left onto path between vineyards. Continue straight until reaching the D29 road	Pass through La Maisonnette	W	128
21	19.5	Cross the D29 road and continue straight on track		W	151
22	19.7	Beside **Le Bédat** continue straight and cross the D31 road	Le Bédat on right	NW	156
23	20.5	Turn left on path that leads to Lamothe	Signpost	S	137

24	21.3	Turn right onto road and descend from **Lamothe**, passing church and picnic area on the left		W	158
25	22.9	Cross the D264 road and continue straight on former railway track leading to Éauze until reaching the D931 road	Signpost	W	127
26	28.6	Turn right onto the D931 road and continue straight to Éauze historic centre	Pass Leclerc supermarket on left	SW	140
27	29.2	Arrive at **Éauze**	Place d'Armagnac, beside Cathedral		162

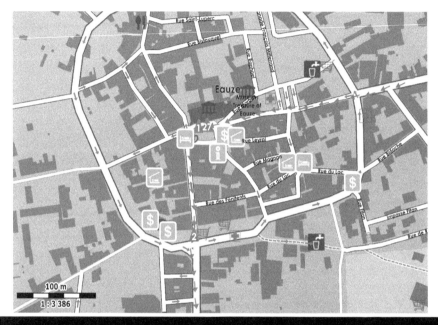

ACCOMODATION & TOURIST INFORMATION

Montréal-du-Gers

Gîte Compostella, (Anita Dann), 10 rue du 14 Juillet, 32250 Montréal-du-Gers, Gers, France; +33(0)5 62 28 67 36; +33(0)6 44 31 82 82; anitadann@hotmail.com; www.gite-compostela.com; €20/pers. (breakfast included), €32/half board; Located off the central square, 14 places in 2 dormitories in old building. English spoken. Former pilgrim.

Gîte la Halte du Rempart, (Françoise and Christian Conort), 11 place de l'Hôtel de Ville, 32250 Montréal-du-Gers, Gers, France; +33(0)5 81 68 10 55; +33(0)6 15 15 34 38; lahaltedurempart@hotmail.fr; www.lahaltedurempart.wix.com; €17/pers. (breakfast included), €9/dinner; 10 places in 1 dormitory. Kitchen.

Gîte Napoléon, (Gabriel Sylvaine and Maria Zago), Boulevard des Pyrénées, 32250 Montréal-du-Gers, Gers, France; +33(0)5 62 29 44 81; +33(0)6 37 55 48 24; armagnac.zago@gmail.com; €15/pers. €5/breakfast, €15-20/dinner; 10-12 places in 2 dormitories. Kitchen.

Carpe Diem, (Micheline and Clause Bertin), Quartier Bitalis, 32250 Montréal-du-Gers, Gers, France; +33(0)5 62 28 37 32; +33(0)6 88 49 57 19; mimibertin@wanadoo.fr; www.carpediem-montreal.fr/; €35/pers. € 59-60/2 pers., €80/3 pers., €20/dinner; Very welcoming B&B with 7 places in 3 rooms. English spoken. Pool.

Lou Prat de la Ressego, (Marylin Mercadier), Chemin de Seviac, 32250 Montréal-du-Gers, Gers, France; +33(0)5 62 29 49 55; +33(0)6 72 94 81 38; marylinweb@neuf.fr; €55/double room; €20/dinner; Lovely and welcoming B&B on the GR®65, about 2km from Montréal, 8 places in 4 rooms. British owner. Reputed for its meals and good atmosphere.

stage 25

Office de Tourisme, Place de l'Hôtel de Ville, 32250 Montreal-du-Gers, Gers, France; +33(0)5 62 29 42 85; contact.montreal@tourisme-tenareze.com; montreal-du-gers.stationverte.com

Lamothe

La Casa d'Elena, (Elena), Lamothe, 32800 Cazeneuve, Gers, France; +33(0)6 50 62 13 46; www.facebook.com/lacasa.delena; €20/pers. (breakfast included); €35/half board; Welcoming and basic hostel with 12 paces in 3 rooms. Kitchen. English spoken. Horses welcome.

Éauze

Maison Béthanie, (Pauline and Marcel), Avenue de Sauboires, 32800 Éauze, Gers, France; +33(0)7 87 72 07 82; Donation (dinner and breakfast included); Located 600m from the church, operated by former pilgrims. 8 places in home with garden. Shared meal. English spoken. Horses welcome. Reservations taken only one day in advance.

Gîte d'Étape Communal, 2 rue Félix Soules, 32800 Éauze, Gers, France; +33(0)5 62 09 85 62; info@tourisme-Éauze.fr; €11/pers.; 23 places, located in the village centre. Check in at the Office de Tourisme. English spoken. Kitchen.

Chez Nadine, (Francis and Nadine Corlaiti), 43 avenue de Sauboires, 32800 Éauze, Gers, France; +33(0)5 62 08 18 37; +33(0)6 50 09 60 42; francis.corlaiti@orange.fr; www.gitecheznadine.com; €25/pers. (sheets and breakfast included), €35/half board; 11 places in 4 rooms. 500m from the village centre. Very welcoming.

Gîte Rabelais, (Mr Claude Thomas), Impasse Rabelais, 32800 Éauze, Gers, France; +33(0)5 62 09 75 22; +33(0)6 73 53 42 43; giterabelais32@orange.fr; €25/pers. €50/2 pers., €5/breakfast; Located in historic centre. 6 places in 3 rooms. English spoken.

Gîte Lou Parpalhou, (Laurence and Patrice Castex), 13 rue du Lac, 32800 Éauze, Gers, France; +33(0)5 62 59 63 59; +33(0)6 25 09 72 84; gitecastex@orange.fr; www.getelouparpalhou.fr; Hostel: €18/pers. €5/breakfast B&B: €35/single; €60/double; Recently and tastefully restored home in the historic centre, with 9 places in 2 rooms (hostel) and 2 B&B rooms. English spoken. Kitchen.

Café de France, Place d'Armagnac, 32800 Éauze, Gers, France; +33(0)5 62 09 80 31; cafedefrance32800@gmail.com; www.cafe-de-france-Éauze.com; B&B:€40/pers. €65/2 pers.; Located in main square, B&B includes 3 rooms and hostel includes 4 places in 3 rooms. English spoken.

Résidence Hôtelière les Tournesols du Gers, (Florence and Michel Nguyen Dat), Le Coupé, 32800 Éauze, Gers, France; +33(0)5 62 08 29 01; +33(0)6 60 36 06 60; lestournesolsdugers@free.fr; www.lestournesolsdugers.fr; €51/double room, €75/3 pers. €100/4 pers., €6/breakfast, €13/dinner; 300 metres from the GR®65, 4 km before Éauze, 10 rooms for 2 to 4 pers. on lake with heated pool.

Office de Tourisme, 2 rue Félix Soules, 32800 Éauze, Gers, France; +33(0)5 62 09 85 62; www.tourisme-Éauze.fr

Cheval Vert Vallée, (Odile and Didier), Route de Condom, 32800 Éauze, Gers, France; +33(0)6 70 51 69 73; chevalvertvallee@orange.fr; www.chevalvertvallee.com; Hostel: €20/pers. (breakfast included), B&B: €30/pers. €60/2 pers., €75/3 pers. (breakfast included); Equestrian centre located 300m from the GR®65 before Éauze, includes dormitory with 6 places and 2 rooms sleeping 2-4 pers. English spoken. Horses welcome. Possibility to organize horse rides.

Landscape before Éauze,

stage 26

ÉAUZE TO LANNE-SOUBIRAN

DISTANCE **28.8km**

ASCENT **596m**

DESCENT **627m**

FROM LE PUY **540km**

TO RONCEVAUX **234km**

Nogaro Cloister

Route - The route is well-marked and uses tracks and asphalt roads, as it crosses gentle vineyards in the heart of the Armagnac region, until reaching the industrial agricultural city of Nogaro. Thereafter, it follows tracks through corn fields and forests to the village of Lanne-Soubiran.

Pointers - **Advance planning:** The route is highly exposed, be sure to have sun protection (hat, sunscreen, etc.).

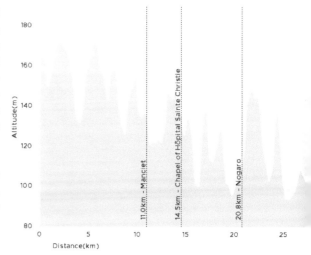

Chapel of the Command Post, Saint Christie Hospital (*Chapelle de la commanderie de l'Hôpital-Sainte-Christie*)

The chapel is the only remaining building of the former Saint Christie command post and hospital, which was probably built in the 12th century by the Knights of Malta. The post was destroyed in 1538 by Protestant troops during the Wars of Religion. Fifty metres west of the chapel, on the right side of the route, is a stone marker with the Cross of Malta. This was one of about 20 markers that fixed the perimeter of the command post, which in 1750 covered 280 hectares.

Nogaro

The economy of Nogaro (popl. 2,000, alt. 100m), a city located between Bordeaux, Toulouse and Bayonne, is based on the wine industry. However, the town's historical centre is the fortified mid-11th century **Church of Saint Nicholas** (*Eglise Saint-Nicolas*), which was organized as a collegiate church, where daily worship was overseen by a college of non-monastic clergy. In 1995, eight 11th century frescoes depicting the martyrdom of Saint Lawrence (a deacon of the early Christian church who was martyred in Rome during Emperor Valerian's persecutions of 258) were discovered in the north apse. In the south apse is a fresco of Christ in Majesty surrounded by the symbols of the four Evangelists and angels. These frescoes were made with a number of important blue-green pigments, including lapis-lazuli (from Afghanistan), azurite (from Germany) and aerinite (local). A Romanesque stone relief above the baptismal font represents a lion woman (*signum leonis*) with crossed legs, a Romanesque symbol that also appears on the southern portal of the Cathedral of Santiago de Compostela. Outside, to the south, are the remains of the cloister, including five delicately carved arches.

The town arena (*arènes*) is also renowned for showcasing the Gascon sport, **Course Landaise**, a traditional form of bullfighting that involves leaping or dodging charging cows. Competitions are held throughout the summer, with a major event held each 14 July.

ROUTE INSTRUCTIONS

Waypoint	Total(km)	Directions	Verification	Compass	Altitude(m)
1	0.0	In **Éauze**, from Place d'Armagnac, turn away from Cathedral left and continue straight on rue Daury		S	162
2	0.1	Cross road and continue straight on avenue des Pyrénées	Signpost	S	166
3	0.4	Pass the Imperial water tower (1870), which supplied drinking water to the city fountains, on the left		SW	163
4	0.7	Turn right on chemin du Soumcide	Opposite Allianz Insurance office	NW	163

5	1.5	Cross road N524 and continue straight on path through vineyards		SW	164
6	2.5	Turn left onto asphalt road, route de Bonnefin	After passing house on the left	SW	168
7	2.8	Continue straight on asphalt road, direction Pennebert	Signpost	SW	173
8	3.1	Turn left onto track, continue straight	After passing farm and tower	SW	163
9	6.5	Turn left and continue straight through vineyards until reaching the D122 road	Cross stream ahead	SW	157
10	8.7	Turn left onto the D122 road and continue straight to the village of Manciet	Signpost	S	127
11	10.8	Turn right before the D931 road, and then use the footbridge to cross left over road. Continue straight towards church		SW	137
12	11.0	Turn right on rue Central (opposite church) and continue straight to leave **Manciet**		SW	141
13	11.3	Merge onto the D931 road and continue straight	Cross river La Douze	SW	124
14	11.9	Turn left onto the D152 road, direction Aignan	Signpost. Pass agricultural facility	S	123
15	12.6	Turn right onto footpath and continue straight through fields until reaching asphalt road	Brown barn ahead	SW	123
16	13.5	Turn right onto asphalt road and then immediately left		W	124
17	14.2	Turn right	Beside vineyards	W	145
18	14.5	Beside **Chapel of Hôpital Sainte Christie** continue straight until reaching the D522 road	Chapel on the right	W	138
19	15.1	Turn left onto a road and continue straight and cross the Midouzon stream		SW	133
20	16.0	Turn right on path that follows stream to the right, then continue straight until reaching road		NW	105
21	16.8	Turn left onto asphalt road and then right onto path. Continue straight		S	134
22	18.7	Turn left and then right, continuing on path until joining the D522 road.		S	129
23	19.4	Turn left onto the D522 road and continue straight through industrial city of Nogaro	Signpost	W	102
24	20.8	At fork keep right and continue straight/climb on D143 road to leave **Nogaro**	**Church of Saint Nicholas** directly behind	W	108
25	21.6	Keep left at fork and then turn immediately right onto track and continue straight	Pass water tower on right	SW	146
26	23.4	Turn left and continue straight towards the Claverie farm		W	109
27	24.4	Turn right and then left on a path (descent towards valley)	Signpost. Cross stream	NW	140
28	25.9	Turn right onto D931 road and continue straight through roundabout		W	92
29	26.7	Turn left onto small road and continue straight to reach Lanne-Soubiran	Signpost. Opposite white house	S	107
30	28.8	Arrive at **Lanne-Soubiran**	Beside church		134

Manciet

Chez Matthieu, (Mathieu Deneyrolles), Rue Centrale, 32370 Manciet, Gers, France; +33(0)6 68 87 78 24; +33(0)6 73 32 50 79; matdeney@hotmail.fr; www.chezmathieumanciet.unblog.fr; €15/pers. €5/breakfast, €32/half board; 12 places in double rooms. Kitchen. English spoken.

Gîte de la Hargue, (Eric and Michèle Texier), Eric and Michèle Texier, 32370 Manciet, Gers, France; +33(0)5 62 08 50 05; +33(0)6 65 54 55 89; eric.texier0449@orange.fr; www.lahargue.com; €30-€50/ pers. €50-€70/double, €60/3 pers., +€15/half board; Lovely country home on large property with pool, located 6.5km after Éauze and before Manciet. English spoken. 8 places in dormitory and 11 places in 5 rooms. Horses welcome. Kitchen.

La Bonne Auberge, (Pepito Sampietro), Le Pesquèrot, 32370 Manciet, Gers, France; +33(0)5 62 08 50 04; labonneauberge.32@orange.fr; €42/pers. €52/2 pers., €79/3 pers., €8/breakfast, €58/half board; Hotel and restaurant located at village exit, reputed for its inventive cuisine using local produce and selection of Armagnac. 14 rooms.

Cravencères

Chambre d'Hôtes, (Stéphanie and Jean-Bernard Ducos), Relais du Haget, 32110 Cravencères, Gers, France; +33(0)5 62 08 54 02; +33(0)6 11 66 13 98; stephanie.brud@wanadoo.fr; €13/pers. €15/dinner, €5/breakfast, €33/half board; B&B: €56/double room, €78/triple room, €15/dinner; Equestrian centre/farm located about 16km after Éauze near the GR®65 (Church of l'hôpital), 10 places in 2 dormitories and 2 rooms for 2-3. Horses welcome.

Sainte-Christie-d'Armagnac

Gîte de la Source, (Jean-Michel Danard), Route de Nogaro, Monneton, 32370 Sainte-Christie-d'Armagnac, Gers, France; +33(0)5 62 69 04 45; +33(0)6 09 31 96 04; gitedelasource.gers@orange.fr; www.lesgitesdelasourcegers.com; €35/half board; B&B:€65/half board, €90/half board 2 pers.; Located 2.5km before Nogaro and 500m from the GR 65, a large estate with 17 places in dormitories for 4, and 2 rooms for 2-3 pers. Pool.

Nogaro

Gîte d'Étape Communal et Associatif, Avenue des Sports, 32110 Nogaro, Gers, France; +33(0)5 62 69 06 15; guy.andree@orange.fr; www.gite-etape-nogaro.fr/; €14/pers. in room, €12/pers. in dormitory, €4/breakfast; 12 places in double rooms, 14 places in dormitory. Basic but welcoming accommodation near airport, on outskirts of town in commercial area. Kitchen.

La Halte du Passant, (Jocelyne Martin), 7 rue Broqué, 32110 Nogaro, Gers, France; +33(0)5 62 08 84 69; +33(0)6 68 58 63 32; martin.haltedupassant@orange.fr; €26/pers. € 42/2 pers., €60/3 pers., €37/half board (upon reservation); 3 rooms in home next to church, with terrace. English spoken.

Office de Tourisme, 77 rue Nationale, 32110 Nogaro, Gers, France; +33(0)5 62 09 13 30; info@nogaro-tourisme.fr; www.nogaro-tourisme.fr

Arblade-le-Haut

L'Arbladoise, (Christian and Dominique Egreteau), Le Haou, 32110 Arblade-le-Haut, Gers, France; +33(0)5 62 09 14 11; +33(0)6 81 88 24 22; larbladoise@gmail.com; www.larbladoise.fr; Hostel: €35/ half board, B&B: €75/half board, €90/half board 2 pers.; On a lovely 19th century Gascon property with garden and pool, located 2.4 km after the church of Nogaro, on an ancient Roman road that is a short cut to the GR®65. Hostel: 9 places in 3 rooms of 2-4 pers. B&B: 2 rooms and 1 cabin. English spoken.

Lanne-Soubiran

Le Presbytère de Lanne Soubiran, (Marinette Piret), Place de l'Eglise, 32110 Lanne-Soubiran, Gers, France; +33(0)5 62 09 70 24; +33(0)6 43 34 99 45; marinette.piret@gmail.com; Dormitory: €15/pers. B&B: €14/dinner, €34/half board, B&B: €88/2 pers. half board.; 14 places in 3 dormitories and 1 double B&B room in a restored and tastefully decorated presbytery with garden. Horses welcome. English spoken.

Gîte d'Étape, (Pierre and Christine Muscato), Maison Labarbe, 32110 Lanne-Soubiran, Gers, France; +33(0)3 96 13 39 31; +33(0)6 66 29 44 55; maisonlabarbe@wanadoo.fr; €15/pers. €5/breakfast, €14/ dinner, €34/half board, B&B: €88/2 pers. half board.; Shared rooms and B&B in regional styled house. English spoken. Kitchen. Horses welcome.

Chambres d'Hôtes, (Thierry Gavard and Frauke Seeling), Domaine de Castagnère, 32110 Lanne-Soubiran, Gers, France; +33(0)5 62 03 82 15; +33(0)6 52 42 91 19; domainedecastagnere@hotmail.fr; www. domainedecastagnere.com; €60/half board, €110/half board 2 pers. €165/half board 3 pers.; B&B on large estate with 5 rooms, located on a former vineyard. English spoken. Horses welcome. Located 800m from GR®65 on shortcut.

DISTANCE	**19.4km**
ASCENT	**283m**
DESCENT	**333m**
FROM LE PUY	**569km**
TO RONCEVAUX	**205km**

Way marking in the Landes Department

Route - The route is well-marked, with no significant climbs, and consists mostly of asphalt roads and some paths, that cross corn fields and forests. Upon approaching the Adour river, corn fields begin to dominate the landscape. The route passes through the industrial city and zone of Barcelonne-du-Gers to arrive at the historic city of Aire-sur-l'Adour, on the Adour river.

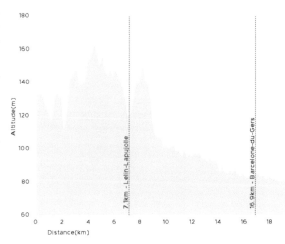

Aire-sur-l'Adour

The town of Aire-sur-l'Adour (popl. 8,280, alt. 70m), with its strategic position on the Ardour river, was an important Roman city, and later a royal city of the Visgoths (5th century). In 506, the Visigoth King Alaric II (484-507) promulgated his *Breviary*, a compilation of Roman laws and texts that applied to certain populations living under his rule. It was during this period that Saint Quitterie is said to have lived. According to legend, Quitterie's father, a Galician prince, wanted her to marry and re-nounce Christianity. Instead, the princess fled to Aire-sur-l'Adour where she was beheaded by the Visigoths. A spring emerged on the spot where she was killed, and its waters were believed to have healing powers (Saint Quitterie's Fountain). At the end of the 11th century, the cathedral was built and Benedictine monks founded the Church of Saint Quitterie and an abbey on the heights of the town. A market is held on Saturday mornings.

Church of Saint Quitterie (*Eglise Sainte-Quitterie*)

The church is dedicated to Saint Quitterie. On the west wall, is the Saint's white marble tomb which has been associated with several miracles. At the far end of the church, are two semi-circular cells, where mentally disturbed people were held before being taken for cure to the Saint's tomb. The foundation of the church, however, predates Saint Quitterie. It was built on the site of a Roman temple of Mars. The laurel-leaf decorated stones in the church's crypt are from the pagan temple. Later, in the 11th century, Benedictine monks became caretakers of Saint Quitterie's tomb, and built the neighbouring abbey to accommodate a growing following.

Shaver-Crandell, A., Gerson, P. L., & Stones, A, p. 105 (1995). *The pilgrim's guide to Santiago de Compostela: A gazetteer.* London: Harvey Miller Publishers.

ROUTE INSTRUCTIONS

Waypoint	Total(km)	Directions	Verification	Compass	Altitude(m)
1	0.0	In **Lanne-Soubiran**, turn right onto D152 road	Pass church on the right	NW	135
2	0.3	Turn left onto small road before white and brown mansard house and con-tinue straight	House	SW	132
3	0.8	At road's end, turn left and con-tinue straight on road/path that leads through fields and forest called "Lande des Bois"	Pay attention to way-marking, as sometimes poorly marked	S	127
4	3.7	Turn left onto asphalt road (away from farmhouse) and then take first right and continue straight		S	138
5	4.5	Turn left onto small road and continue straight		S	162
6	4.9	Turn left and continue straight, direc-tion Lelin-Lapujolle	Signpost and pass farms of Bi-det and La Grange on left	SE	151
7	7.1	Enter village of **Lelin-Lapujolle**. Keep right, passing church on the left to leave village	Signpost and church	SW	123
8	7.5	Turn right onto D169 road and con-tinue straight		NW	130
9	7.9	Turn left onto asphalt road and contin-ue straight passing through vineyards and fields	Passing on the left last house (beige) of the village	SW	139

LANNE-SOUBIRAN TO AIRE-SUR-L'ADOUR

10	9.0	Turn right (houses) and then left onto small road passing through fields, until reaching road		W	130
11	11.1	Turn right before railway tracks and continue straight	Railway tracks to the left	NW	98
12	13.6	Turn left. Cross railway tracks and the D935 road, and continue straight through fields	Railway tracks and D935	SW	95
13	14.1	Turn right at oak tree, direction Barcelonne-du-Gers, and continue straight	Signpost	W	88
14	16.3	Turn right on road towards Barcelone-du-Gers, then keep left on boulevard du Midi	Signpost and pass lavoir on left	NW	82
15	16.9	In **Barcelone-du-Gers** turn right on rue de Casamont and then left on D512/Rue de l'Hôpital at Place de la Garlande. Continue straight to leave village	Pass church on the right	N	86
16	17.4	Turn left onto rue du Beret and then right onto chemin des Moncaux		S	84

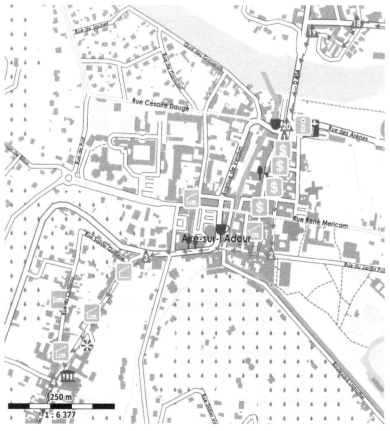

17	18.1	Turn right onto rue des Saligats, and then left onto avenue du 4 Septembre. Continue straight		N	83
18	19.1	Turn left at Place de la Liberté, and then right on Impasse Frédéric Lévrier	Turn before Hôtel-Restaurant Les Platanes	SW	84
19	19.2	Turn left and cross bridge to enter Aire-sur-l'Adour centre	Bridge	SW	81
20	19.4	Arrive at **Aire-sur-l'Adour**	Place Général de Gaulle		80

ACCOMODATION & TOURIST INFORMATION

Lelin-Lapujolle

Gîte d'Étape, (Véronique and Philippe Biérent), La Grange À Dubarry, 32400 Lelin-Lapujolle, Gers, France; +33(0)5 62 69 64 82; +33(0)6 27 35 84 13; contact@la-grange-a-dubarry.fr; www.la-grange-a-dubarry.fr; €15/pers. €5/breakfast, €33/half board; 300m off the GR®65, restored farmhouse with 12 places in 1 room and 2 dormitories. English spoken. Horses welcome.

Arblade-le-Bas

Gîte d'Étape Belardine, (Pierre Guillaume and Véronique Mariotti), Bélardine, 32720 Arblade-le-Bas, Gers, France; +33(0)5 62 69 06 14; +33(0)7 89 57 33 30; contact@belardine.fr; www.belardine.fr; €18/pers. (breakfast included), €52/double room, €31/half board, €13/dinner (upon reservation); On a lovely restored farm, 3 rooms of 2-4 pers. Kitchen. English spoken. Horses welcome. Located 2.5km after Lelin-Lapujolle on a short cut to the GR®65.

Barcelonne-du-Gers

La Bastide du Cosset, (Florence and Freddy Fior), 11 place de la Garlande, 32720 Barcelonne-du-Gers, Gers, France; +33(0)6 33 80 50 95; info@bastideducosset.com or freddy.fior@wanadoo.fr; www. bastideducosset.com or www.hospitaletducosset.com; Hostel: €16/pers. €4/breakfast, €32/half board, B&B: €60-€120/double room, €102-€145/half board 2 pers.; Located in the city centre, agreeable hostel includes 14 places in shared rooms and B&B with 6 rooms. English spoken. Kitchen.

Aire-sur-l'Adour

Hospitalet Saint Jacques, (Odile and André), 21 rue Félix Despagnet, 40800 Aire-sur-l'Adour, Landes, France; +33(0)5 58 03 26 22; www.saintjacques-hospitalet.fr; €13.50/pers. €4.50/breakfast, €7/dinner; Run by pilgrims and reserved for pilgrims on foot with credentials. Home with garden located 500m from city centre. 2 shared rooms. English spoken. Kitchen.

Chapelle des Ursulines, 40 rue Félix Despagnet, 40800 Aire-sur-l'Adour, Landes, France; +33(0)5 58 52 09 01; +33(0)6 08 37 18 26; chapelledesursulines@gmail.com; www.chapelledesursulines.eklablog.fr; €19/pers. €5/breakfast, €12/dinner, €36/half board.; Located in a converted chapel on the GR®65 when exiting the city, 12 places in 2 dormitories. Donkeys can be attached in nearby pasture.

Hôtel de la Paix, 7 rue Carnot, 40800 Aire-sur-l'Adour, Landes, France; +33(0)5 58 71 60 70; +33(0)6 81 39 50 02; hoteldelapaix.40@wanadoo.fr; www.hoteldelapaix40.fr; Rooms: €17/pers. (breakfast included); Dormitory: €14/pers. (breakfast and sheets included); Located in the city centre, a family run hotel for pilgrims that is worn but charming. 7 single and double rooms and 1 dormitory with 9 places. English spoken. Kitchen.

La Maison des Pèlerins, (Isabelle and Alejandro), 4 rue du Général Labat, 40800 Aire-sur-l'Adour, Landes, France; +33(0)5 58 71 68 07; +33(0)7 80 39 36 58; lamaisondespelerins@gmail.com; www. lamaisondespelerins.tk; €15/pers. €4.50/breakfast, €14/dinner, € 33.50/half board; Located in the city centre, and run by former pilgrims who know the Chemin well, includes 15 places in 5 rooms. English spoken.

Relais Sainte Quitterie, (Jean Philippe and Mirian), 32 rue Félix Despagnet, 40800 Aire-sur-l'Adour, Landes, France; +33(0)5 58 71 69 37; +33(0)6 29 85 97 83; jip_v@hotmail.fr; www.pelerins.fr.nf/; €20/pers. (breakfast included), €35/half board.; Located on the GR®65 in a charming restored school house, with terrace and pool. 15 places in 5 shared rooms. English spoken.

Chambre d'Hôtes au Gré de l'Adour, (Christine Lavie), 24 route de Duhort, 40800 Aire-sur-l'Adour, Landes, France; +33(0)5 58 52 39 79; +33(0)6 32 96 58 96; duhort40@orange.fr; €23/pers. (breakfast included), €13/dinner , €36/half board; Located on the banks of the Ardour river, 6 minutes from the city centre, calm environment with 5 places in 2 shared rooms. English spoken. Horses welcome.

Le Mas, (Pascale Bertho), 17 rue du Château, 40800 Aire-sur-l'Adour, Landes, France; +33(0)5 58 71 91 26; +33(0)3 61 54 43 68 2; pascale.bertho757@orange.fr; www.le-mas.net/; €83/half board, €115/half board 2 pers. €162/half board 3 pers., €216/half board 4 pers.; 5 luxury rooms in a lovely home 50m from the GR®65 and the Church of Sainte Quitterie, with garden, pool and yard. Horses welcome. English spoke.

Office de Tourisme, 1962 place du 19 Mars, 40800 Aire-sur-l'Adour, Landes, France; +33(0)5 58 71 64 70; accueil-eugenie@tourisme-aire-eugenie.fr; www.tourisme-aire-eugenie.fr

DISTANCE **33.8km**

ASCENT **768m**

DESCENT **616m**

FROM LE PUY **589km**

TO RONCEVAUX **186km**

Pimbo Collegiate Church

Route - Leaving Aire-sur-l'Adour, the way markings are different, and include a white/yellow/blue arrow. The route is, however, well-marked and follows mainly asphalt roads, as it crosses endless corn fields in this highly agricultural area.

Pointers - **Advance planning: The** route is exposed, be sure to have sun protection (hat, sunscreen, etc.). **Stage length:** This and the next two stages in the Béarn and Basque region tend to be longer due the scarcity of accommodation and distance between villages.

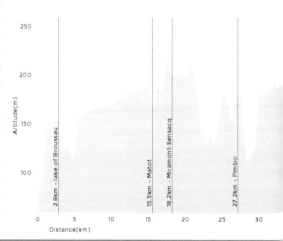

CULTURAL DISCOVERIES

Pimbo
A document from the 13th century sets out the *paréage,* or terms, for the creation of the *bastide* of Pimbo (popl. 200, alt. 150m). Specifically, an agreement was reached between the abbot and canons of the collegiate church, on the one hand, and King Henry III of England, on the other. The *bastide,* which developed along the narrow ridge of Pimbo, linked the church and the castle and granted inhabitants religious and military protection. The Collegiate Church of Saint-Barthélemy, founded in the 12th century, is Romanesque.

Arzacq-Arraziguet
While there is not a great deal to visit in Arzacq-Arraziguet (popl. 1,000, alt. 120m), the village is welcoming. In the 13th-14th century, probably due to its strategic position near the border of the Béarn region and its important market, a *bastide* was built, of which only a tower (known as the *tour de peich*) remains. A market is held each Saturday morning.

stage 28

Waypoint	Total(km)	Directions	Verification	Compass	Altitude(m)
1	0.0	From Place du Général de Gaulle, in **Aire-sur-l'Adour**, continue (away from river) on rue Gambetta		S	82
2	0.3	Turn right on rue Henri Labeyrie, then left on avenue des Pyrénées/D834 to begin climb out of city		W	85
3	0.6	Turn left on rue Félix Despagnet and climb hill to leave city		W	89
4	1.0	Pass church of Saint Quitterie on left and continue straight on rue du Mas		S	111
5	1.6	Turn left onto avenue des Pyrénées. Then turn right at roundabout on the D2/rue Nelson Mandela		S	151
6	2.1	Turn left on rue Georges Fraisse and then left on rue du Jardinet. Continue straight		SW	156
7	2.8	Turn right onto chemin du Brousseau, which leads to the **lake of Broussau**		SW	157
8	3.4	Turn left onto path that goes around the perimeter of the lake		S	135
9	4.5	Turn left onto the D456 road. Go through underpass of the A65 highway		W	121
10	5.0	Turn right onto a small road (running parallel to power line), which then veers left		NW	119
11	6.1	Turn left on small local road (Voie Communale de Lourine)		SW	160
12	7.2	Turn right and then immediately left on road		W	166
13	9.3	Turn right on the D62 road, cross stream, and then left on route de Pitocq	Pass agricultural facility to the right	W	169
14	14.5	Turn right onto path, and continue straight		W	186
15	14.8	Turn left onto small road (chemin de Saint Pé) that passes through corn fields. Continue straight until reaching Matot		S	187
16	15.5	In **Matot** turn right onto road and continue straight. Cross the Bahus stream as well as the D11 road		NW	178
17	17.5	Turn left, keep to the right and head towards Miramont-Sensacq centre	Signpost	S	218
18	18.2	After passing through **Miramont-Sensacq** turn left onto the D314 road and continue straight		SE	202
19	20.3	Turn right. At road's end turn right again. Continue straight (climbs and descents) until the village of Sensacq		SW	201
20	23.1	Turn right towards church, then take first right and continue straight		N	131
21	24.0	Turn left and continue straight to the D111 road.		W	131
22	25.2	Turn right onto the D111 road and then left on path through woods. Continue straight until reaching village of Pimbo		NW	179
23	27.2	Turn left and continue straight through village of **Pimbo**	Pass church on the left	SE	179
24	27.5	Turn right direction Espenaturel	Signpost	SE	189
25	27.7	Turn right onto chemin du Pèlerin and descend towards valley		W	182
26	28.7	Cross Le Gabas stream and continue straight		SW	112
27	30.1	Turn right and immediately left onto chemin de Lassalle	Signpost	W	182

28	31.4	Turn left and then right onto the D32 road and continue straight towards Arzacq-Arraziguet	SE	188
29	33.1	Turn right onto Côte de Camot and then left onto the D944 road	SW	199
30	33.6	At roundabout, keep straight on the D946 road, Pass Carrefour supermarket on the right to reach the town centre.	SW	234
31	33.8	Arrive at **Arzacq-Arraziguet** town centre		233

ACCOMODATION & TOURIST INFORMATION

Miramont-Sensacq

Gîte Piphane, (Bruno Pecassou Bacque and Elise Arreule), Lieu Dit Piphane, 40320 Miramont-Sensacq, Landes, France; +33(0)5 58 79 95 57; +33(0)6 85 94 15 60; elisearreule@hotmail.com; €35/half board.; Located approximately 1 km after Miramont and 50m from the GR®65, restored cottage with 4 places in 2 rooms, kitchen and garden. English spoken.

Gîte d'Étape Communal, Mairie de Miramont Sensacq, 40320 Miramont-Sensacq, Landes, France; +33(0)5 58 79 94 06; +33(0)5 58 79 91 23; miramont.mairie@wanadoo.fr; €12/pers. (dinner and breakfast included); 20 places. Kitchen.

Ferme de Marsan, (Bernard and Dominique Darnaudery), Quartier Bestit, 40320 Miramont-Sensacq, Landes, France; +33(0)5 58 79 94 93; +33(0)6 84 78 07 25; contact@lafermedemarsan.com; Rooms €38/2 pers. dormitory: €13/pers., €3/breakfast; 300m from the GR®65 on a working farm with pool, 10 places in dormitory and 6 double rooms in separate building. Local and farm products sold on site. Kitchen. Horses welcome.

La Maison du Bos, (Corinne Favre), 378 Chemin Dubos, 40320 Miramont-Sensacq, Landes, France; +33(0)5 58 79 93 18; +33(0)6 42 79 84 26; info@maisondubos.com; www.maisondubos.com; €75/half board, €105/half board 2 pers. €157.50/half board 3 pers.; Refined B&B with 5 rooms in a restored 18th century stone house with terrace an pool on 9 hectare property. Horses welcome.

Pimbo

Ferme de Nordland, (Family Passicos), Chemin de Mahaourat, Chuteou, 40320 Pimbo, Landes, France; +33(0)5 58 44 49 80; +33(0)6 75 97 34 23; earl.nordland@orange.fr; www.ferme-de-nordland.com; €21/pers. €6/breakfast, €43/half board.; Located less than 2 km from the GR before Pimbo. Two modern and fully equipped cottages for 2 and 5 pers. on working farm that sells local produce, particularly fois gras.

Gîte d'Étape Communal, Au Bourg, 40320 Pimbo, Landes, France; +33(0)5 58 44 46 57; +33(0)5 58 44 49 18; gitedepimbo@hotmail.fr; €13/pers. (breakfast included); €18/half board; Located in the village. 18 places in dormitory. Kitchen. Horses welcome.

Chez Louis and Virginie, (Louis and Virginie Gautret), Le Bourg, 40320 Pimbo, Landes, France; +33(0)5 58 44 48 06; +33(0)6 52 82 95 92; ni_lou@hotmail.fr; €60/ half board, €90/half board 2 pers.; 3 room B&B in the village of Pimbo. Horses welcome.

Maison Couhet, (Irène Theux), Le Bourg, 40320 Pimbo, Landes, France; +33(0)5 58 44 49 59; +33(0)6 84 98 21 64; stheux@gmail.com; www.chambres-hotes-pimbo.e-monsite.com; €40/half board.; Located in village below the church, 2 rooms on first floor of large house, with garden and terrace.

Arzacq-Arraziguet

Centre d'Accueil Communal, (Karine Desclaux and Didier Laccassagne), Place du Marcadieu, 64410 Arzacq-Arraziguet, Pyrénées Atlantiques, France; +33(0)5 59 04 41 41; centreaccueil@arzacq.com; www.arzacq.com; Hostel: €11/pers. breakfast €4/pers., €26/half board, €12/dinner; Located in village centre, large hostel with 35 places in shared rooms of 2-6 and 1 dormitory for 10. Kitchen. English spoken.

Chambre d'Hôtes Dulucq, (Huguette Dulucq), Place du Marcadieu, 64410 Arzacq-Arraziguet, Pyrénées Atlantiques, France; +33(0)5 59 04 46 12; +33(0)7 85 32 81 26; dulucqhuguette@gmail.com; €36/pers. €72/2 pers., €45/half board, €72/half board 2 pers.; Located in village, 9 places in 4 double rooms in home with terrace and garden. Horses welcome.

La Maison d'Antan, (Jean-Pierre Guerin-recoussine), 1 place de la République, 64410 Arzacq-Arraziguet, Pyrénées Atlantiques, France; +33(0)5 59 04 53 01; lamaison.dantan@orange.fr; www.lamaison-dantan.com; €115/2 pers. €148/2 half board; Located in the village centre, 4 rooms in an elegant 15th century restored country home with terrace and garden. English spoken.

Maison Gibardeü, (Véronique Pantaignan), Place Marcadieu, 64410 Arzacq-Arraziguet, Pyrénées Atlantiques, France; +33(0)5 59 04 41 48; +33(0)6 32 37 45 44; didier.tapy@aliceadsl.fr; €34-€44/double room; €38-€55/half board per person; €67-€88/half board 2 pers.; Located about 2km from the village, 6 places in 3 rooms on 1st floor of a charming 18th century house with garden. Horses welcome.

Office de Tourisme, 45 place de la République, 64410 Arzacq-Arraziguet, Pyrénées Atlantiques, France; +33(0)5 59 04 59 24; ot.soubestre@wanadoo.fr; www.tourisme-arzacq-morlanne.com

stage 29

DISTANCE **33.8km**

ASCENT **688m**

DESCENT **714m**

FROM LE PUY **622km**

TO RONCEVAUX **152km**

Caubin Chapel

Route - This stage is relatively flat, and the route continues to follow tracks and asphalt roads through corn fields and pastures as it enters the Béarn region and approaches the Pyrenees mountains.

Pointers - **Advance planning:** The route is highly exposed, be sure to have sun protection (hat, sunscreen, etc.).

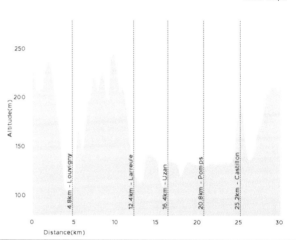

CULTURAL DISCOVERIES

Larreule

In the 10th century, an important and wealthy Benedictine abbey was founded in Larreule (popl. 420, alt. 200m), which in Gascon means "the rule," and refers to the Benedictine rule (the rules promulgated by Saint Benedict in the 6th century to govern monastic life and which integrated prayer, manual labour and study into a daily routine). However, by the end of the 18th century, the last monks left the abbey, the monastery and hospital buildings were demolished and their stone sold. The parish church is the sole vestige of this once important abbey.

Arthez-de-Béarn

Before the village of Arthez-de-Béarn, on the left is the **Caubin Chapel** (*Chapelle de Caubin*), which is all that remains of an important 12th century Knights of Malta command post. The chapel, which is Romanesque, was likely built upon the orders of Gaston IV, Viscount of Béarn upon his safe return from the first crusade. Of note are the capitals and the 14th century tomb of Baron Guilhem Arnaud d'Andoins, a local ruler. A market is held in Arthez on Saturday mornings.

Waypoint	Total(km)	Directions	Verification	Compass	Altitude(m)
1	0.0	In **Arzacq-Arraziguet**, head down the narrow passage (chemin de Saint-Jacques) to leave the village. Continue straight on the path to Arzacq lake	Next to Crédit Agricole bank	W	233
2	0.4	Turn left on chemin du Barada, and continue around the perimeter of the lake		SW	227
3	1.5	Turn left passing through woods and continue straight on path	Walking away from lake	SW	213
4	2.1	Turn right onto small road (chemin de Cabirou) and continue straight. Pass Vignes, and the farms of Cabalette and Cabirou.	Ahead, pass stone cross on the left	W	236
5	4.2	Cross the Le Luy de France river and continue straight to Louvigny		SW	148
6	4.8	Turn left and pass through **Louvigny**		S	103
7	6.0	Turn left onto chemin de Pedebignes and climb	Pass red shed and bench on the right	SE	157
8	8.6	Turn right onto chemin de l'Eglise and continue straight to Fichous-Riumayou	Cross the La Rance river	SW	231
9	9.9	Pass church and cemetery on the right, and turn left onto D79/Route de Fichous.		SE	245
10	10.0	Turn right onto D278/Route de Larreule and continue straight until Larreule	Turn before Basketball court. Signpost "Larreule"	W	246
11	12.4	In **Larreule** pass stone cross on left, and continue straight on route de Mazerolles	Ahead, cross the Le Luy de Béarn river	SW	130
12	13.5	Turn left and continue straight. At fork keep right (head towards farm)		S	116
13	13.9	Turn right on Route d'Uzan and continue straight through corn fields until reaching village of Uzan	Signpost	NW	143
14	16.2	Turn right at church/cemetery, and then turn right onto the D49 road		NW	115
15	16.4	In **Uzan** turn left onto La Carrère, direction Géus d'Arzacq and keep left at intersection (cross)	Signpost	W	133
16	16.8	Turn right onto Cami de la Lebe, passing through corn fields, until reaching Géus-d'Arzacq	Signpost and oak tree	NW	134
17	18.4	Turn right (passing church on right) and then keep left at fork on Cami de Compostelle		N	128
18	20.3	Turn left onto road and then right to enter Pomps		SW	132
19	20.8	In **Pomps**, turn left at stone cross		W	130
20	21.0	Turn left after bridge onto Route dou Pebe and continue straight (attention, poorly marked)	Bridge	S	129
21	22.4	Turn right on track after dilapidated barn and continue straight		SW	131
22	23.5	Turn left onto D269 road, cross Le Lech river and keep left on principal road until reaching Castillon		W	135
23	25.2	Cross road (D269) in **Castillon** and continue straight	Pass brown cross on the left	SW	202
24	26.0	Turn left onto the D269 road and continue straight towards Arthez-de-Béarn		SW	161

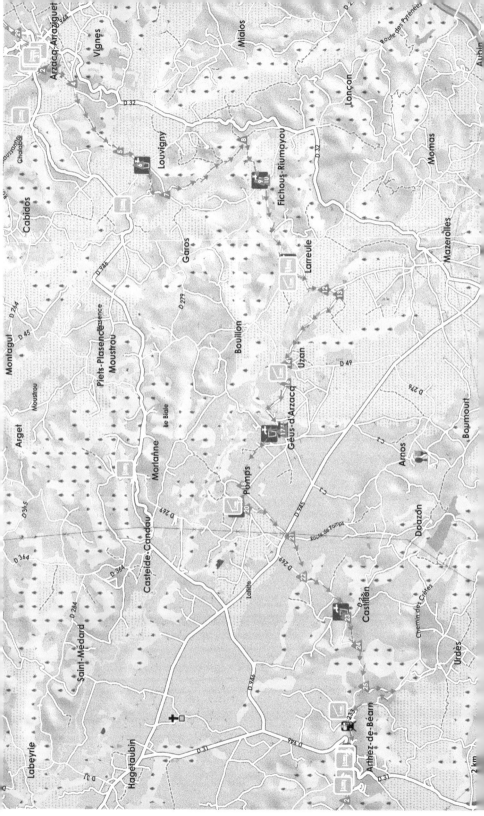

| 25 | 27.0 | Turn left onto chemin de Benicet and then right onto the D233 road to enter Arthez-de-Béarn | | S | 149 |
| 26 | 30.2 | Arrive at **Arthez-de-Béarn** centre | Place du Palais | | 211 |

ACCOMODATION & TOURIST INFORMATION

Louvigny

Ferme la Houn de Lacoste, (Jean-Michel Lacadée), 1 route d'Orthez, 64410 Louvigny, Pyrénées Atlantiques, France; +33(0)5 59 04 42 73; +33(0)6 80 42 68 94; jeanmichel.lacadee@hotmail.fr; €42/half board, €84/half board 2 pers.; Located on a beautiful working farm 500m from the village of Louvigny, and run by a family of musicians. 4 rooms. Dinner prepared with local products. English spoken. Horses welcome.

Larreule

Gîte l'Escale, (Patricia Bourda), 1 route de Mazerolles, 64410 Larreule, Pyrénées Atlantiques, France; +33(0)5 59 81 49 24; +33(0)6 32 02 25 48; alain.patricia64@orange.fr; Dormitory: €12/pers. €4/breakfast, €28/half board, B&B: €43/pers., €56/2 pers., €12/dinner; Located on a restored farm on the GR®65. Includes 3 double rooms (B&B), and 1 dormitory sleeping 9. Horses welcome.

Uzan

Gîte d'Étape Perarnaud, (Mr and Mrs Perarnaud), Carpan, 64370 Uzan, Pyrénées Atlantiques, France; +33(0)5 59 81 65 76; +33(0)6 82 97 47 29; bernard.perarnaud@wanadoo.fr; €12/pers. €4/breakfast, €30/half board; Located in the village on the GR, welcoming hostel with 8 places in 4 rooms.

Morlanne

Ferme Auberge Grandguillotte-Lauzet, (Cécile Grandguillotte Lauzet), 33 Carrère du Château, 64370 Morlanne, Pyrénées Atlantiques, France; +33(0)5 59 81 61 28; cecile.grandguillotte@wanadoo.fr; €52/2 pers. €40/half board, €16/dinner; 4 places in two rooms on working farm with welcoming hosts. Located approximately 3 km from GR®65.

Pomps

Centre d'Accueil Communal, 1 route de Billère, 64370 Pomps, Pyrénées Atlantiques, France; +33(0)5 59 81 60 61; +33(0)6 84 91 94 00; mairie-de-pomps@orange.fr; €11/pers. €4/pers., €10/dinner, €25/half board; Rudimentary accommodation. 18 places in dormitory. Horses welcome.

Arthez-de-Béarn

Gîte de la Boulangerie Broussé, (Myriam and Bertrand Broussé), 13 la Carrère, 64370 Arthez-de-Béarn, Pyrénées Atlantiques, France; +33(0)5 59 67 74 46; bertrand.brousse@wanadoo.fr; www.boulangerie.gite.over-blog.com; €13/pers. €6/breakfast, €13/dinner (upon reservation); Located close to village on the GR®65, 4 rooms for 1-3 pers. in 18th century building. English spoken. Accommodation for horses possible.

Gîte en Coussina, (Myriam and Bertrand Broussé), 13 la Carrère, 64370 Arthez-de-Béarn, Pyrénées Atlantiques, France; +33(0)5 59 67 78 78; +33(0)7 81 00 09 64; murielle.arris@neuf.fr; €13/pers. €6/breakfast, €13/dinner (upon reservation), €31/half board; Located before village and 150m from GR®65, cottage with 6 places, operated by friendly couple. English spoken. Horses welcome.

Maison des Pèlerins, Mairie d'Arthez-de-Béarn, 52 rue la Carrère, 64370 Arthez-de-Béarn, Pyrénées Atlantiques, France; +33(0)5 59 67 45 62; +33(0)3 55 96 77 43 2; mairie.arthezdebearn@wanadoo.fr; €10/pers.; Located on the GR®65, renovated hostel with 24 places in rooms of 2 to 5, near village centre and commerce. View on the Pyrenees mountains. English spoken. Horses welcome. Kitchen.

Domaine de la Carrère, (Fritz Kisby and Mike Ridout), 54 rue la Carrère, 64370 Arthez-de-Béarn, Pyrénées Atlantiques, France; +33(0)5 24 37 61 24; info@domaine-de-la-carrere.fr; www.domaine-de-la-carrere.fr; €85-€125/1-2 pers. €30/dinner; Luxury B&B located on the GR®65 in village centre, in a beautifully restored and decorated 17th century historic residence with gardens and pool. English spoken.

Chambre d'Hôtes Maison en Paille, (Claude Segond), 42 Ter rue du Bourdalat, 64370 Arthez-de-Bearn, Pyrénées Atlantiques, France; +33(0)6 99 36 41 24; segondc@yahoo.fr; €23/pers. €15/dinner; Located at village exit, 8 places in 3 rooms in a straw bale house. Warm welcome and lovely views. English spoken.

Chambre d'Hôtes Prat, (Jean- Marc and Françoise Prat), 3 Chemin de Peyroulet, 64370 Arthez-de-Béarn, Pyrénées Atlantiques, France; +33(0)5 59 67 40 94; +33(0)6 21 93 28 63; jeanmarc.prat@orange.fr; €30/pers. €45/half board; 3km from the village centre with garden, 2 double rooms. English spoken. Horses welcome.

DISTANCE **31.9km**

ASCENT **763m**

DESCENT **846m**

FROM LE PUY **653km**

TO RONCEVAUX **122km**

Navarrenx

Route - The route is well-marked and follows small country roads and paths through fields and small forests. It passes over a chain of hills that is regularly cut by rivers, so that the route includes several climbs, descents and bridges, before arriving at the beautiful fortified city of Navarrenx.

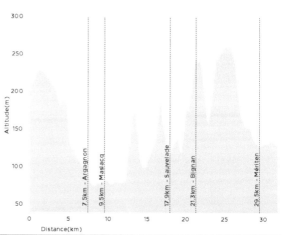

CULTURAL DISCOVERIES

Oratory of Notre-Dame-de-Muret

A short walk off the GR®65 is the Byzantine-styled oratory of Notre-Dame-de-Muret (1936). It commemorates one of the oldest sanctuaries in Béarn, which was built in the 11th century by Raymond Le Vieux, bishop of Gascony.

Sauvelade

Sauvelade (popl. 265, alt. 115m) once housed an important monastery. In 1127, in thanks for having survived the wars against the Moors in Spain, Gaston IV, Viscount of Béarn, made a donation to the Benedictine monks that were living in a nearby forest (called *silva lata*) so that they might build a monastery dedicated to Mary. In the 13th century, the Benedictine monastery was taken over by Cistercian monks and later sold during the French Revolution. All that remains of the monastery is the Church of Saint James the Greater (*Eglise Saint-Jacques-le-Majeure*), which was built from local sandstone in the unusual shape of a Greek cross (as opposed to a Latin cross). Today the church is owned by the State and is used for local functions.

Navarrenx

The city of Navarrenx (popl. 1,060, alt. 120m), which sits on the Gave d'Oloron river, is classified as one of the most beautiful villages in France and is also one of the region's oldest *bastides* or fortified cities. The current ramparts, however, were designed and built in the first half of the 16th century by Italian military engineer, Fabrizio Siciliano, on orders of the King of Navarre who sought to refortify the original 14th century walls. The conversion of Jeanne d'Albert (Queen Regent of Navarre, mother of King Henry IV and leader of the French Protestants) to Calvinism plunged the region into the religious wars that pitted Catholics against Protestants. But Navarrenx's fortifications withstood a three month siege by Catholic armies in 1569. The city was never conquered.

Next to the Tourist Office is La Maison du Cigare, the only company to make cigars using 100% French tobacco (visits on weekdays). A market is held every Wednesday morning.

ROUTE INSTRUCTIONS

Waypoint	Total(km)	Directions	Verification	Compass	Altitude(m)
1	0.0	From **Arthez-de-Béarn**, stay straight on rue la Carrère through village	Pass church on the left	SW	212
2	1.2	At fork keep right on chemin du Bosc	Stone cross	NW	226
3	4.8	Turn left on route de l'Eglise and continue straight until reaching Argagnon	Signpost	SW	187
4	7.5	Beside **Argagnon** turn left onto the D817 road. Then ahead cross the D817 (caution), the bridge over the river (Gave de Pau) and the A64 highway. Stay on the D275 road, direction Maslacq		S	99
5	9.5	In **Maslacq**, turn left onto rue du Fronton and then left onto the D9 road		SE	82
6	10.2	Cross the Le Geu river and turn left on the road that runs parallel to the Cave de Pau river.		S	82
7	13.1	At top of steep climb turn right and continue straight	**Sanctuary de Muret** to the left	S	152
8	13.3	Cross the D9/Route de Maslacq and continue straight on track		SW	172
9	13.4	Turn left and then right on chemin Saubade. Continue straight		SE	170
10	14.4	Cross stream (Le Geu) and continue straight		S	100

11	15.8	Turn right on route de Sauvelade, direction Sauvelade		N	125
12	17.9	Turn left onto the C110 road and continue straight through **Sauvelade**		S	115
13	18.9	Turn right onto Camino de Compostela and continue straight		S	135
14	21.3	Enter hamlet of **Bignan** and keep right	Signpost	W	240
15	21.9	At fork keep left on the Camino de Berduqueu	Signpost	N	244
16	22.2	Turn left on Matheu Bacot road		W	233
17	24.0	Turn left onto Camino de Sentier Jouan, and continue straight		S	247
18	25.6	Turn right on road and continue straight		SW	258
19	27.2	Keep to right on road that runs parallel to the Le Lucq stream, and leads to Méritein	Stream to the left	SW	173
20	28.5	At fork, keep left and continue straight towards Méritein		W	153
21	29.0	Turn left and continue straight	Pass church on right	SW	133
22	29.5	In **Méritein** turn left on the D947 road, then (at cross) turn left onto chemin de la Biasse	Pass through residential area and underpass	S	129
23	31.0	Turn right onto avenue de Mourenx		SW	135
24	31.5	Turn right onto avenue de France and proceed through town on main road, rue Saint-Germain		NW	129
25	31.9	Arrive at **Navarrenx** centre	Place des Casernes		129

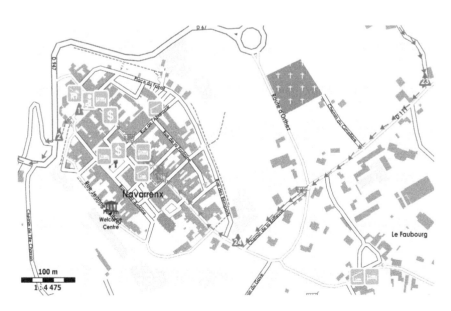

Argagnon

Arrêt et Aller, (Linda and Andrew Jones), 190 route de Pédauque, 64300 Argagnon, Pyrénées Atlantiques, France; +33(0)5 59 09 37 35; +33(0)6 79 56 98 37; glyn34@hotmail.com; €35/pers. (in room for 4) half board,€75/2 pers. half board (double room), €10/dinner; B&B with 3 rooms located 3km after Arthez-de-Béarn, about 250m from the GR®65, on a lovely 18th century Bearnise styled farmhouse with large property. Owned by an English couple. English spoken. Horses welcome.

Maslacq

Gîte d'Étape-Chambres la Halte, (Chantal Pouchou), 35 rue la Carrère, 64300 Maslacq, Pyrénées Atlantiques, France; +33(0)5 59 67 30 85; +33(0)6 45 33 68 23; gite.lahalte@laposte.net; €20/pers. (breakfast included), €50/double room, €69/triple room, €88/room for 4.; Located in the village on the GR®65 in a Bearnaise styled house. Very welcoming hosts. 5 places in dormitory and 9 places in 3 rooms. English spoken. Horses welcome.

La Ferme du Bicatou, (Evelyne and Philippe Gantet), 8 rue de l'Ecole, 64300 Maslacq, Pyrénées Atlantiques, France; +33(0)5 59 67 62 17; +33(0)6 63 74 02 56; phil.gantet@gmail.com; €20-25/pers. €35/2 pers. (mobile home), €13/dinner; 2 comfortable rooms in a warm family home and 1 mobile home.

Sauvelade

Ecogîte la Maison du Grillon, (Jef Blanchard and Lili), 1559 route Deu Lavarth, 64150 Sauvelade, Pyrénées Atlantiques, France; +33(0)5 59 09 34 30; +33(0)6 76 27 36 38; oustau.grigt@gmail.com; https://www.facebook.com/eco.gite.oustau.grigt; €21/pers. (breakfast included), €35/half board, €16/organic dinner; 10 places in renovated home with dormitory and 4-pers. rooms. Garden. English spoken. Next to a bistrot serving regional specialities. Call in advance to confirm that they can accept guests for a single night.

Gîte Nadette, (Bernadette Godfroy), 998 Camin de Capdelas, 64150 Sauvelade, Pyrénées Atlantiques, France; +33(0)5 59 38 48 79; +33(0)6 87 29 13 70; gitenadette@laposte.net; www.gitenadette.com; Dormitories: €17/pers. (breakfast included), €32/half board, B&B: €60/half board, €95/half board 2 pers. €120/half board 3 pers., €5/pool; Located 2km from the GR®65 after the Abbaye de Sauvelade in a lovely 18th century stone house with pool and terrace. 8 places in 2 dormitories and 2 double rooms. English spoken. Accommodation for horses with advance notice.

Bugnein

Gîte, (Henry and Patricia Chalret du Rieu), Le Grand Saule, 64190 Bugnein, Pyrénées Atlantiques, France; +33(0)5 59 67 33 39; pouchka55@yahoo.fr; €48/double room, €15/pers. in triple room; Lovely 19th century property and home in Bearnais style, with one double and triple room. English spoken.

Navarrenx

L'Alchimiste, (Jean-Gaétan Pélisse), 10 rue de l'Abreuvoir, 64190 Navarrenx, Pyrénées Atlantiques, France; +33(0)9 67 03 26 84; +33(0)6 32 78 13 76; alchimistesurlechemin@hotmail.fr; www.alchimistesurlechemin.com; Donation (dinner and breakfast included); 11 places in 5 rooms. English spoken. Very welcoming.

Gîte Communaux de Navarrenx, Mairie, place d'Armes, 64190 Navarrenx, Pyrénées Atlantiques, France; +33(0)5 59 66 10 22; mairie.navarrenx@wanadoo.fr; €13/pers.; 54 places in basic accommodation located in the village centre on the GR®65. Check-in at café Le Dahu, 23 rue Saint-Germain.

Le Cri de la Girafe, (Maria Laullon and Fabian Tumpling), 12 rue du Faubourg, 64190 Navarrenx, Pyrénées Atlantiques; France; +33(0)5 59 66 24 22; contact@lecridelagirafe.fr; www.lecridelagirafe.fr; Dormitory: €21/pers. €12/dinner, €35/half board, B&B: €30-€33/double room, €42-€45/half board; 8 places in dormitory and 6 places in 3 double rooms. Courtyard and garden. Horses welcome. English spoken.

Chambres d'Hôtes Lasarroques, (Monique and Jean Lasarroques), 4 place d'Armes, 64190 Navarrenx, Pyrénées Atlantiques, France; +33(0)5 59 66 27 59; +33(0)7 80 00 37 77; lasarroques.monique@orange.fr; www.chambres-hotes-lasarroques.com; €55/pers. €60/2 pers., €90-€120/studio; 3 tastefully decorated rooms in a welcoming home and 4 places in a studio apartment with kitchen.

Le Relais du Jacquet, (Régis Gabastou), 42 rue de Saint Germain, 64190 Navarrenx, Pyrénées Atlantiques, France; +33(0)5 59 66 57 25; +33(0)6 75 72 89 33; regis.gabastou@orange.fr; www.chambre-hotes-navarrenx.com; €45/pers. €52/2 pers., €82/3 pers., €59/pers. half board, €90/2 pers. half board, €126/triple half board; Located on the main street in the village centre, 5 rooms in historic building, welcoming host and former pilgrim. English spoken.

Le Commerce, Place des Casernes, 64190 Navarrenx, Pyrénées Atlantiques, France; +33(0)5 59 66 50 16; hotel.du.commerce@wanadoo.fr; www.logishotels.com/fr/hotel/hotel-le-commerce-1009?partid=661; €62.50/pers. €75/2 pers., €8/breakfast, €78/half board, €120/2 pers. half board; Centrally located, agreeable hotel with 10 spacious rooms. English spoken.

Office de Tourisme, Place des Casernes, 64190 Navarrenx, Pyrénées Atlantiques, France; +33(0)5 59 38 32 85; navarrenx@bearndesgaves.com; www.tourisme-bearn-gaves.com

Castetnau-Camblong

Domaine de Lespoune, (Mr and Mrs Everaert), 20 Camblong, 64190 Castetnau-Camblong, Pyrénées Atlantiques, France; +33(0)5 59 66 24 14; contact@lespoune.fr; www.lespoune.fr; €69-€89/2 pers. €109-€139/3 pers., €149/4 pers., €25/dinner; B&B in 18th century home with 8 rooms 250m from Castetnau-Camblong and GR®65. English spoken. Horses welcome.

Basque Landscape © Alexia Adamski

BASQUE COUNTRY

The French Basque region (French: *Pays basque français*, Basque: *Iparralde* (the northern side)) is centred around the Western Pyrenees mountains and makes up the northeastern part of the Basque country, which totals seven provinces in Spain and France.

The climate is wet and the region sparsely populated (less than 300,000 inhabitants compared with about two million in Basque Spain). Most people live in the coastal cities of Bayonne (the capital of French Basque country) and glamorous Biarritz (a major surfing destination). Inland, on the foothills of the Pyrenees, sheep are extensively grazed for cheese production.

The region boasts a history that dates to pre-Roman times, a distinct architectural style (like the white red-shuttered farm houses), musical traditions (namely choral singing), sports (*pelote*) and foods (like sheep cheese (*Ossaulraty*), red chilies (*piment rouges*), paprika-flavoured sausages and Bayonne ham). *Euskara*, the ancient Basque language that survived Roman conquest, is spoken by a minority of the population and remains at risk of disappearing. Descending deeper into the region, red, white and green Basque flags become more common.

DISTANCE **19.2km**

ASCENT **455m**

DESCENT **477m**

FROM LE PUY **684km**

TO RONCEVAUX **90km**

Basque Landscape © Alexandra Huddleston

Route - The route is well-marked, with limited climbs and follows mostly small country roads and some paths through fields (corn), small forests, and over gentle hills and streams. Enter the French Basque country by crossing the Saison river after the village of Charre.

Pointers - **Backtracking:** The village of Aroue is located approximately 300 metres off the GR®65. Backtrack from there to rejoin the main route.

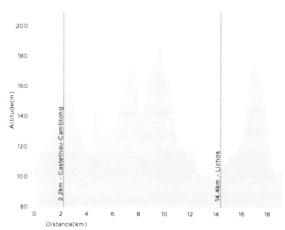

CULTURAL DISCOVERIES

Church of Saint Stephen (*Eglise Saint-Etienne*)

While the Church in Aroue has been rebuilt, certain Romanesque features were reused in the sacristy. Notably, there is a relief sculpture above the sacristy door that has been interpreted as a hunting scene or as an early depiction of Saint James the Moor-slayer. Other figures include a woman and serpent (interpreted as Eve) and a man carrying a large stone (which could be a depiction of a traditional Basque stone lifting competition).

See Shaver-Crandell, A., Gerson, P. L., & Stones, A, p. 119 (1995). The pilgrim's guide to Santiago de Compostela: A gazetteer. London: Harvey Miller Publishers.

Waypoint	Total(km)	Directions	Verification	Compass	Altitude(m)
1	0.0	From Place des Casernes, in **Navarrenx**, head (left) south-west and pass through historic gate Saint-Antoine		SW	129
2	0.1	Turn left onto the D947 road and cross the Gave d'Oloron river		SW	129
3	0.3	Turn right and continue straight on D115/Impasse des Lambrits. Continue straight through roundabout	Signpost.	NW	106
4	1.6	Turn right onto the D815 road. Then turn left onto path and finally keep right onto the D815 road and head to Castetnau-Camblong	Signpost. Ahead pass town hall (*Mairie*) on left	NW	128
5	2.2	In **Castetnau-Camblong** turn left onto rue des Debantets and continue straight		W	155
6	2.9	Turn left onto small road and continue straight	Stone cross. Ahead Cross stream "Le Lausset"	SW	155
7	3.9	Turn right and continue straight through woods.		W	124
8	4.5	Turn right and continue straight until reaching small road		NW	125
9	5.0	Turn left onto road and continue straight		W	130
10	6.4	Turn right onto path		W	138
11	7.6	At fork turn left		S	168
12	9.6	Cross the D115 road and continue straight on route de Saint-Jacques towards Lichos		SW	186
13	12.7	Turn right on route du Saison/D244 and then turn left and go through underpass. Turn left on path running parallel to the D23 road	Cross **Le Saison River,** enter Basque country.	NW	103
14	13.8	Turn right onto track (after river), and proceed to Lichos centre		SW	99
15	14.4	In **Lichos**, turn left and then right	Church	SW	104
16	14.7	Turn right onto Lou Brousta and continue straight	Cross the Le Borlaas stream and the D2023 road	NW	106
17	16.8	At intersection, turn left	Farm Bouhaben	SW	167
18	17.5	Turn right and then take stairs left to rejoin the D11		W	162
19	18.0	Turn right onto the D11 road and continue straight towards Ferme Bohoteguia (on left)		NW	148
20	19.2	Continue straight to arrive at **Aroue** (off the GR®65)	Village visible at top of hill		108

Lichos

Gîte Loumpré, (Angèle Loumpré), Le Village, 64130 Lichos, Pyrénées Atlantiques, France; +33(0)5 59 28 81 39; +33(0)6 31 90 92 41; jeanmarie.loumpre@sfr.fr; €19/pers. €5/breakfast, €38/half board.; Apartment with 2-6 places located in the village after the public school, on the GR®65.

Chambres d'Hôtes Haïtzpean, (Marie-Reine and Emile Hontaas), 23 route Départementale, 64130 Lichos, Pyrénées Atlantiques, France; +33(0)5 59 28 29 45; +33(0)6 67 66 73 09; frhs@voila.fr; €20/pers. €38/ half board; 5 double rooms. Horses welcome.

Aroue-Ithorots-Olhaïby

Gîte d'Étape Communal d'Aroue, (Mrs Cécile Darritchon), Ancienne École, 64120 Aroue-Ithorots-Olhaïby, Pyrénées Atlantiques, France; +33(0)5 59 65 95 54; gite.aroue@wanadoo.fr; €10/pers.; 12 places in former school house. Basic accommodation. Groceries available for purchase. Horses welcome.

Ferme Bohoteguia, (Mrs Simone Barneix), Maison Bohoteguia, 64120 Aroue-Ithorots-Olhaïby, Pyrénées Atlantiques, France; +33(0)5 59 65 85 69; +33(0)6 75 83 82 61; bohoteguia@aol.com; www.ferme-bohoteguia.com; €11/pers.; €30-€36/half board; 27 places in 8 rooms of 1-6 pers. in a welcoming renovated (2013) farmhouse.

Gîte d'Étape Familial Bellevue, (Marie-Paule and Marcel Gégu), Maison Bellevue, 64120 Aroue-Ithorots-Olhaïby, Pyrénées Atlantiques, France; +33(0)5 59 65 70 19; +33(0)6 16 48 63 65; gegubellevue@yahoo.fr; €11/pers. €4/breakfast; 1.5km before Aroue. 14 places in double rooms. Kitchen. Welcoming. English spoken. Pool.

Basque Landscape

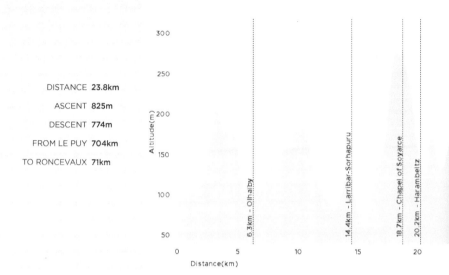

DISTANCE **23.8km**

ASCENT **825m**

DESCENT **774m**

FROM LE PUY **704km**

TO RONCEVAUX **71km**

Route - The route is well-marked, with gentle climbs over the green hills, forests and sheep pastures, typical of the Basque country. The Pyrenees mountains are clearly in view, especially from the beautiful viewpoint at the Chapel of Soyarce.

Pointers - **Culture:** The section of the GR®65 from Arroue to Ostabat is on the UNESCO world heritage list. **Shortcut:** Possibility to bypass Larribar-Sorhapuru by taking a short cut through Uharte-Mixe, which reconnects to the GR®65 north of Harambletz.

CULTURAL DISCOVERIES

Chapel of Saint Nicholas (Chapelle Saint-Nicolas)

The Chapel of Saint Nicholas in Harambeltz (Basque: *haram* valley and *belzt* dark), is a recently restored Romanesque chapel dating from the 12th century. It is all that remains of a former priory and hospital.

Waypoint	Total(km)	Directions	Verification	Compass	Altitude(m)
1	0.0	Before **Aroue**, turn left onto the D11 road, direction St Palais and continue straight	Château de Joantho (brown and red) and iron cross on left	S	108
2	2.2	Turn right on serpentine path that climbs		W	119
3	5.0	Turn sharply left and continue on path		NW	175
4	5.9	Turn right onto a small road, direction Olhaïby		N	104
5	6.3	In **Olhaïby**, turn left and continue on road	Turning away from village	W	100
6	7.3	Turn right and head towards Casab-onne		NW	120
7	7.6	Turn right and head towards Jaurrib-erria		NW	131
8	8.3	Turn left and continue straight		SW	132
9	10.7	Turn right direction Benta		NW	192
10	10.9	Turn left and continue descent until reaching the D242 road	Pass farm Benta	SW	182
11	12.2	Turn right onto the D242 road and continue straight		NW	104
12	12.7	Continue straight on the D242 road	Turn left for short-cut through Uhart Mixe	NW	92
13	13.2	At fork keep left, direction Larribar-Sorhapuru		NW	85
14	14.4	Keep left and cross **Larribar-Sorhap-uru**	Pass town-hall (*Mairie*) and church on the right	W	128
15	14.9	Cross the D933 road and continue straight		NW	98
16	15.7	Cross bridge over the Bidouze river and continue straight on path that climbs west to Hiriburia		NW	64
17	16.9	Turn left and continue straight on road that climbs to plateau, direction Chap-el of Soyarce	Signpost	S	150
18	18.7	Turn left towards **Chapel of Soyarce**		SE	280
19	18.8	Turn right on path that descends to-wards Harambeltz. Attention poorly marked	Near information board	S	283
20	19.5	Keep right and descend towards vil-lage of Harambeltz		S	246
21	20.2	Turn right and descend through village of **Harambeltz**	Pass **Chapel of Saint Nicholas** on the right	SW	149
22	20.4	Keep right on road that cuts through forest, and crosses the Harambeltzko Erreka stream. Continue straight		SW	148
23	21.4	Turn left and continue straight on path		SE	176
24	22.0	Keep right and cross the Ibidiak Erreka stream		S	133
25	22.2	Turn right and continue straight		W	130
26	23.0	Turn left onto track and continue straight to village of Ostabat-Asme	Signpost and stone marker	SW	169

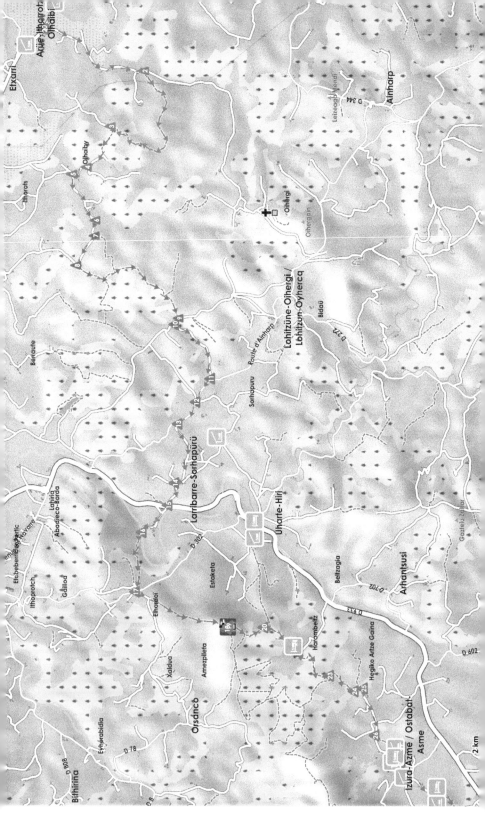

| 27 | 23.6 | Turn right (after the Ospitalia Hostel) to enter village centre | | W | 127 |
| 28 | 23.8 | Arrive at **Ostabat** | Village centre | | 141 |

ACCOMODATION & TOURIST INFORMATION

Larribar-Sorhapuru

Gîte À la Ferme, (Famille Castillon), Ferme Arosteguia, 64120 Larribar-Sorhapuru, Pyrénées Atlantiques, France; +33(0)5 59 65 27 94; +33(0)6 27 71 69 82; contact@arosteguia.com; €15/pers. €30/half board; 5 rooms on farm located on shortcut to GR®65 passing through Uhart-Mixe. English spoken. Horses welcome.

Uhart-Mixe

Gîte de l'Escargote, (Arnaud), Le Bourg, 64120 Uhart-Mixe, Pyrénées Atlantiques, France; +33(0)5 59 65 60 00; +33(0)6 16 33 72 13; ostatua64@hotmail.com; www.augitedelescargot.com; €35/half board; 7 places in 2 dormitories and 3 double rooms located on shortcut to GR®65 passing through Uhart-Mixe. Horses welcome.

Harambeltz

Maison d'Hôtes Etchetoa, (Jean Pierre Loustalot), Harambeltz, 64120 Ostabat-Asme, Pyrénées Atlantiques, France; +33(0)6 17 90 45 59; loustalot.jean@laposte.net; €50/double room, Dormitory: €20/pers. (breakfast included), €15/dinner; Beautiful and spacious B&B on authentic Basque farm, with welcoming hosts serving traditional Basque cuisine. Located 4 km before Ostabat next to the Chapel Saint Nicolas. 1 double room and 1 dormitory for 4.

Ostabat-Asme

Gîte Aïre-Ona, (Françoise Irigoin), Le Bourg, 64120 Ostabat-Asme, Pyrénées Atlantiques, France; +33(0)5 59 37 88 75; +33(0)6 33 65 77 15; gite.aire-ona@live.fr; www.aireona-gite-ostabat.fr/; €15-€18/pers. €5/breakfastvvvv; Modern, high quality, fully renovated gîte with 4 rooms in village centre. English spoken. Kitchen.

Gite d'Étape Burgosaharia, (Valérie Harismendy), Quartier Asme, 64120 Ostabat-Asme, Pyrénées Atlantiques, France; +33(0)5 59 65 46 69; +33(0)6 72 68 13 24; pilival@free.fr; €24/pers. (breakfast included); Located 2km from the GR®65, 6 places in 3 rooms.

Gîte d'Etape Ospitalia, (Mr Etcheparreborde), Maison Aneteia, 64120 Ostabat-Asme, Pyrénées Atlantiques, France; +33(0)5 59 37 83 17; +33(0)6 10 04 65 75; €13/pers.; A former hospital converted into a hostel with 10 places in 3 rooms. Located at entrance to village. Basic and somber accommodation. Kitchen.

Gîte d'Étape Izarrak, (Mr and Mrs Eyharts), Ferme Gaineko Etxea, 64120 Ostabat-Asme, Pyrénées Atlantiques, France; +33(0)5 59 37 81 10; +33(0)6 72 73 78 56; lucie.eyharts@wanadoo.fr; www.gites-de-france-64.com/ostabat-compostelle/; B&B: €36-€44/half board; Located 1km from Ostabat on the way, 19 places in rooms or dormitories on a restored farm, terrace swimming pool and spa. English spoken. Horses welcome.

Auberge Ametzanea, (Marie-Hélène and Daniel Arbeletche), Ametzanea, 64120 Ostabat-Asme, Pyrénées Atlantiques, France; +33(0)5 59 37 85 03; +33(0)5 59 37 81 56; danielantxo@wanadoo.fr; €36/half board, €12/dinner, €5/breakfast; 3 rooms in auberge located in village centre. Accommodation for horses possible.

DISTANCE **22.5km**

ASCENT **625m**

DESCENT **613m**

FROM LE PUY **728km**

TO RONCEVAUX **47km**

Hiker on path to St-Jean-Le-Vieux © Alexia Adamski

Route - The route is well-marked, generally flat, and uses primarily asphalt roads and tracks as it makes its way deeper into the Basque country to the foot of the Pyrenees, Saint-Jean-Pied-de-Port. The route passes through typical Basque villages and green pastures.

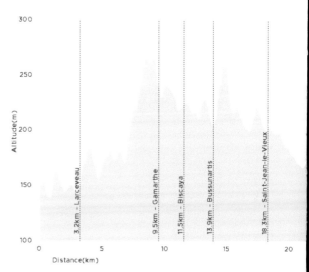

Saint-Jean-le-Vieux

Saint Jean-le-Vieux (popl. 870, alt. 200m) occupies a strategic position at the entrance of the Cize plain. Around 15 BC, Romans built a camp here, at the foot of the Pyrenees on the road between Bordeaux and Astorga (Spain). Archaeological excavations have unearthed Roman baths and other objects that can be seen at the local museum.

The **Chapel of Saint Peter of Usakoa** (*Chapelle Saint-Pierre d'Usakoa*) has a beautiful Romanesque tympanum from the 12th century, which predates the destruction of the city by Richard the Lionheart in 1177. Thereafter, the city was rebuilt nearby on more easily defensible site - Saint-Jean-Pied-de-Port.

St-Jean-Pied-de-Port © Alexandra Huddleston

Saint-Jean-Pied-de-Port

Located at the foot of the pass over the Pyrenees mountains, St-Jean-Pied-de-Port (Basque: *Donibane Garazi*, popl. 1500, alt. 160m) has served as a commercial, military and religious crossroads. It is also the last stop in France on the Way of Saint James.

Dominating the village from atop the Mendiguren hill is the 17th century **Citadel** (*Citadelle*), which was built on the site of the former fortress of the Kings of Navarre. From there, the cobblestone street, rue de la Citadelle, descends to the **Church of Our Lady at the End of the Bridge** (*Eglise Notre-Dame-du-Bout-du-Pont*), a 14th century Gothic church on the banks of the Nive river. According to legend, King Sancho VII of Navarre founded the church to commemorate his victory over the Moors in the battle of Las Navas de Tolosa (1212), a turning point in the Christian reconquest of Spain.

There is a pilgrim welcome centre at 39, rue de la Citadelle. The village holds a lively farmers market on Monday mornings.

ROUTE INSTRUCTIONS

Waypoint	Total(km)	Directions	Verification	Compass	Altitude(m)
1	0.0	Continue straight on main street in **Ostabat**	Pass town-hall (*Mairie*) on the right	W	141
2	0.1	At fork turn right onto smaller road and continue straight towards Burgo-saharia	Road passes between stone walls	SW	154
3	2.8	Turn right onto the D933 road and continue straight		SW	150
4	3.2	Enter **Larceveau** (signpost) and turn right onto route de Saint-Palais	Signpost	SW	144
5	3.7	Keep right on road and continue straight through fields and typical white and red houses		W	170

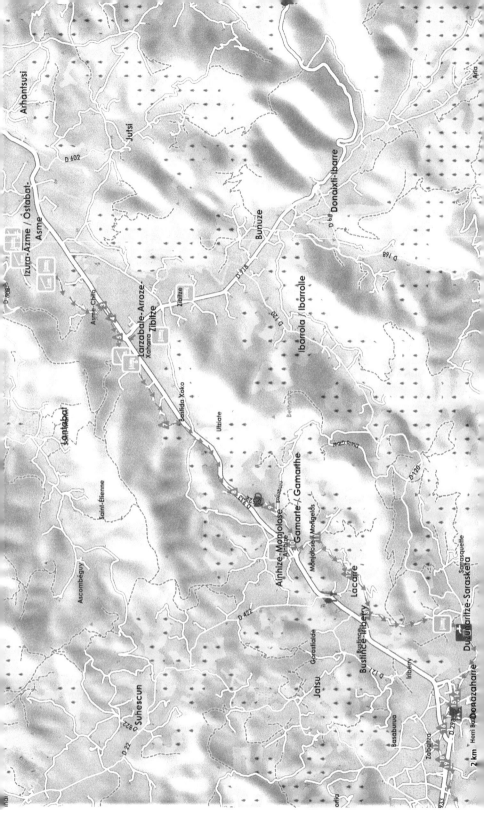

6	4.4	Continue straight on road towards Bastida Choko	White house with red shutters and stone wall on right	SW	177
7	6.0	Cross stream (Arlako Erréka) and turn left towards the D933 road. Continue on the track that runs parallel to the D933		SW	175
8	8.6	Cross the D933 road and head south on the D522 towards Gamarthe		SW	268
9	9.5	At **Gamarthe**, turn left and then right to rejoin the D522 road. Continue straight until reaching the D933 road		E	255
10	10.7	Turn left onto the D933 road. Then take first left towards Biscaya	Signpost	SW	234
11	11.5	In **Biscaya**, turn right and continue straight	Stream to the left	SW	223
12	12.7	Turn left and climb hill	Signpost	S	216
13	13.9	Turn left into the hamlet of **Bussunartis**		S	212
14	18.0	Turn left and then right to Saint-Jean-le-Vieux	Signpost	SW	205
15	18.3	In **Saint-Jean-le-Vieux**, cross the D2933 road and continue straight through square. Turn left after Bar Sotua and continue straight to the D933 road		NW	202
16	18.9	Cross the D933 road and keep left	Signpost	NW	197
17	19.4	Turn left towards the D933 road		SW	198
18	19.7	Turn left and then right on the D933 road		S	191
19	19.9	Cross the D933 road, and turn left and then right. Then keep right, passing church on the left and cross the Le Laurhibar river		SW	185
20	21.8	Cross the D401 road and veer right	Citadel to the left	W	177
21	22.2	Pass through historic gates of Saint Jean Pied de Port. Continue straight on rue de la Citadelle		W	200
22	22.5	Arrive at **Saint-Jean-Pied-de-Port**	Beside church of Notre-Dame-du-Bout-du-Pont		187

ACCOMODATION & TOURIST INFORMATION

Larceveau-Arros-Cibits

Gite d'Étape Paradis, (Marie-Claire and Pierre), Mais Mendiondoua, 64120 Larceveau-Arros-Cibits, Pyrénées Atlantiques, France; +33(0)5 59 37 82 67; +33(0)6 81 43 12 47; pierreparadis64@aol.com; €25/pers. (breakfast included), €12/dinner; Located 1.5km after Larcevau, 6 places in 2 rooms.

Chambre d'Hôtes Arantzeta, (Mrs. Michèle Ampo), Quartier Cibits, 64120 Larceveau-Arros-Cibits, Pyrénées Atlantiques, France; +33(0)5 59 37 37 26; +33(0)6 81 17 92 54; ampochristophe@aol.com; www.arantzeta.fr/; €48/pers. €57-€63/2 pers., €18/dinner; Located about 1.5km from village, 3 rooms in very welcoming B&B. English spoken.

Chambre d'Hôtes, (Chantal and Christian Isaac), Oyhanartia, 64120 Larceveau-Arros-Cibits, Pyrénées Atlantiques, France; +33(0)5 59 37 88 16; contact@oyhanartia.com; www.chambre-d-hote-pays-basque.com; €65-68/pers. €70-€78/2 pers., €30/dinner; Lovely B&B with 5 rooms, 2 km from the GR®65. Horses welcome.

Maison Bichta Eder, (Mrs Danielle Daressy-Jouanolou), Quartier Chaharra, 64120 Larceveau-Arros-Cibits, Pyrénées Atlantiques, France; +33(0)5 59 37 49 24; +33(0)6 86 67 77 91; etapealarceveau@gmail.com; www.etapealarceveau.e-monsite.com; €20/pers. €10/dinner, €5/breakfast; 2 rooms in family home located on the GR®65. English spoken. Horses welcome.

Aïnhice-Mongelos

Domaine de Schiltenea, (Schiltenea), Route de l'Eglise, 64220 Aïnhice-Mongelos, Pyrénées Atlantiques, France; +33(0)5 59 37 22 56; albanne.t.sandras@gmail.com; €35/pers. €50/2 pers., €20/dinner; B&B with 2 rooms in a 18th century home with garden. English spoken. Accommodation for horses.

Bussunarits-Sarrasquette

Maison Etxekonia, (Mrs. Marie Eliçagaray), Ferme Etxekonia, 64220 Bussunarits-Sarrasquette, Pyrénées Atlantiques, France; +33(0)5 59 37 00 40; €45/pers. €55/2 pers., €80/3 pers., €18.50/dinner; B&B on farm located on GR®65 1.5km before Saint-Jean-le-Vieux. 4 rooms. Horses welcome.

Saint-Jean-Pied-de-Port

Refuge Accueil Paroissial/ Maison Kaserna, 43 rue d' Espagne, 64220 Saint-Jean-Pied-de-Port, Pyrénées Atlantiques, France; +33(0)5 59 37 65 17; €10-€15/Donation (breakfast and dinner included);.

Gîte Azkorria, 50 rue de la Citadelle, 64220 Saint-Jean-Pied-de-Port, Pyrénées Atlantiques, France; +33(0)5 59 37 00 53; +33(0)6 21 16 94 76; gite.azkorria50@orange.fr; www.hebergements-pays-basque.fr; €27/pers. (breakfast and sheets included); Located in the village centre, on the GR®65. 14 places in rooms of 2 or 4.

Gîte Beilari, 40 rue de la Citadelle, 64220 Saint-Jean-Pied-de-Port, Pyrénées Atlantiques, France; +33(0)5 59 37 24 68; info@beilari.info; www.beilari.info; €30/half board; Located in the village centre on the GR®65, with garden and terrace. 18 places in various sized rooms. Communal dinner. English spoken.

Gîte Ultreia, 8 rue de la Citadelle, 64220 Saint-Jean-Pied-de-Port, Pyrénées Atlantiques, France; +33(0)6 80 88 46 22; dodo.ultreia@gmail.com; www.ultreia64.fr; €16-€17/pers. €44-€48/double room, €5/breakfast; Located in the village centre on the GR®65. Comfortable and tastefully decorated hostel with 15 places in rooms of 2, 4 or 7. English spoken.

Gîte Zazpiak Bat, (Mr and Mrs. Lopépé), 13 Bis route Maréchal Harispe, 64220 Saint-Jean-Pied-de-Port, Pyrénées Atlantiques, France; +33(0)5 59 49 10 17; +33(0)6 75 78 36 23; giteguill.lopepe@gmail.com; www.gite-zazpiak-bat.com; €23-€38/pers. €5/breakfast; Located 1 km from the village centre on the GR®65. 18 places in rooms of 1 to 3. Terrace. Kitchen. English spoken.

L'Auberge du Pèlerin, 25 rue de la Citadelle, 64220 Saint-Jean-Pied-de-Port, Pyrénées Atlantiques, France; +33(0)5 59 49 10 86; +33(0)6 78 44 62 10; contact@aubergedupelerin.com; www.aubergedupelerin.com; €17/pers. €5/breakfast, €36/half board; Located in the village centre, on the GR®65 in an 18th century building. 43 places in rooms of 2 or 6.

Refuge Municipal des Pèlerins (Associatif), 55 rue de la Citadelle, 64220 Saint-Jean-Pied-de-Port, Pyrénées Atlantiques, France; +33(0)6 17 10 31 89; avn64@yahoo.fr; €10/pers.; 32 places. Reservations not accepted.

Maison Donamaria, 1 Chemin d'Olhonce, 64220 Saint-Jean-Pied-de-Port, Pyrénées Atlantiques, France; +33(0)5 59 37 02 32; +33(0)6 61 90 29 21; info@donamaria.fr; www.donamaria.fr; €60/pers. €70/2 pers., €90/3 pers., €115/4 pers.; Top ranked B&B near village centre. Pool. English spoken.

Maison Ziberoa, 3 route d'Arneguy, 64220 Saint-Jean-Pied-de-Port, Pyrénées Atlantiques, France; +33(0)5 59 37 75 25; +33(0)6 61 23 59 44; maisonziberoa@ziberoa.com; www.ziberoa.com; €60/pers. €75/2 pers., €100/3 pers, €125/4 pers.; Top ranked B&B located in village centre. English spoken.

Maison Errecaldia, (Tim and Louisa Proctor), 5 Chemin de la Porte Saint Jacques, 64220 Saint-Jean-Pied-de-Port, Pyrénées Atlantiques, France; +33(0)5 59 49 17 02; +33(0)6 47 80 87 32; tim@errecaldia.com; www.errecaldia.com; €55/pers. €75/2 pers.; Located before entering the village old town centre on the GR®65, 3 rooms. English spoken.

Refuge Esponda, 9 rue du Trinquet, 64220 Saint-Jean-Pied-de-Port, Pyrénées Atlantiques, France; +33(0)6 79 07 52 52; lavillaesponda@sfr.fr; €50-€70/double.; Located near village centre.

Office de Tourisme, 14 place Charles de Gaulle, 64220 Saint-Jean-Pied-de-Port, Pyrénées Atlantiques, France; +33(0)5 59 37 03 57; saint.jean.pied.de.port@wanadoo.fr; www.saintjeanpieddeport-paysbasque-tourisme.com

Uhart-Cize

La Coquille Napoléon, (Lorna and Bixente Eguiazabal), Route Napoléon, 64220 Uhart-Cize, Pyrénées Atlantiques, France; +33(0)6 62 25 99 40; lacoquillenapoleon@bbox.fr; www.lacoquillenapoleon.simplesite.com; €15/pers. €3/breakfast, €12/dinner; 10 places in dormitory, 1 km after Saint-Jean-Pied-de-Port on the GR®65. Horses welcome. English spoken.

SAINT-JEAN-PIED-DE-PORT TO RONCEVAUX

DISTANCE **24.2m**

ASCENT **1574m**

DESCENT **333m**

FROM LE PUY **801km**

TO RONCEVAUX **24km**

Hiker in St-Jean-Pied-de-Port © Alexia Adamski

Route - The crossing of the Pyrenees, is one of the most beautiful stages of the French Way of Saint James. The route climbs rapidly from Saint Jean to its peak of 1420 metres. It is extremely well-marked, and generally follows the Route Napoleon/D 428 for about 15km until turning off onto a path to cross into Spain and then descends by a track into Roncevaux.

Pointers - While the weather in the Pyrenees is highly variable, avoid undertaking this stage in rain or foggy conditions, as visibility can be an issue. It is also worthwhile to await nice weather, in order to take advantage of the spectacular views.

Choice of Routes: If the weather has turned, from Col de Lepoeder consider taking the tarmacked road into Roncevaux, as opposed to the track, which

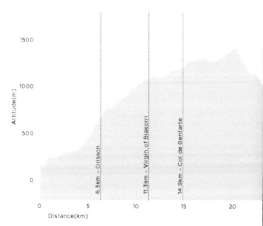

can be slippery. This alternative route is the GR®12, which switchbacks to Puerto de Ibañeta before reaching Roncevaux. **Advance planning:** If you don't plan on stopping for lunch in Orisson, you should shop for lunch the evening before in Saint-Jean as there are no groceries on the route.

Virgin of Biakorri

The lovely small Virgin of Biakorria (Basque: blowing winds, alt. 1055m) was placed on this outcrop of rock near the Route de Napoléon by shepherds from Lourdes. Note the beautiful panoramic views.

Virgin of Biakorri © Alexia Adamski

Roncevaux

Roncevaux (Basque: *Orreaga,* Spanish: *Roncevalles,* alt. 1,057m) became famous for Charlemagne's stunning defeat at the **Battle of Roncevaux Pass** in the evening of 15 August 778, which was evoked in the 11th century French literary work, the *Song of Roland.* While retreating from Moor-controlled Spain and passing through the narrow and wooded Roncevaux Pass, Charlemagne's rear guard was ambushed by attacking Basque forces. A number of high ranking officers were killed, including Roland, the governor of the French area known as Breton March. A monument and chapel in Roncevaux Pass commemorate the battle.

Below Roncevaux Pass, is the former monastery and hospital complex ***Collégiale de Roncevaux.*** As the first stop after crossing the Pyrenees, since the Middle Ages it has played an important role in receiving pilgrims. The complex, which has been modified many times since its founding in the 12th century, was historically managed by Augustinian monks, and includes the *Real Colegiata de Santa María*, one of the earliest examples of Spanish gothic church architecture. The church altar has a medieval statue of *Nuestra Señora de Roncevalles*, which commemorates Mary's apparition in the Middle Ages. The cloister (14th century) contains the enormous tomb of King Sancho VII of Navarre, who was more than seven feet tall and a hero of the decisive battle of *Las Navas de Tolosa* (*1212*).

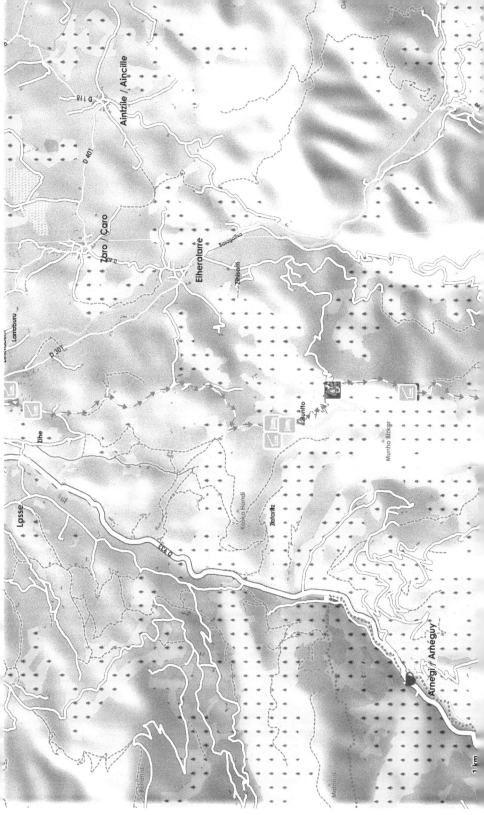

Waypoint	Total(km)	Directions	Verification	Compass	Altitude(m)
1	0.0	In **Saint-Jean-Pied-de-Port**, from church, cross the bridge over the Nive River and continue straight on rue de l'Espagne		SW	186
2	0.2	Leave Saint-Jean by passing through Spanish Gate and continuing straight on route de Saint-Michel/D301		S	171
3	0.4	Turn left onto D428/Route Napoleon, which climbs for about 16km to the Spanish border		SW	172
4	0.9	Continue on route Napolean	Signpost	S	222
5	5.4	Turn left onto footpath that is a short-cut and switchbacks before rejoining the D428 road		S	519
6	6.3	Rejoin the D428 road, turning left and continue climb through **Orisson**		E	687
7	11.3	Bear right beside **Virgin of Biakorri**	Parking area on the left	W	1097
8	14.9	Turn right (cross) off the D428 road and climb on rocky trail. Pass the **Col de Bentarte** and the Fountain of Roland and continue following the French/Spain border, until turning right on forest road		S	1221
9	18.7	Keep left ontrack. Then descend right on rocky trail before emergency point		SW	1308
10	20.5	Turn left on trail that descends steeply through forest. At fork turn right onto forest road and cross the stream. The alternative route through Puerto de Ibañeta (Roncevaux Pass) departs to the right on asphalt road, after the emergency point.	Signpost	SW	1423
11	24.2	Arrive at **Roncevaux**. The alternative route through Puerto de Ibañeta (Roncevaux Pass) rejoins the main route at the foot of the the monastery of Roncevaux	Beside the monastery		940

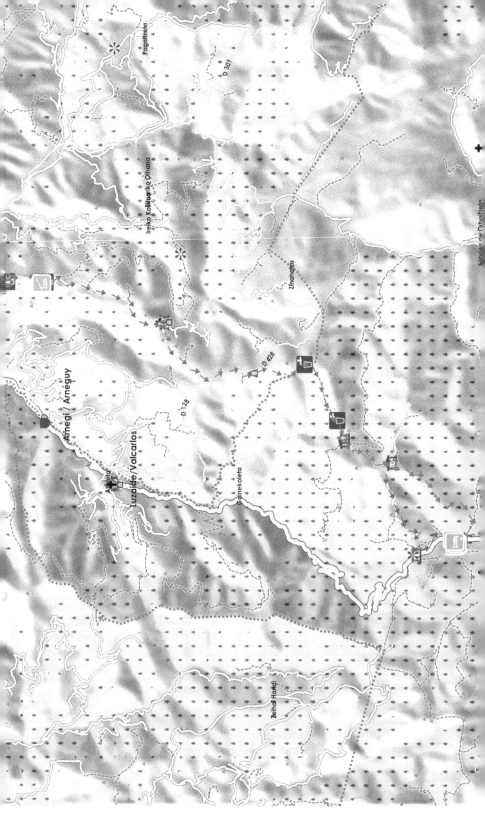

DISTANCE **9.7km**

ASCENT **32m**

DESCENT **507m**

Hiker at rest, Pyrenees

Route - The alternative route from Col de Lepoeder to Roncevaux should be taken if rain or fog make the main track difficult to navigate or slippery. The route is well-marked with the white-red way markings of the GR®12. From Col de Lepoeder, it follows mostly an asphalt road that switchbacks descending to Puerto de Ibañeta (or Roncevaux Pass), where in 778 a battle took place between Charlemagne and Basque forces, which was later recounted in the Song of Roland. (Note the Char-

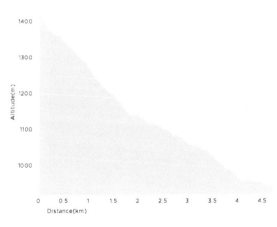

lemagne monument (1934)). From the chapel at Roncevaux Pass, the route crosses through a fenced garden and descends by footpath to the monastery of Roncevaux.

Waypoint	Total(km)	Directions	Verification	Compass	Altitude(m)
1	0.0	Turn right to take the GR12 variant on road	Signpost	S	1421
2	4.7	End of the route	Beside the monastery		947

ACCOMODATION & TOURIST INFORMATION

Honto

La Ferme Ithurburia, (Mrs. Ourtiague), Route Napoléon, 64220 Saint-Michel, Pyrénées Atlantiques, France; +33(0)5 59 37 11 17; +33(0)6 80 53 00 46; jeann.outiague@orange.fr; www.gites-de-france-64.com/ferme-ithurburia; €50/pers. €55/2 pers., €75/3 pers., €85/4 pers., €18/dinner; Hostel: €16/pers., €36/half board, €6/breakfast; Located 5 km after Saint-Jean. B&B includes 14 places in 5 rooms and hostel has 19 places in 5 rooms. No kitchen.

La Ferme Gaineko Etchea, (Marie-Agnès and Jean-Noel Harispe), Route Napoléon, 64220 Saint-Michel, Pyrénées Atlantiques, France; +33(0)5 59 11 20 64; michel.harispe@gmail.com; €30/half board; 5 places in 2 rooms on a working sheep farm located 5 km after Saint-Jean. Very welcoming, with beautiful views. Kitchen.

Orisson

Refuge Auberge Orisson, (Jean-Jacques Etchandy), Chemin de Saint-Jacques de Compostelle, 64220 Uhart-Cize, Pyrénées Atlantiques, France; +33(0)5 59 49 13 03; +33(0)6 81 49 79 56; refuge.orisson@wanadoo.fr; www.refuge-orisson.com; €35/half board; Located in the Basque mountains, 9 kilometres after Saint-Jean-Pied-de-Port, 28 places in rooms or dormitories, with restaurant and bar. English spoken.

Roncevaux

Albergue de Peregrinos, (Edurne and Mari Sol), Real Colegiata de Roncesvalles, 31650 Roncesvalles, Navarra, Spain; +34 948 760 000; +34 948 760 029; info@alberguederoncesvalles.com; www.alberguederoncesvalles.com; €12/pers.; Renovated and modernized in 2011, massive hostel with more than 183 places. Possibility to celebrate mass at 8 p.m. English spoken.

Casa Sabina, Carretera de Francia, 31650 Roncesvalles, Navarra, Spain; +34 494 876 001 2; www.casasabina.es/; €45/pers. €55/double room; 10 places in 5 double rooms. English spoken.

Hotel Roncesvalles, C.Nuestra Señora de Roncesvalles, 14,, 31650 Roncesvalles, Navarra, Spain; +34 948 760 105; info@hotelroncesvalles.com; www.hotelroncesvalles.com; €66-€80/double, €56-70/double, €95-€115/triple, €95-150/apartments for 3-6 pers. €10/breakfast; Beautiful and welcoming hotel in fully renovated monastery (part of main complex). English spoken.

Office of Tourism, Antiguo Molino, Nuestra Señora de Roncesvalles, 31650 Roncevaux, Navarra, Spain; +34 948 760 301; turismo@navarra.es; www.turismo.navarra.es

Real Colegiata de Santa María, Roncevaux

Lightfoot Guides to the Way of St James

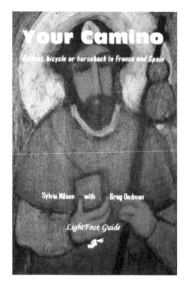

Our Camino planning guide, Your Camino on foot, bicycle or horseback in France and Spain a complete planning guide for walking, riding or cycling a Camino route.

Over 300 pages, 18 chapters with everything you need to know to plan your Camino.

Information on over 30 different routes, how to get to the start, packing lists, budgets, training, walking with children, dogs or donkeys. For cyclists and people with disabilities.

Written by Sylvia Nilsen

Lightfoot Guide to Slackpacking the Camino Frances

Slackpacking the Camino with beds booked and baggage transferred doesn't mean that you won't get blisters, tendonitis, aching muscles and a funny tan! You will have to hike up the same mountain paths in the sun or rain, wobble down the same rocky descents, and struggle through the same boot-clinging mud and sludge with all the other pilgrims. The main difference is that your daypack will only weigh about 3kg instead of the average 7kg, and knowing that you have a bed and a hot shower waiting for you at the end of the day means plenty of time to have breakfast, to smell the wildflowers along the way, enjoy a leisurely lunch and wait for an interesting church or museum to open, instead of racing to queue for a bed in a pilgrim dormitory. Slackpacking the Camino Frances provides all the information and advice you'll need to plan your perfect Camino.

Written by Sylvia Nilsen

Camino Lingo

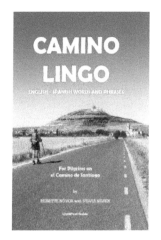

If you only take one Spanish phrase book or dictionary with you on the Camino this is it! The Lightfoot Guide: Camino Lingo, English – Spanish Words and Phrases for Pilgrims on el Camino de Santiago contains all the Spanish words you'll need to walk a pilgrimage in Spain. No complicated verb conjugations or rules on diphthongs and grammar. This is a 'cheats' guide to speaking Spanish on the Camino. Over 650 English/Spanish words relating specifically to the Camino pilgrimage with simplified pronunciation – including a few curse words should you need them!

Written by Reinette Novoa with Sylvia Nilsen

The LightFoot Guides to the Three Saints' Way

For anyone contemplating starting their "Camino" in England these two books will lead you from Winchester via the Mont Saint Michel to join one of the four main tributaries of the "Camino" in France the Via Turonensis.

The name, **Three Saint's Way,** has been created by the authors of the LightFoot guide, but is based on the three saints associated with this pilgrimage: St Swithin, St Mchael and St James. Far from being a single route, it is in fact a network of intersecting routes: **The Millenium Footpath Trail** starting in Winchester and ending in Portsmouth, England, the **Chemin Anglais** to **Mont St Michel** and the **Plantagenet Way to St Jean d'Angely**, where it intersects with the Via Turonensis carrying pilgrims from Paris, the benelux countrie and Scandanavia.

All of the Lightfoot Guides are available at www.pilgrimagepublications.com or from your favourite book store.

Lightning Source UK Ltd.
Milton Keynes UK
UKHW051107060223
416527UK00011B/495

9 782917 183373